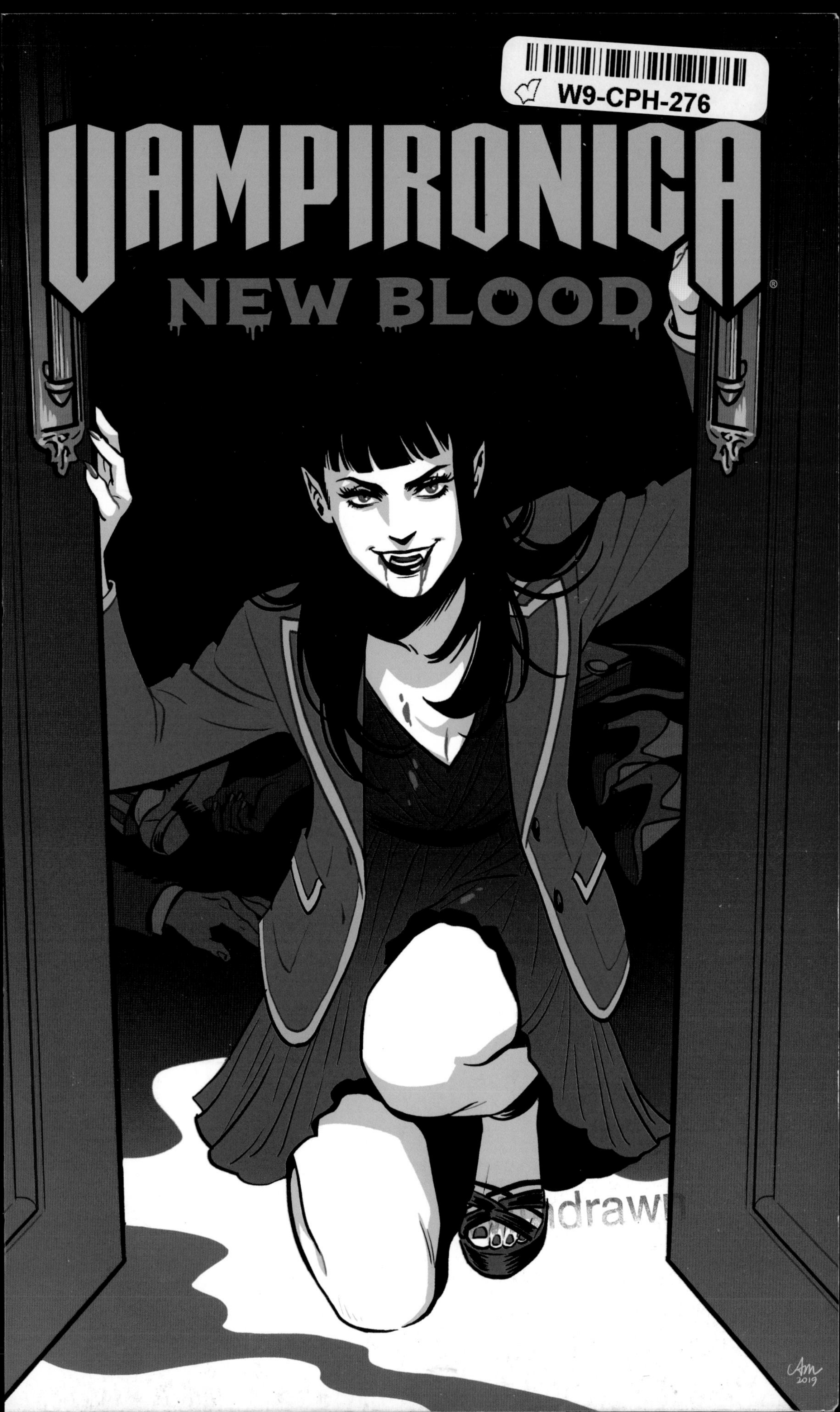
VAMPIRONICA®
NEW BLOOD
Am 2019

VAMPIRONICA
NEW BLOOD ®

Story by
FRANK TIERI &
MICHAEL MORECI

Art by
AUDREY MOK
JOE EISMA (ISSUE 4, P16-25)

Lettering by
JACK MORELLI

Coloring by
MATT HERMS (ISSUES 1,3,4)
LEE LOUGHRIDGE (ISSUE 2)

Graphic Design
KARI McLACHLAN

Rendering by
RYAN JAMPOLE (ISSUE 4, P16-25)

Creative Consultant
JESSE GOLDWATER

Editors
ALEX SEGURA &
JAMIE L. ROTANTE

Co-President
MIKE PELLERITO

Associate Editor
STEPHEN OSWALD

Assistant Editor
VINCENT LOVALLO

Editor-in-Chief
VICTOR GORELICK

Publisher
JON GOLDWATER

PREVIOUSLY...

Veronica Lodge is popular, beautiful, rich, and fashionable. She's also a bloodsucking vampire. And it's not just Veronica, either. Riverdale's teen socialite descends from a long line of vampires... something she didn't learn until she came face-to-face with Ivan, an evil, centuries-old vampire who had her parents, Hiram and Hermione Lodge, under his command. While trying to escape from the vampire hellscape that was once her loving home, she was given refuge by fellow student and teen genius Dilton Doiley. Together, they were able to successfully thwart Ivan's tactics and stop him from turning the rest of Riverdale into his vampire army. However, Veronica realized that there was another master vampire pulling the strings back at Lodge Mansion. After facing horrible traps and illusions, Veronica heroically defeated the master vampire (or at least who she *believed* to be the master) and saved the town!

But Veronica's paranormal nightmare was just one possible scenario. In another world, another *Riverdale*, one of her friends was dealing with his own horror story. Jughead Jones was grappling with learning that he too descended from a long line of monsters—however, his lineage was werewolves. Fortunately, there's no way their two worlds could meet, and that's for the best, as vampires and werewolves have been enemies since Riverdale was first colonized. *Unfortunately* for them, however, a young woman named Jinx Holliday, who just so happens to be the daughter of Satan, cast a spell using one of her father's occult books, which brought two universes together.

Before another all-out vampire vs. werewolf war started, the residents of Riverdale were confronted with an uncomfortable truth: if there were two different versions of Riverdale, who's to say there aren't even more than that? And Jinx proved that to be true when all of the realities came crashing together, meaning they all could individually be affected by this collision. No one knew what to do or how to prevent it and set things right.

Enter: Sabrina Spellman. The teen witch tasked Jugwolf and Vampironica to find the Book of Lucifer, the only thing that could restore order. Unfortunately, it was long buried with the first (and most powerful) vampire ever in Riverdale... and that resting place? Right under Riverdale High School! They were able to successfully retrieve the book and set things right, but not before Veronica learned a harsh truth: that evil, historic vampire was Sir Francis Lodge, her ancestor.

Now Veronica is back in her own vampire reality with the knowledge that her ancestry is filled with evil. It's up to her to manage her family's past while still confronting the struggles of being a teen bloodsucker.

CHAPTER ONE

COVER ART BY **AUDREY MOK**

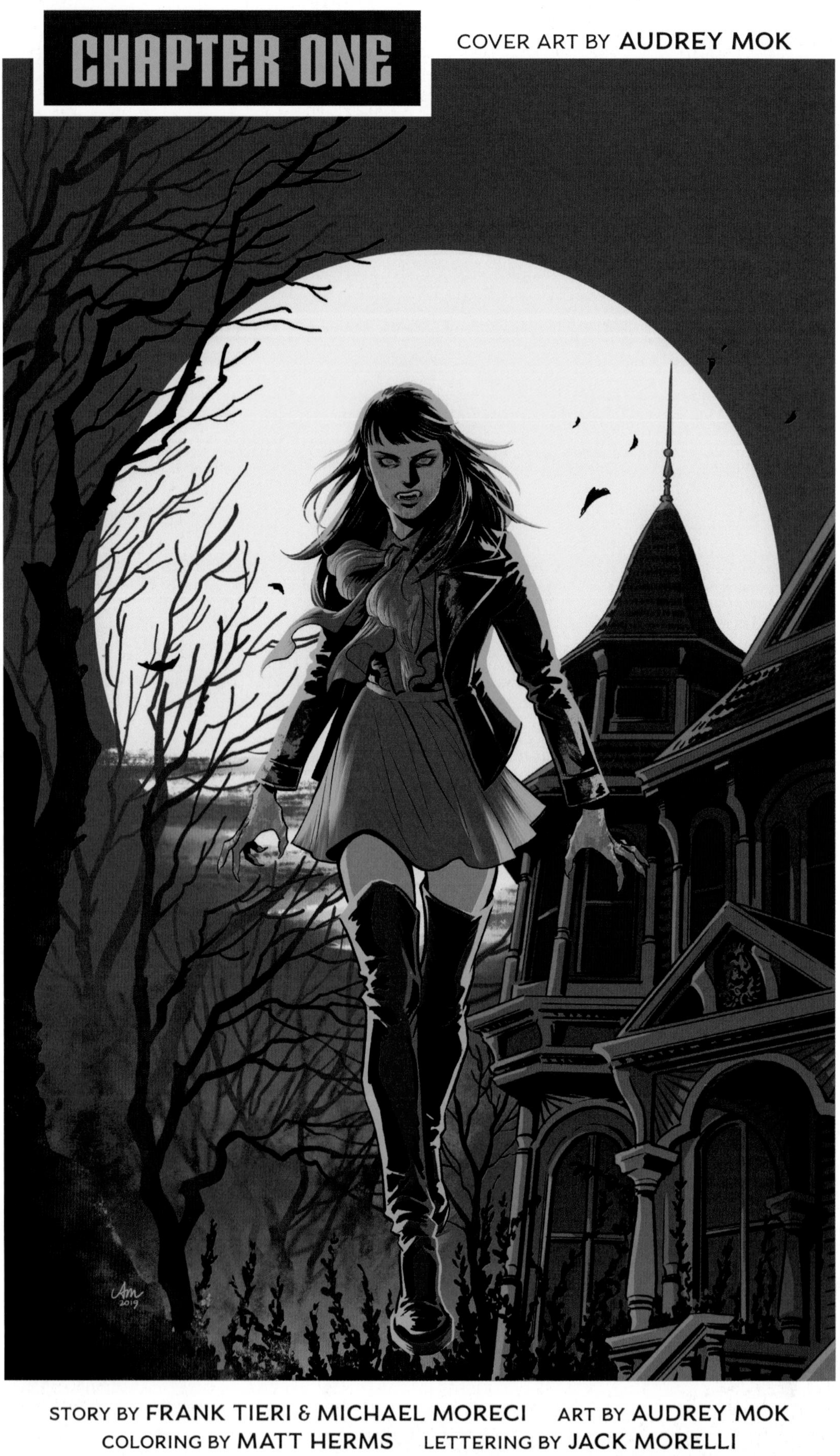

STORY BY **FRANK TIERI & MICHAEL MORECI** ART BY **AUDREY MOK**
COLORING BY **MATT HERMS** LETTERING BY **JACK MORELLI**

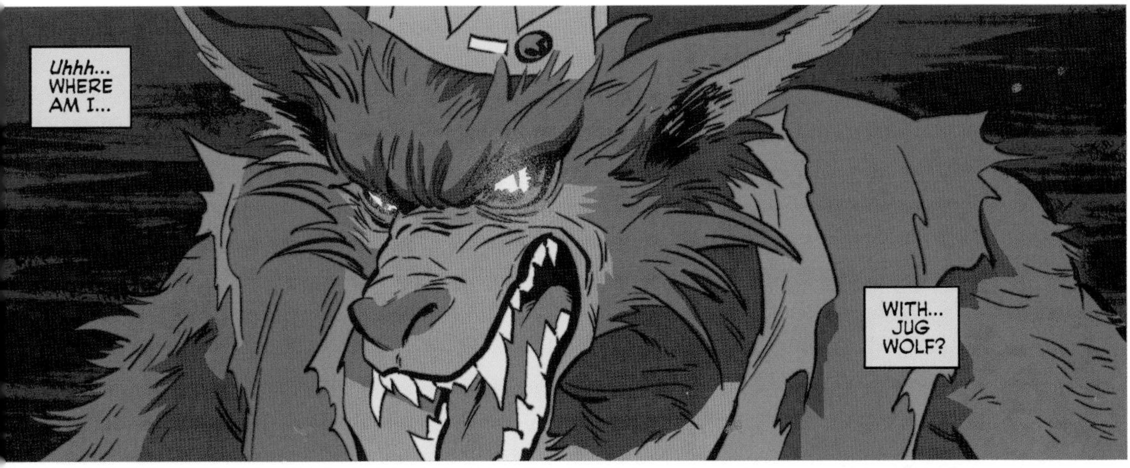
Uhhh... WHERE AM I...
WITH... JUG WOLF?
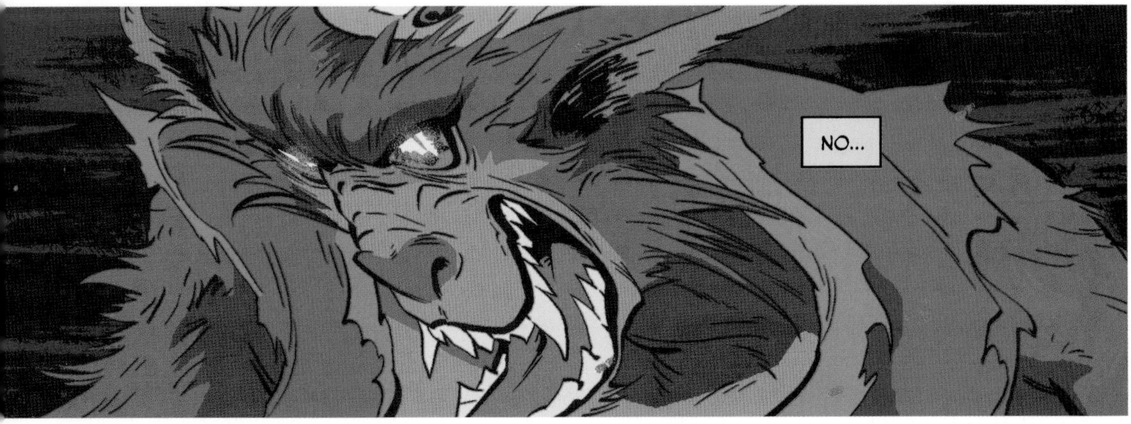
NO...
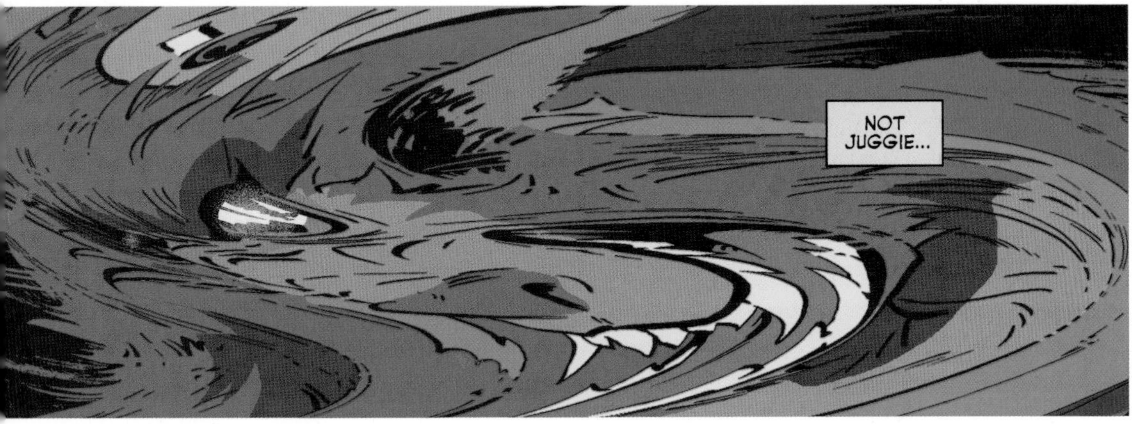
NOT JUGGIE...
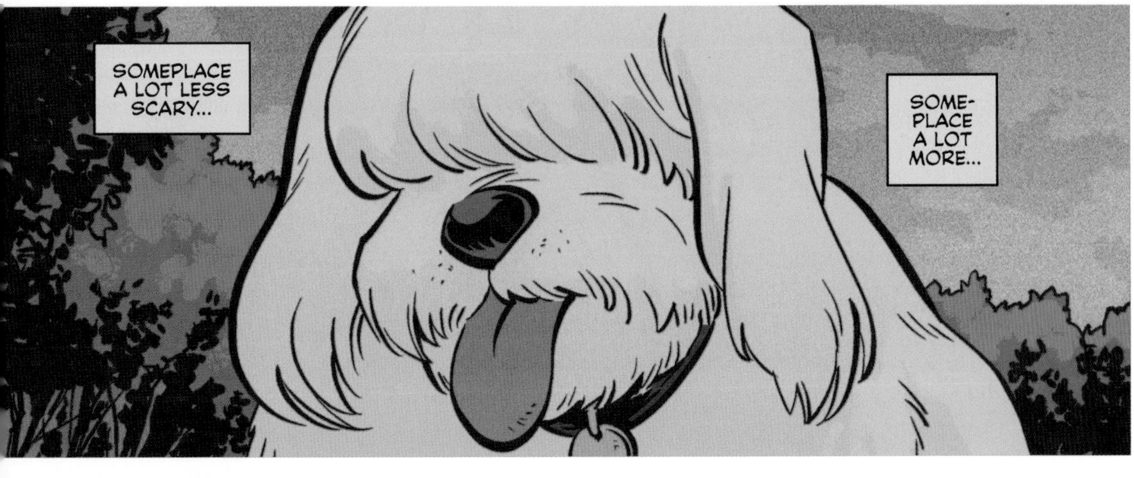
SOMEPLACE A LOT LESS SCARY...
SOME-PLACE A LOT MORE...

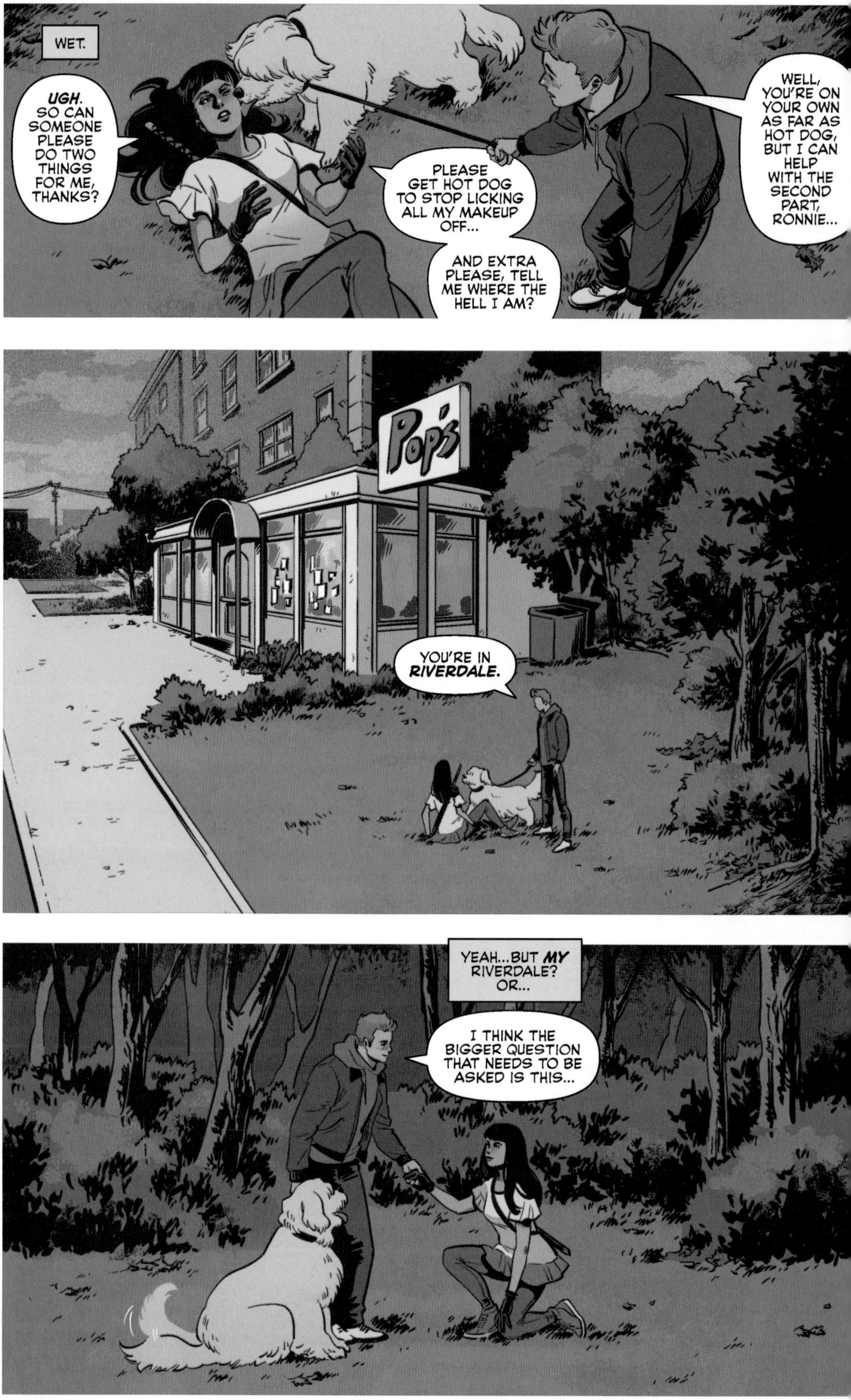
WET.
UGH. SO CAN SOMEONE PLEASE DO TWO THINGS FOR ME, THANKS?
PLEASE GET HOT DOG TO STOP LICKING ALL MY MAKEUP OFF...
AND EXTRA PLEASE, TELL ME WHERE THE HELL I AM?
WELL, YOU'RE ON YOUR OWN AS FAR AS HOT DOG, BUT I CAN HELP WITH THE SECOND PART, RONNIE...
Pop's
YOU'RE IN RIVERDALE.
YEAH...BUT MY RIVERDALE? OR...
I THINK THE BIGGER QUESTION THAT NEEDS TO BE ASKED IS THIS...

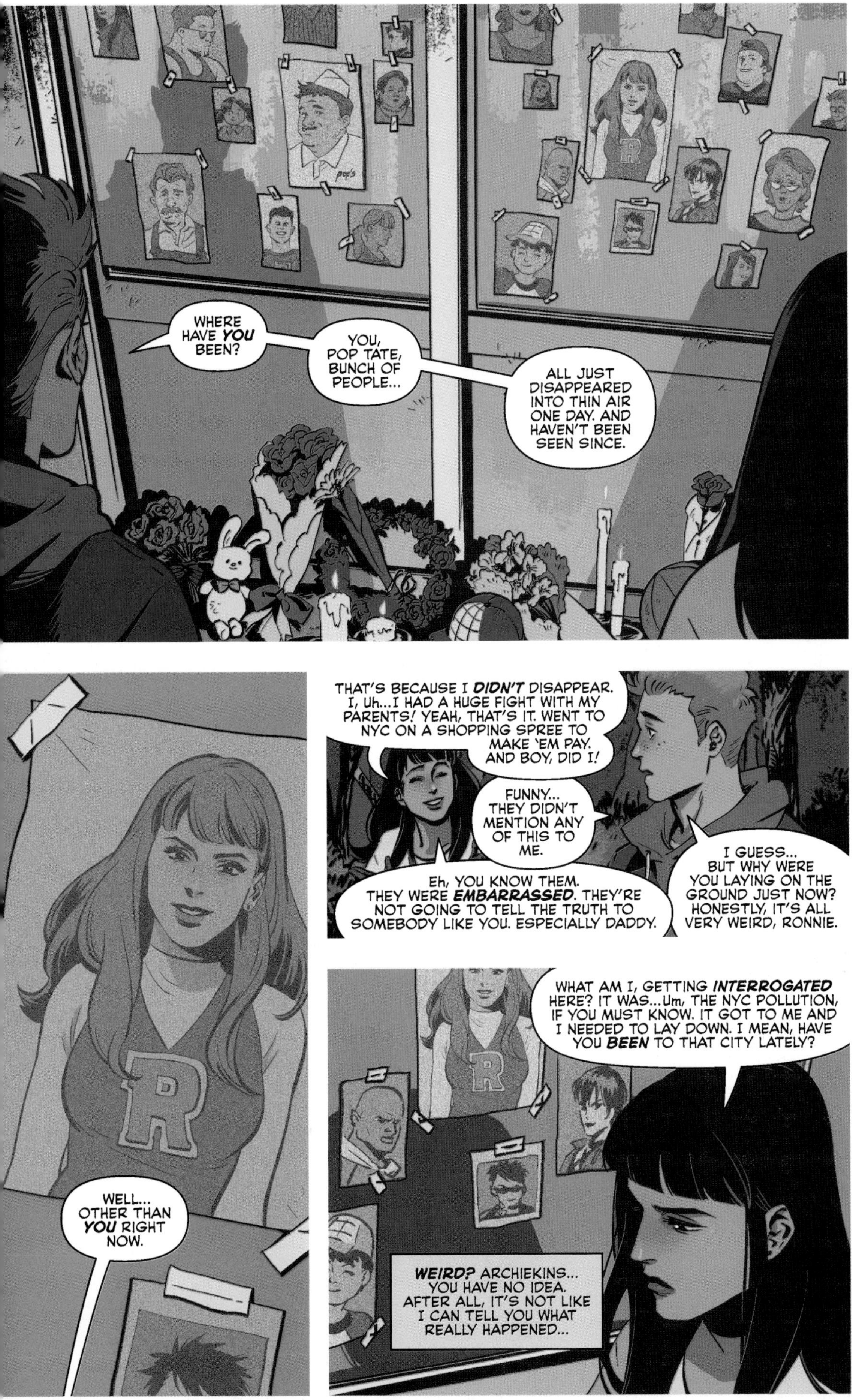

WHERE HAVE YOU BEEN?
YOU, POP TATE, BUNCH OF PEOPLE...
ALL JUST DISAPPEARED INTO THIN AIR ONE DAY. AND HAVEN'T BEEN SEEN SINCE.
WELL... OTHER THAN YOU RIGHT NOW.
THAT'S BECAUSE I DIDN'T DISAPPEAR. I, Uh...I HAD A HUGE FIGHT WITH MY PARENTS! YEAH, THAT'S IT. WENT TO NYC ON A SHOPPING SPREE TO MAKE 'EM PAY. AND BOY, DID I!
FUNNY... THEY DIDN'T MENTION ANY OF THIS TO ME.
Eh, YOU KNOW THEM. THEY WERE EMBARRASSED. THEY'RE NOT GOING TO TELL THE TRUTH TO SOMEBODY LIKE YOU. ESPECIALLY DADDY.
I GUESS... BUT WHY WERE YOU LAYING ON THE GROUND JUST NOW? HONESTLY, IT'S ALL VERY WEIRD, RONNIE.
WHAT AM I, GETTING INTERROGATED HERE? IT WAS...Um, THE NYC POLLUTION, IF YOU MUST KNOW. IT GOT TO ME AND I NEEDED TO LAY DOWN. I MEAN, HAVE YOU BEEN TO THAT CITY LATELY?
WEIRD? ARCHIEKINS... YOU HAVE NO IDEA. AFTER ALL, IT'S NOT LIKE I CAN TELL YOU WHAT REALLY HAPPENED...

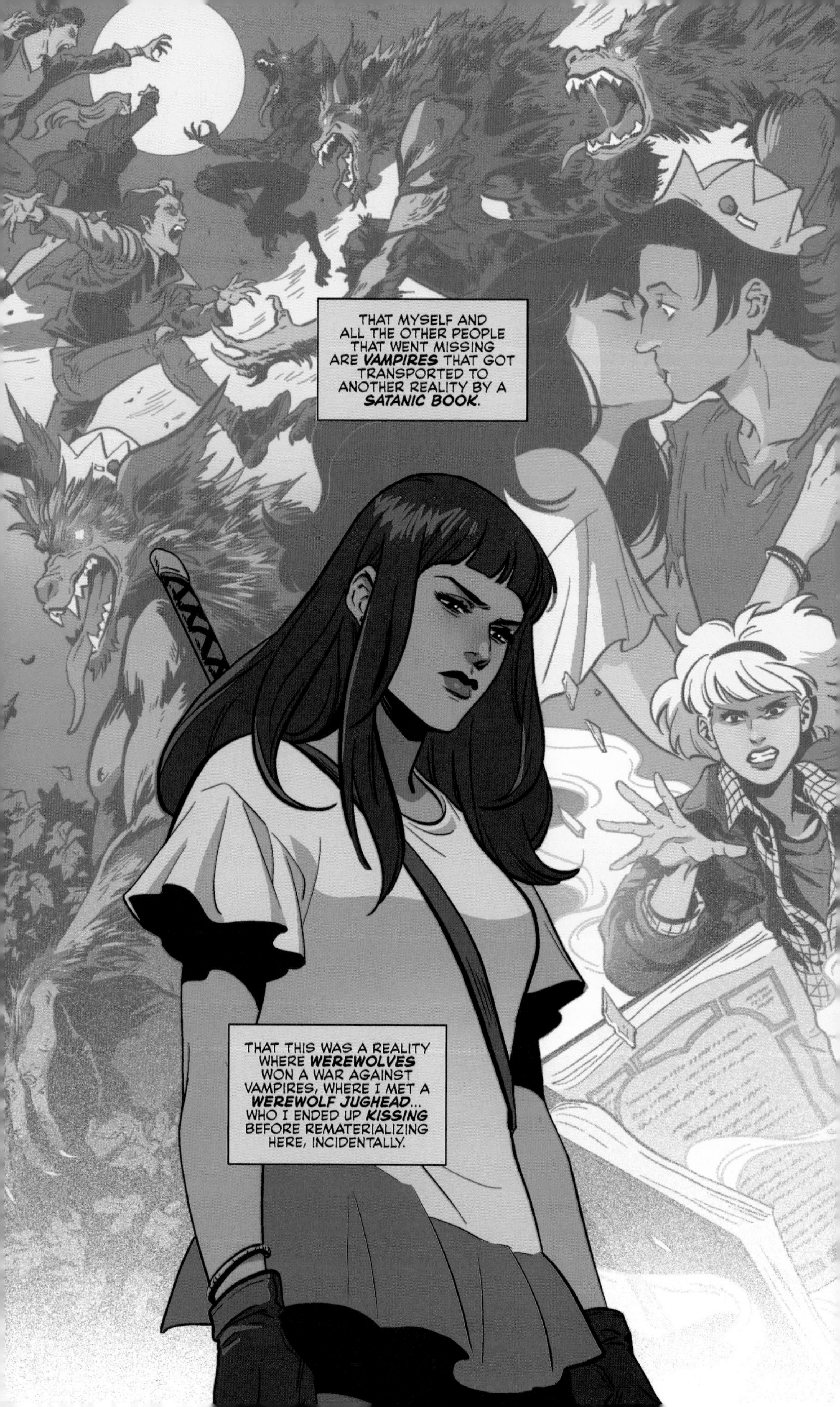
THAT MYSELF AND ALL THE OTHER PEOPLE THAT WENT MISSING ARE VAMPIRES THAT GOT TRANSPORTED TO ANOTHER REALITY BY A SATANIC BOOK.
THAT THIS WAS A REALITY WHERE WEREWOLVES WON A WAR AGAINST VAMPIRES, WHERE I MET A WEREWOLF JUGHEAD... WHO I ENDED UP KISSING BEFORE REMATERIALIZING HERE, INCIDENTALLY.

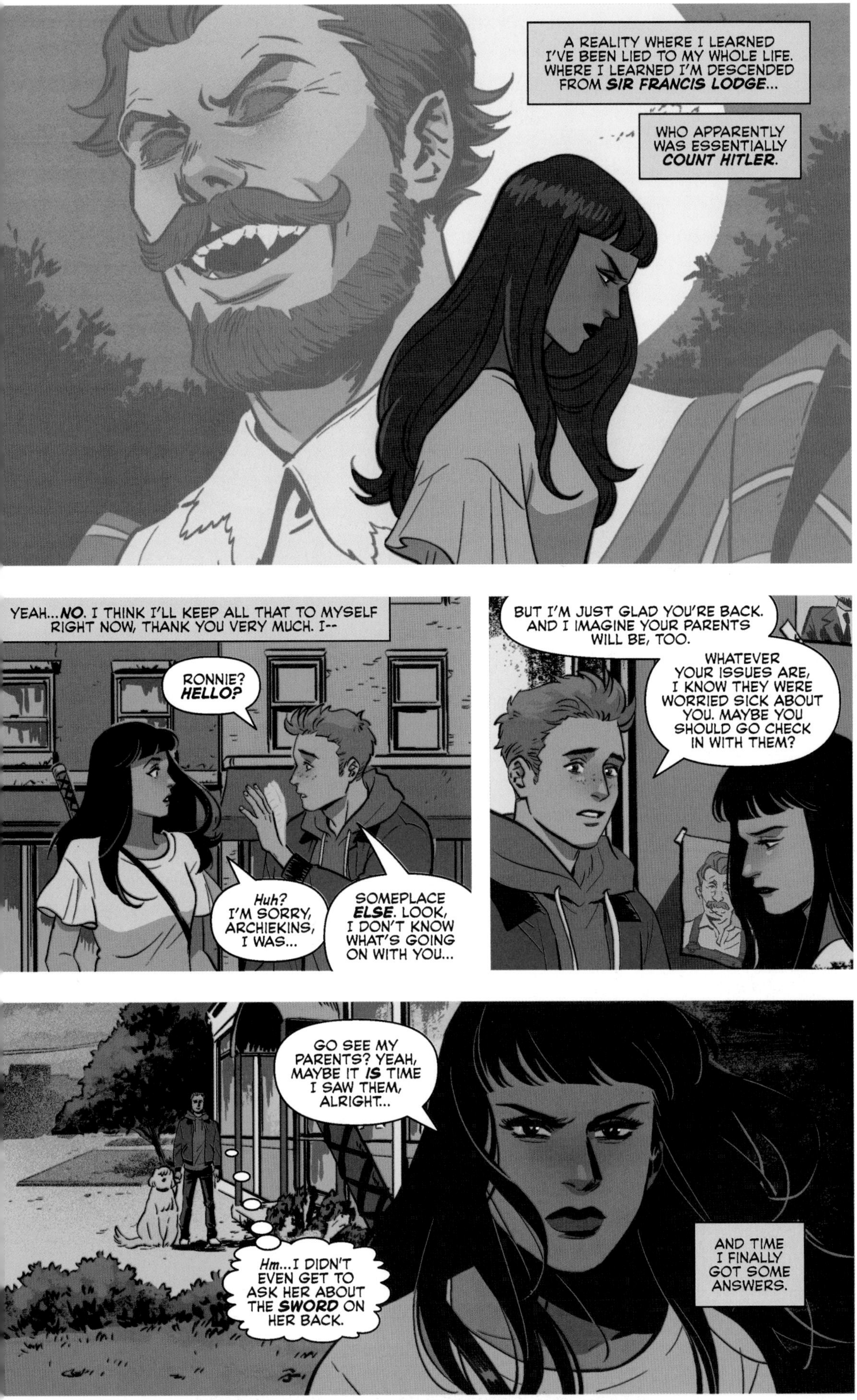
A REALITY WHERE I LEARNED I'VE BEEN LIED TO MY WHOLE LIFE. WHERE I LEARNED I'M DESCENDED FROM SIR FRANCIS LODGE...
WHO APPARENTLY WAS ESSENTIALLY COUNT HITLER.
YEAH...NO. I THINK I'LL KEEP ALL THAT TO MYSELF RIGHT NOW, THANK YOU VERY MUCH. I--
RONNIE? HELLO?
Huh? I'M SORRY, ARCHIEKINS, I WAS...
SOMEPLACE ELSE. LOOK, I DON'T KNOW WHAT'S GOING ON WITH YOU...
BUT I'M JUST GLAD YOU'RE BACK. AND I IMAGINE YOUR PARENTS WILL BE, TOO.
WHATEVER YOUR ISSUES ARE, I KNOW THEY WERE WORRIED SICK ABOUT YOU. MAYBE YOU SHOULD GO CHECK IN WITH THEM?
GO SEE MY PARENTS? YEAH, MAYBE IT IS TIME I SAW THEM, ALRIGHT...
Hm...I DIDN'T EVEN GET TO ASK HER ABOUT THE SWORD ON HER BACK.
AND TIME I FINALLY GOT SOME ANSWERS.

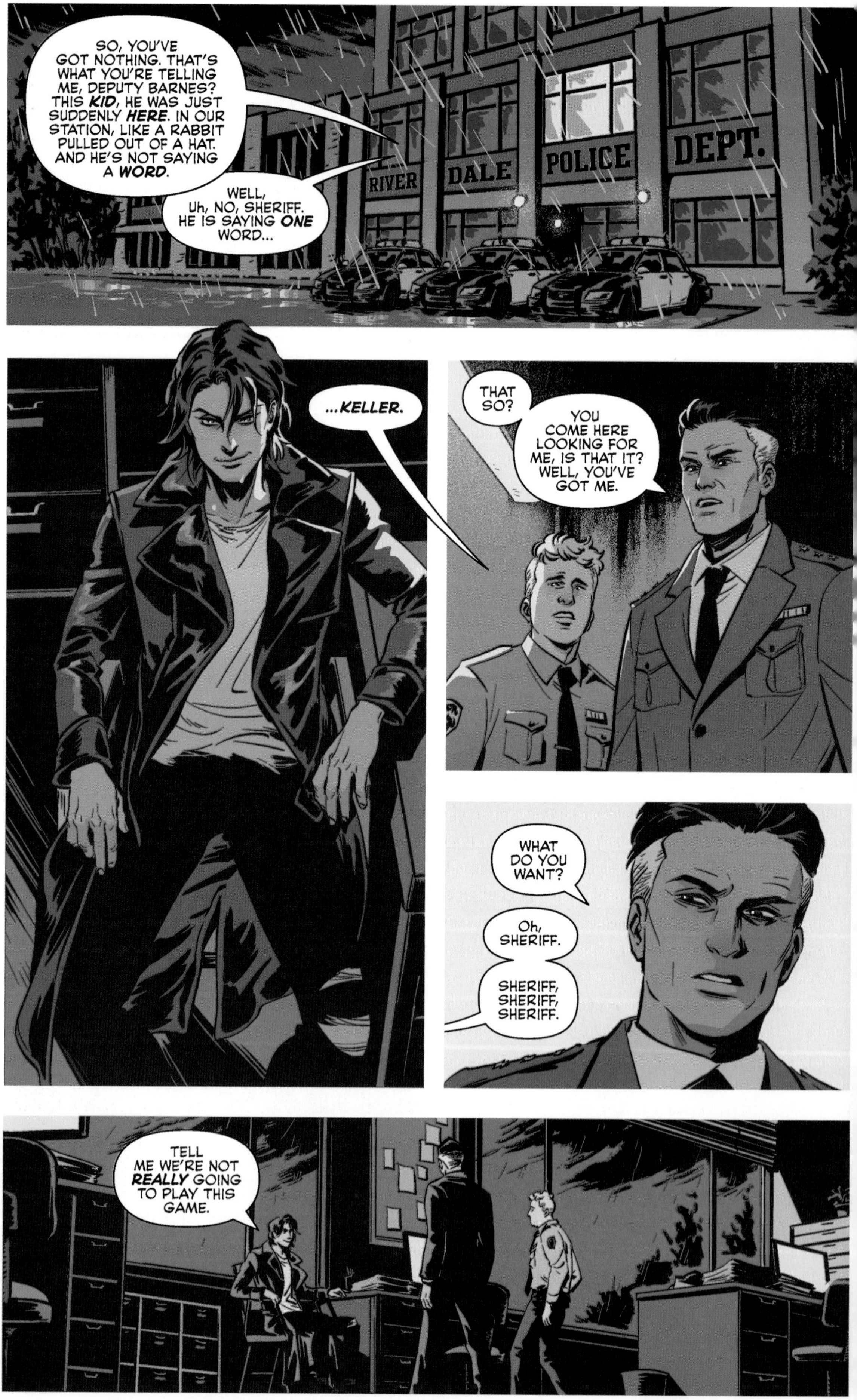
SO, YOU'VE GOT NOTHING. THAT'S WHAT YOU'RE TELLING ME, DEPUTY BARNES? THIS KID, HE WAS JUST SUDDENLY HERE. IN OUR STATION, LIKE A RABBIT PULLED OUT OF A HAT. AND HE'S NOT SAYING A WORD.
WELL, Uh, NO, SHERIFF. HE IS SAYING ONE WORD...
RIVER DALE POLICE DEPT.
...KELLER.
THAT SO?
YOU COME HERE LOOKING FOR ME, IS THAT IT? WELL, YOU'VE GOT ME.
WHAT DO YOU WANT?
Oh, SHERIFF.
SHERIFF, SHERIFF, SHERIFF.
TELL ME WE'RE NOT REALLY GOING TO PLAY THIS GAME.

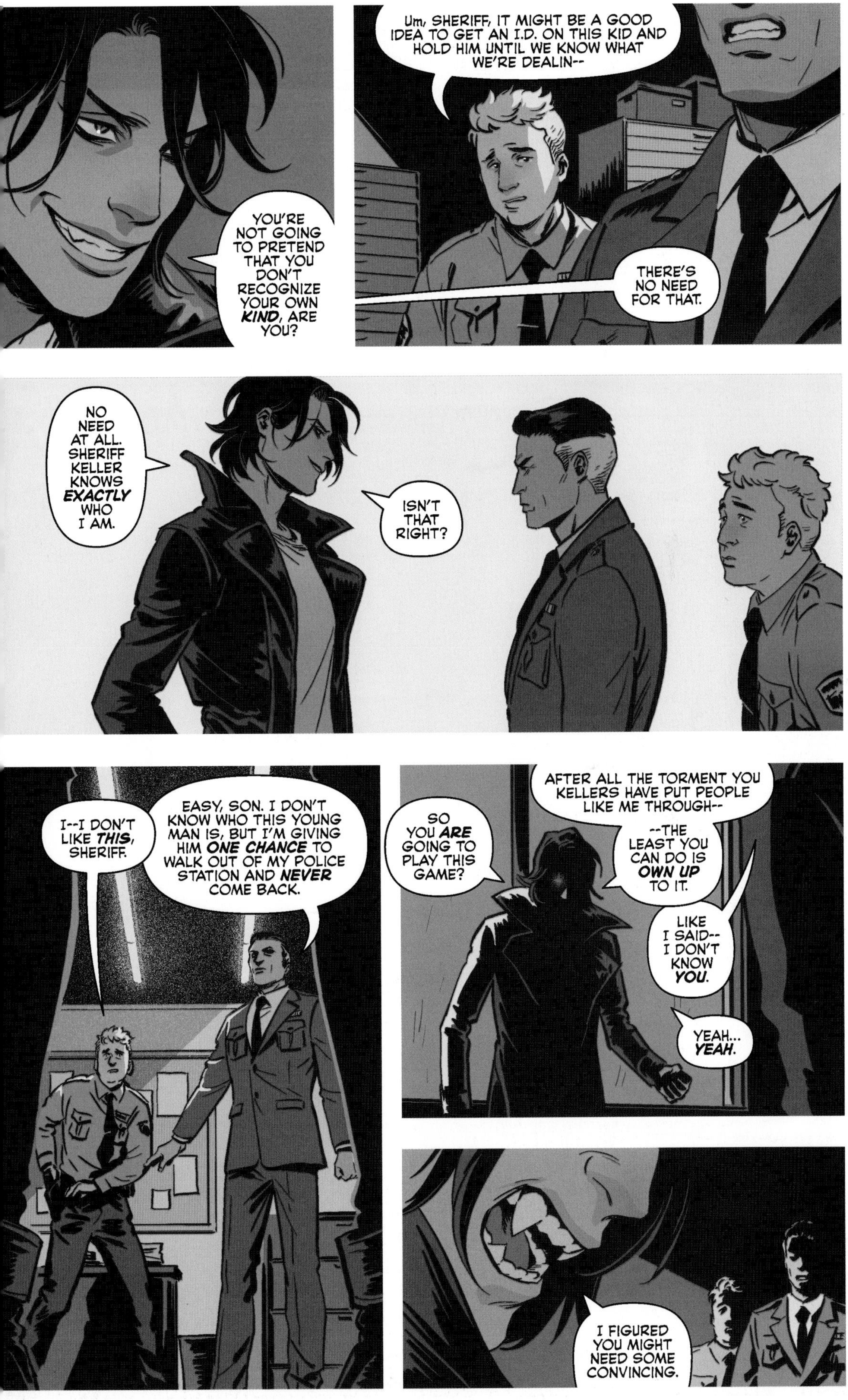

YOU'RE NOT GOING TO PRETEND THAT YOU DON'T RECOGNIZE YOUR OWN KIND, ARE YOU?
Um, SHERIFF, IT MIGHT BE A GOOD IDEA TO GET AN I.D. ON THIS KID AND HOLD HIM UNTIL WE KNOW WHAT WE'RE DEALIN--
THERE'S NO NEED FOR THAT.
NO NEED AT ALL. SHERIFF KELLER KNOWS EXACTLY WHO I AM.
ISN'T THAT RIGHT?
I--I DON'T LIKE THIS, SHERIFF.
EASY, SON. I DON'T KNOW WHO THIS YOUNG MAN IS, BUT I'M GIVING HIM ONE CHANCE TO WALK OUT OF MY POLICE STATION AND NEVER COME BACK.
SO YOU ARE GOING TO PLAY THIS GAME?
AFTER ALL THE TORMENT YOU KELLERS HAVE PUT PEOPLE LIKE ME THROUGH--
--THE LEAST YOU CAN DO IS OWN UP TO IT.
LIKE I SAID-- I DON'T KNOW YOU.
YEAH... YEAH.
I FIGURED YOU MIGHT NEED SOME CONVINCING.

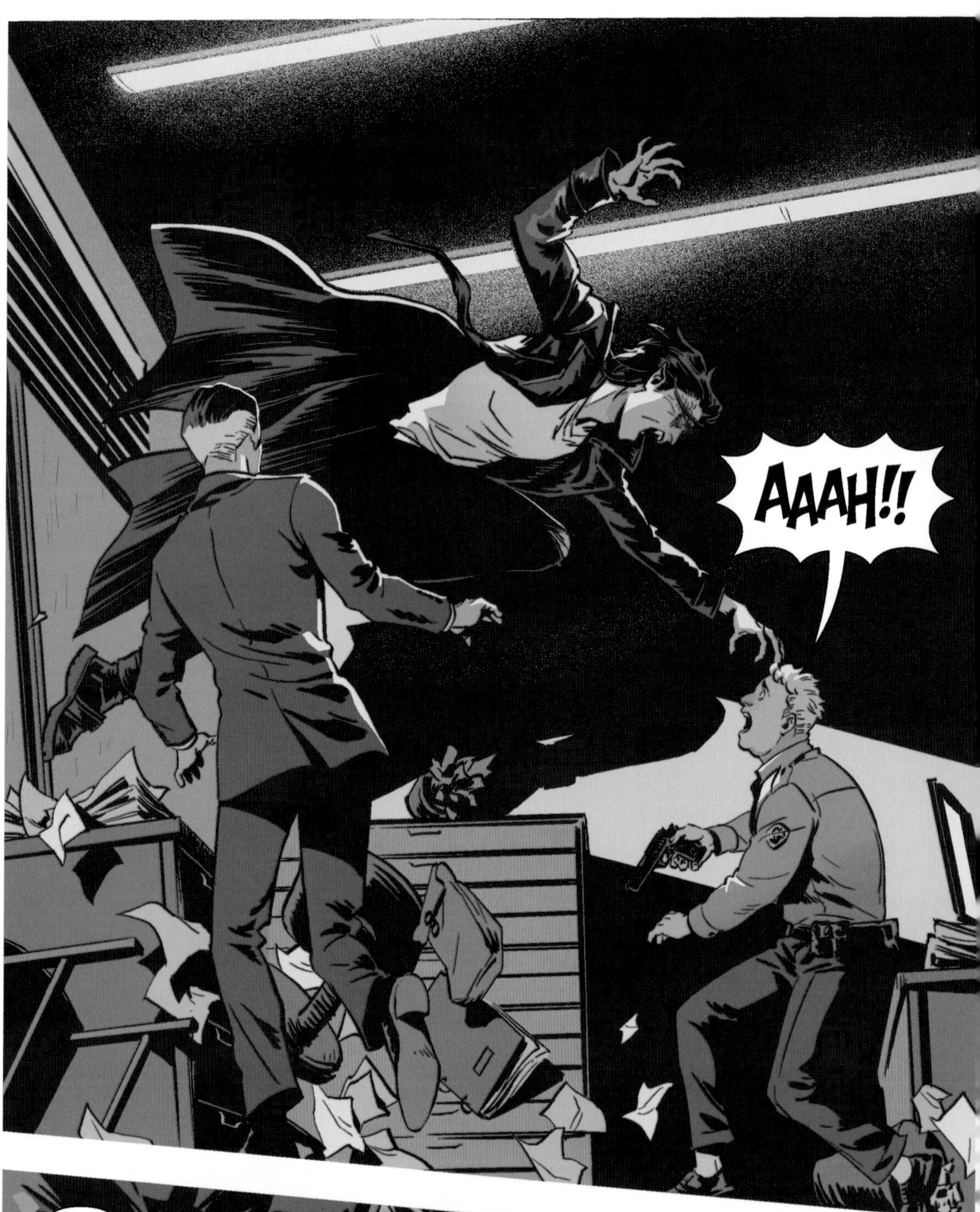
AAAH!!

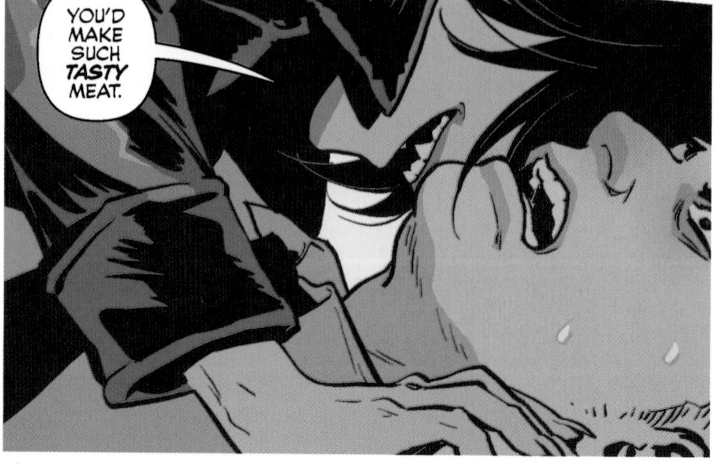
YOU'D MAKE SUCH *TASTY* MEAT.

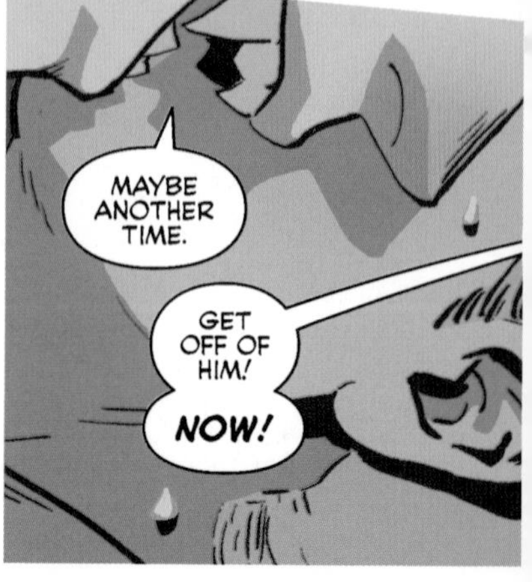
MAYBE ANOTHER TIME.
GET OFF OF HIM! *NOW!*

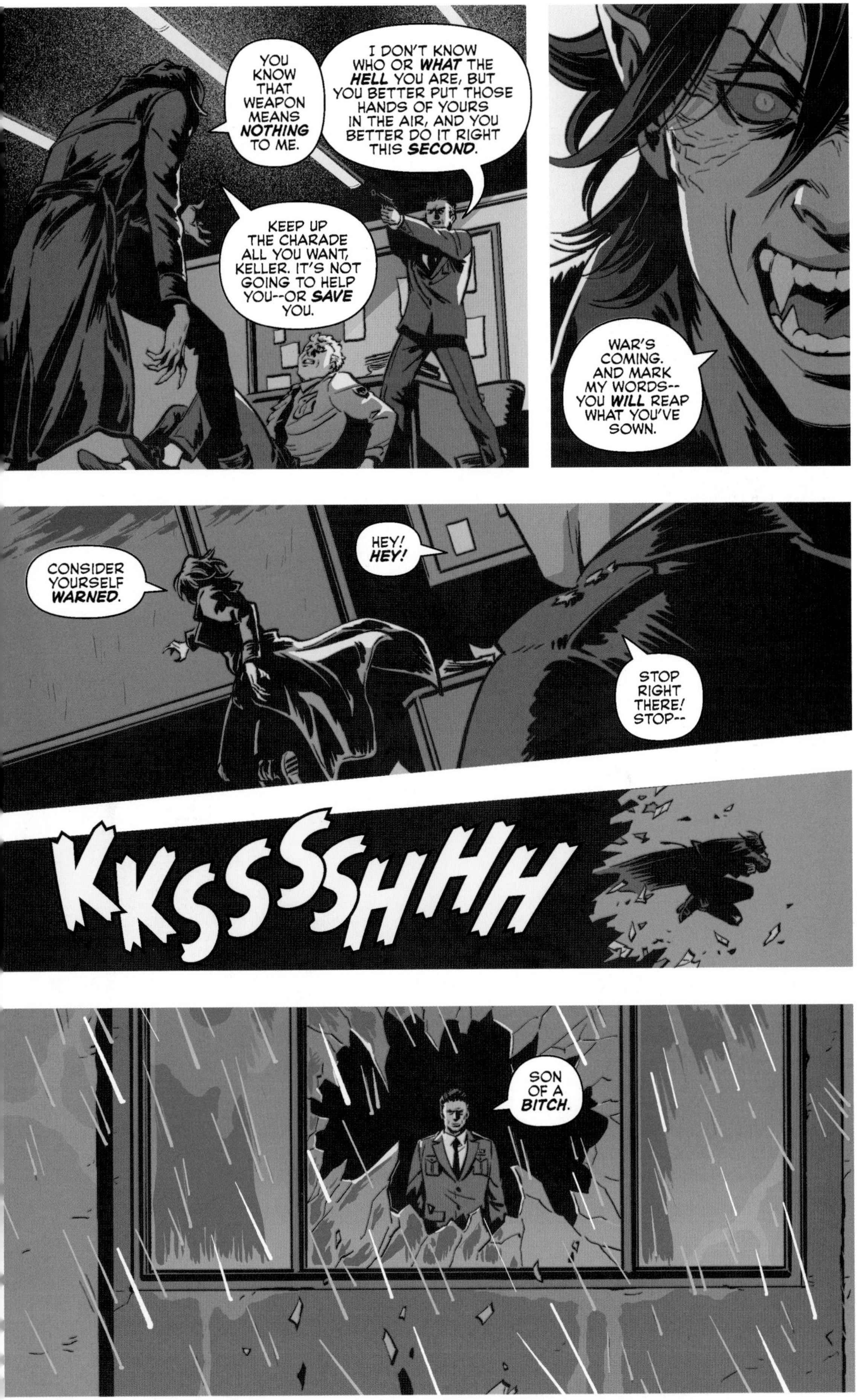
YOU KNOW THAT WEAPON MEANS NOTHING TO ME.
I DON'T KNOW WHO OR WHAT THE HELL YOU ARE, BUT YOU BETTER PUT THOSE HANDS OF YOURS IN THE AIR, AND YOU BETTER DO IT RIGHT THIS SECOND.
KEEP UP THE CHARADE ALL YOU WANT, KELLER. IT'S NOT GOING TO HELP YOU--OR SAVE YOU.
WAR'S COMING. AND MARK MY WORDS-- YOU WILL REAP WHAT YOU'VE SOWN.
CONSIDER YOURSELF WARNED.
HEY! HEY!
STOP RIGHT THERE! STOP--
KKSSSSHHH
SON OF A BITCH.

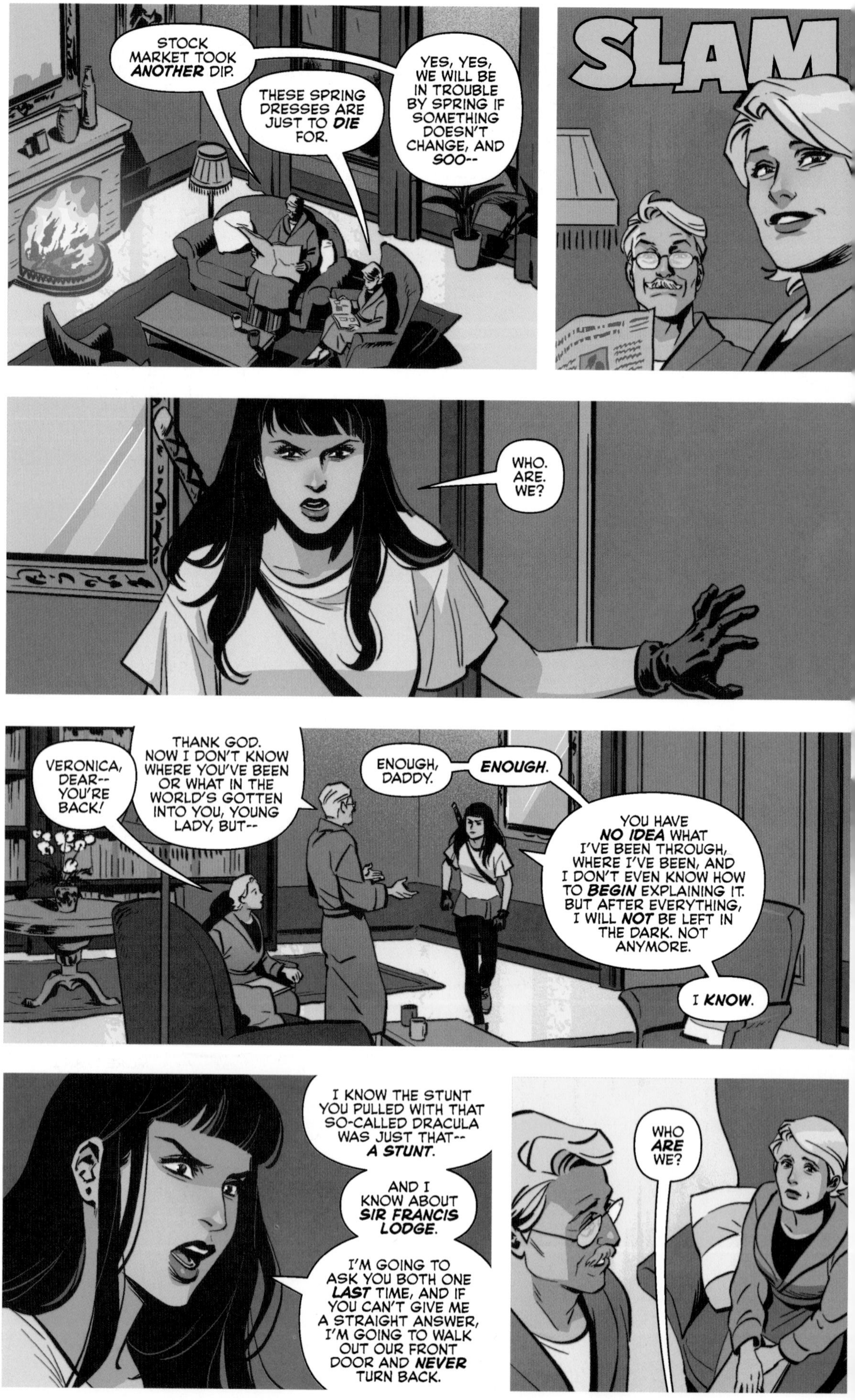

STOCK MARKET TOOK **ANOTHER** DIP.
THESE SPRING DRESSES ARE JUST TO **DIE** FOR.
YES, YES, WE WILL BE IN TROUBLE BY SPRING IF SOMETHING DOESN'T CHANGE, AND **SOO**--
SLAM
WHO. ARE. WE?
VERONICA, DEAR-- YOU'RE BACK!
THANK GOD. NOW I DON'T KNOW WHERE YOU'VE BEEN OR WHAT IN THE WORLD'S GOTTEN INTO YOU, YOUNG LADY, BUT--
ENOUGH, DADDY.
ENOUGH.
YOU HAVE **NO IDEA** WHAT I'VE BEEN THROUGH, WHERE I'VE BEEN, AND I DON'T EVEN KNOW HOW TO **BEGIN** EXPLAINING IT. BUT AFTER EVERYTHING, I WILL **NOT** BE LEFT IN THE DARK. NOT ANYMORE.
I **KNOW**.
I KNOW THE STUNT YOU PULLED WITH THAT SO-CALLED DRACULA WAS JUST THAT-- **A STUNT**.
AND I KNOW ABOUT **SIR FRANCIS LODGE**.
I'M GOING TO ASK YOU BOTH ONE **LAST** TIME, AND IF YOU CAN'T GIVE ME A STRAIGHT ANSWER, I'M GOING TO WALK OUT OUR FRONT DOOR AND **NEVER** TURN BACK.
WHO **ARE** WE?

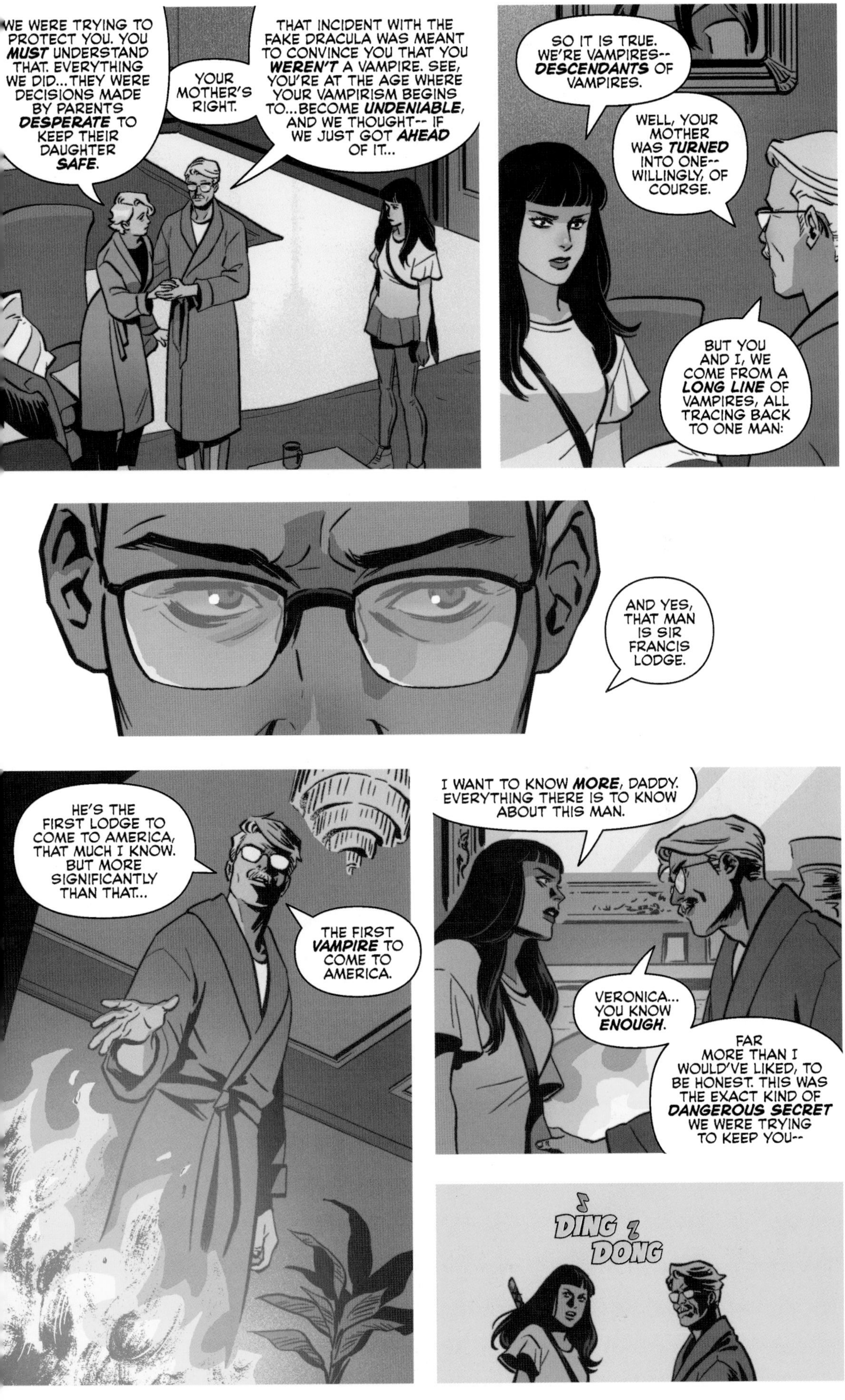
WE WERE TRYING TO PROTECT YOU. YOU MUST UNDERSTAND THAT. EVERYTHING WE DID...THEY WERE DECISIONS MADE BY PARENTS DESPERATE TO KEEP THEIR DAUGHTER SAFE.
YOUR MOTHER'S RIGHT.
THAT INCIDENT WITH THE FAKE DRACULA WAS MEANT TO CONVINCE YOU THAT YOU WEREN'T A VAMPIRE. SEE, YOU'RE AT THE AGE WHERE YOUR VAMPIRISM BEGINS TO...BECOME UNDENIABLE, AND WE THOUGHT-- IF WE JUST GOT AHEAD OF IT...
SO IT IS TRUE. WE'RE VAMPIRES-- DESCENDANTS OF VAMPIRES.
WELL, YOUR MOTHER WAS TURNED INTO ONE-- WILLINGLY, OF COURSE.
BUT YOU AND I, WE COME FROM A LONG LINE OF VAMPIRES, ALL TRACING BACK TO ONE MAN:
AND YES, THAT MAN IS SIR FRANCIS LODGE.
HE'S THE FIRST LODGE TO COME TO AMERICA, THAT MUCH I KNOW. BUT MORE SIGNIFICANTLY THAN THAT...
THE FIRST VAMPIRE TO COME TO AMERICA.
I WANT TO KNOW MORE, DADDY. EVERYTHING THERE IS TO KNOW ABOUT THIS MAN.
VERONICA... YOU KNOW ENOUGH.
FAR MORE THAN I WOULD'VE LIKED, TO BE HONEST. THIS WAS THE EXACT KIND OF DANGEROUS SECRET WE WERE TRYING TO KEEP YOU--
DING
DONG

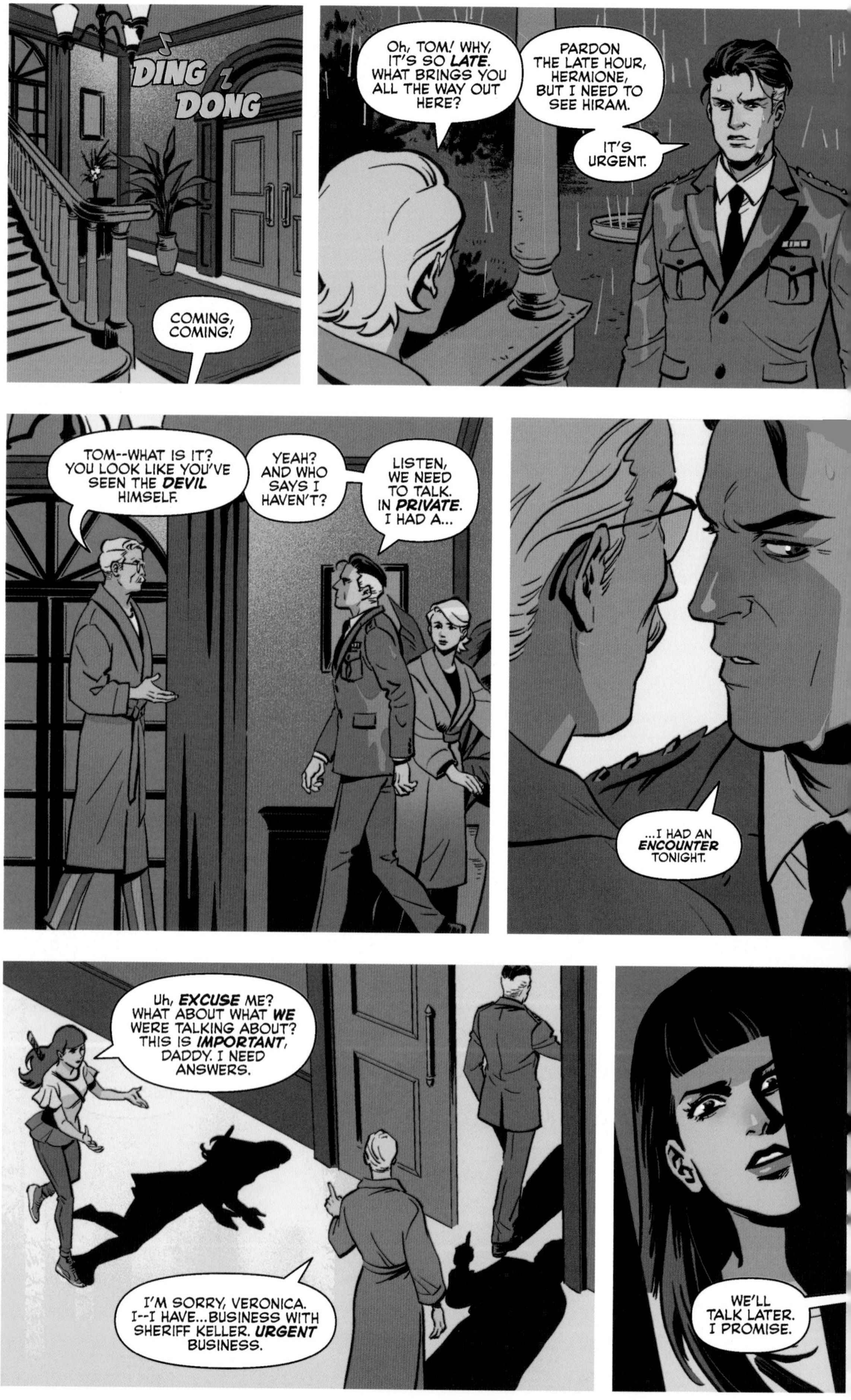
DING
DONG
COMING, COMING!
Oh, TOM! WHY, IT'S SO LATE. WHAT BRINGS YOU ALL THE WAY OUT HERE?
PARDON THE LATE HOUR, HERMIONE, BUT I NEED TO SEE HIRAM.
IT'S URGENT.
TOM--WHAT IS IT? YOU LOOK LIKE YOU'VE SEEN THE DEVIL HIMSELF.
YEAH? AND WHO SAYS I HAVEN'T?
LISTEN, WE NEED TO TALK. IN PRIVATE. I HAD A...
...I HAD AN ENCOUNTER TONIGHT.
Uh, EXCUSE ME? WHAT ABOUT WHAT WE WERE TALKING ABOUT? THIS IS IMPORTANT, DADDY. I NEED ANSWERS.
I'M SORRY, VERONICA. I--I HAVE...BUSINESS WITH SHERIFF KELLER. URGENT BUSINESS.
WE'LL TALK LATER. I PROMISE.

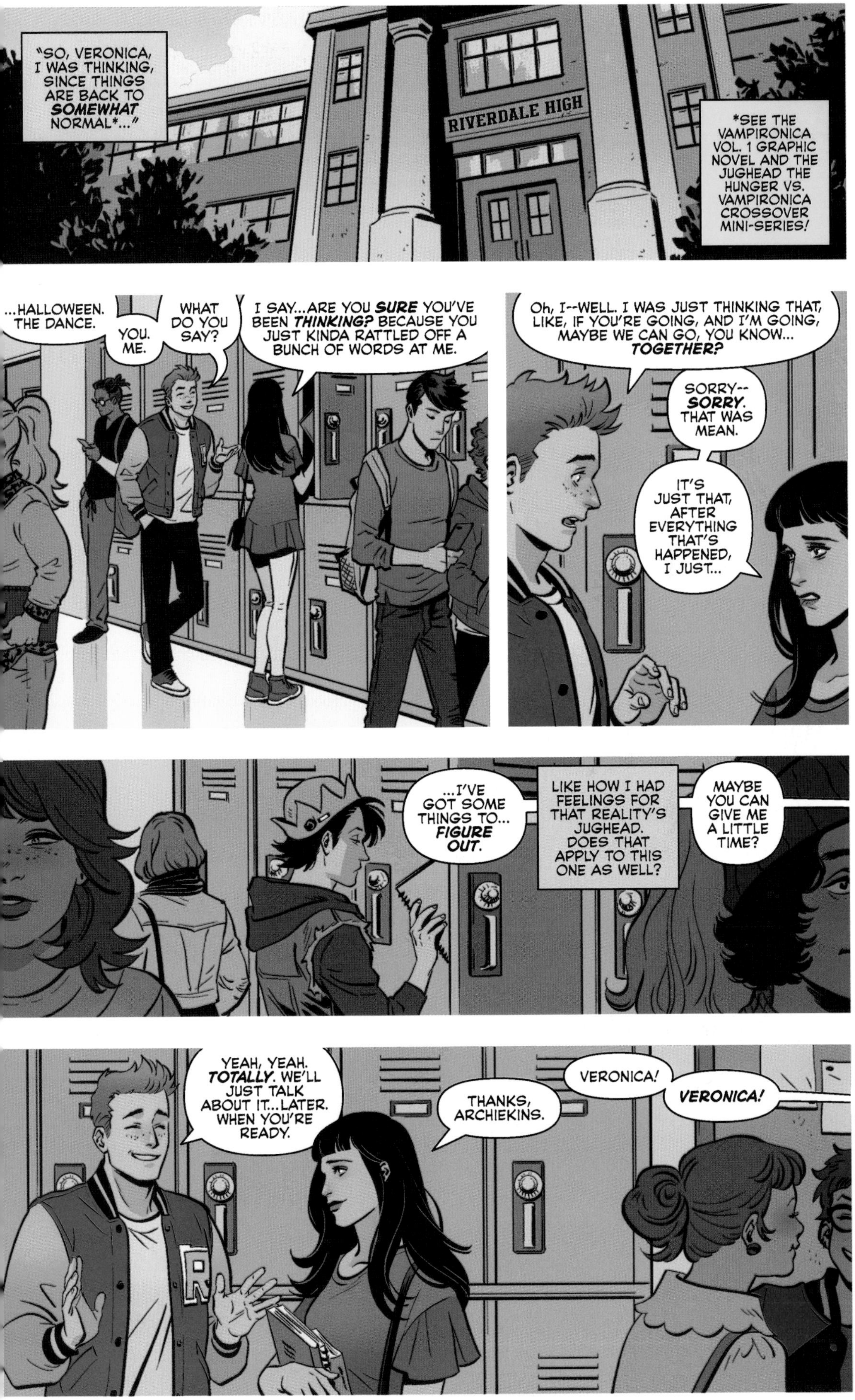
"SO, VERONICA, I WAS THINKING, SINCE THINGS ARE BACK TO *SOMEWHAT* NORMAL*..."
RIVERDALE HIGH
*SEE THE VAMPIRONICA VOL. 1 GRAPHIC NOVEL AND THE JUGHEAD THE HUNGER VS. VAMPIRONICA CROSSOVER MINI-SERIES!
...HALLOWEEN. THE DANCE.
YOU. ME.
WHAT DO YOU SAY?
I SAY...ARE YOU *SURE* YOU'VE BEEN *THINKING?* BECAUSE YOU JUST KINDA RATTLED OFF A BUNCH OF WORDS AT ME.
Oh, I--WELL. I WAS JUST THINKING THAT, LIKE, IF YOU'RE GOING, AND I'M GOING, MAYBE WE CAN GO, YOU KNOW... *TOGETHER?*
SORRY-- *SORRY*. THAT WAS MEAN.
IT'S JUST THAT, AFTER EVERYTHING THAT'S HAPPENED, I JUST...
...I'VE GOT SOME THINGS TO... *FIGURE OUT*.
LIKE HOW I HAD FEELINGS FOR THAT REALITY'S JUGHEAD. DOES THAT APPLY TO THIS ONE AS WELL?
MAYBE YOU CAN GIVE ME A LITTLE TIME?
YEAH, YEAH. *TOTALLY*. WE'LL JUST TALK ABOUT IT...LATER. WHEN YOU'RE READY.
THANKS, ARCHIEKINS.
VERONICA!
VERONICA!

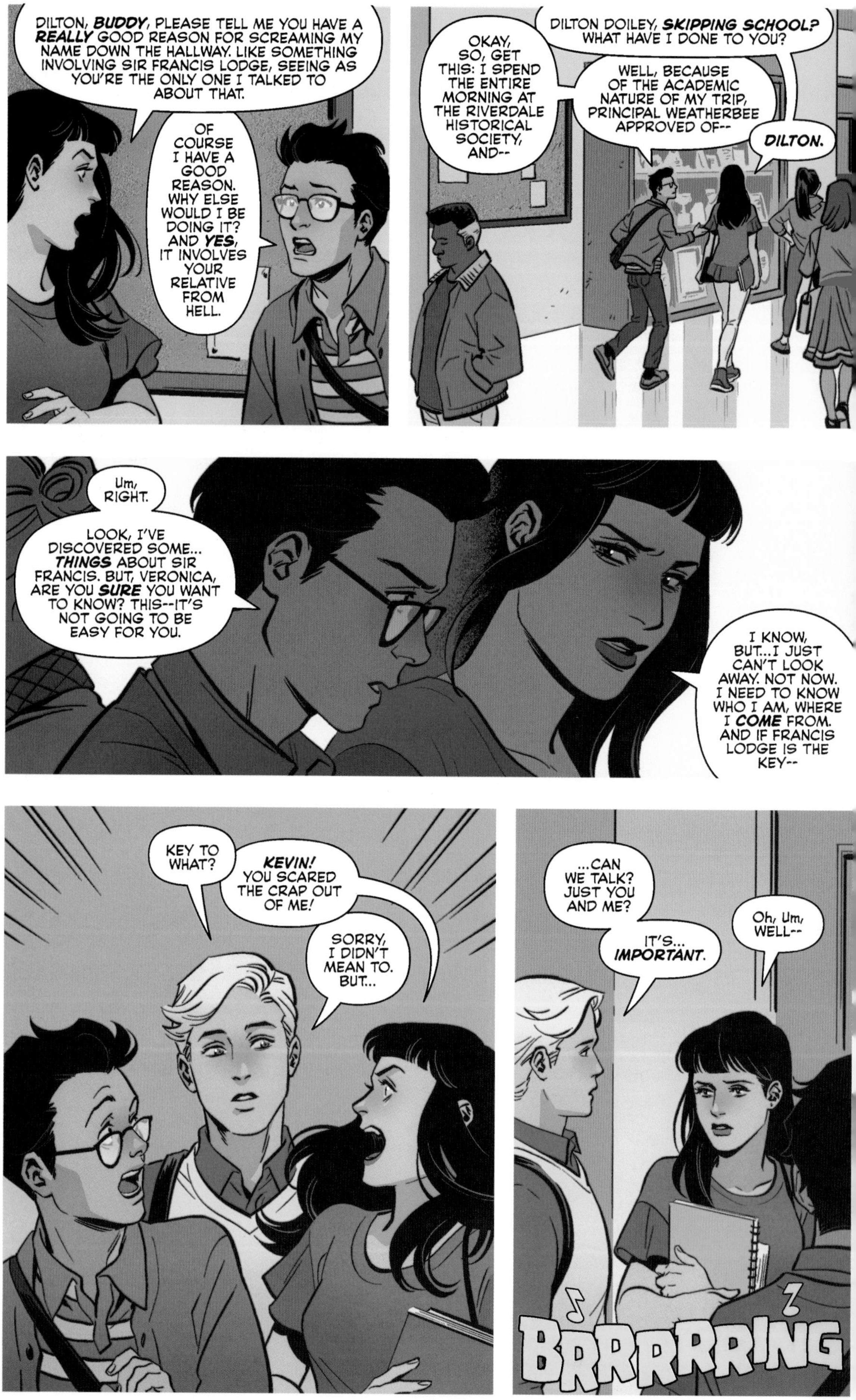
DILTON, **BUDDY**, PLEASE TELL ME YOU HAVE A **REALLY** GOOD REASON FOR SCREAMING MY NAME DOWN THE HALLWAY. LIKE SOMETHING INVOLVING SIR FRANCIS LODGE, SEEING AS YOU'RE THE ONLY ONE I TALKED TO ABOUT THAT.
OF COURSE I HAVE A GOOD REASON. WHY ELSE WOULD I BE DOING IT? AND **YES**, IT INVOLVES YOUR RELATIVE FROM HELL.
OKAY, SO, GET THIS: I SPEND THE ENTIRE MORNING AT THE RIVERDALE HISTORICAL SOCIETY, AND--
DILTON DOILEY, **SKIPPING SCHOOL?** WHAT HAVE I DONE TO YOU?
WELL, BECAUSE OF THE ACADEMIC NATURE OF MY TRIP, PRINCIPAL WEATHERBEE APPROVED OF--
DILTON.
Um, RIGHT.
LOOK, I'VE DISCOVERED SOME... **THINGS** ABOUT SIR FRANCIS. BUT, VERONICA, ARE YOU **SURE** YOU WANT TO KNOW? THIS--IT'S NOT GOING TO BE EASY FOR YOU.
I KNOW, BUT...I JUST CAN'T LOOK AWAY. NOT NOW. I NEED TO KNOW WHO I AM, WHERE I **COME** FROM. AND IF FRANCIS LODGE IS THE KEY--
KEY TO WHAT?
KEVIN! YOU SCARED THE CRAP OUT OF ME!
SORRY, I DIDN'T MEAN TO. BUT...
...CAN WE TALK? JUST YOU AND ME?
IT'S... **IMPORTANT**.
Oh, Um, WELL--
BRRRRRING

SORRY, KEV. GOTTA GET TO CLASS. MAYBE LATER?

ALL RIGHT, EVERYONE. SETTLE DOWN.

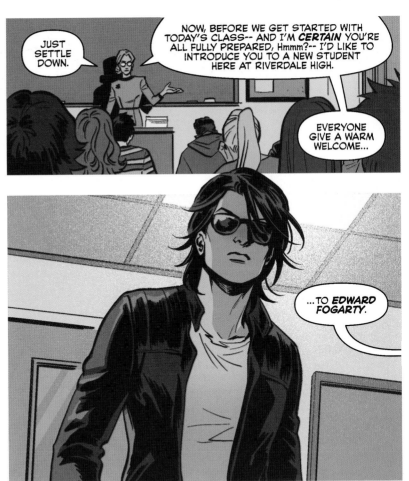

JUST SETTLE DOWN.

NOW, BEFORE WE GET STARTED WITH TODAY'S CLASS-- AND I'M *CERTAIN* YOU'RE ALL FULLY PREPARED, Hmmm?-- I'D LIKE TO INTRODUCE YOU TO A NEW STUDENT HERE AT RIVERDALE HIGH.

EVERYONE GIVE A WARM WELCOME...

...TO *EDWARD FOGARTY.*

HEY.

YOU KNOW ME? KNOW WHO I AM?

I USED TO *BE* RIVERDALE, SAME AS YOU. THEY NEVER TALK ABOUT ME?

MAYBE ONE DAY THEY'LL TALK ABOUT THE KID WHO GOT DETENTION IN HIS FIRST FIVE MINUTES OF SCHOOL.

COME ON. THINK *REAL* HARD.

THEY USED TO CALL ME *FANGS.*

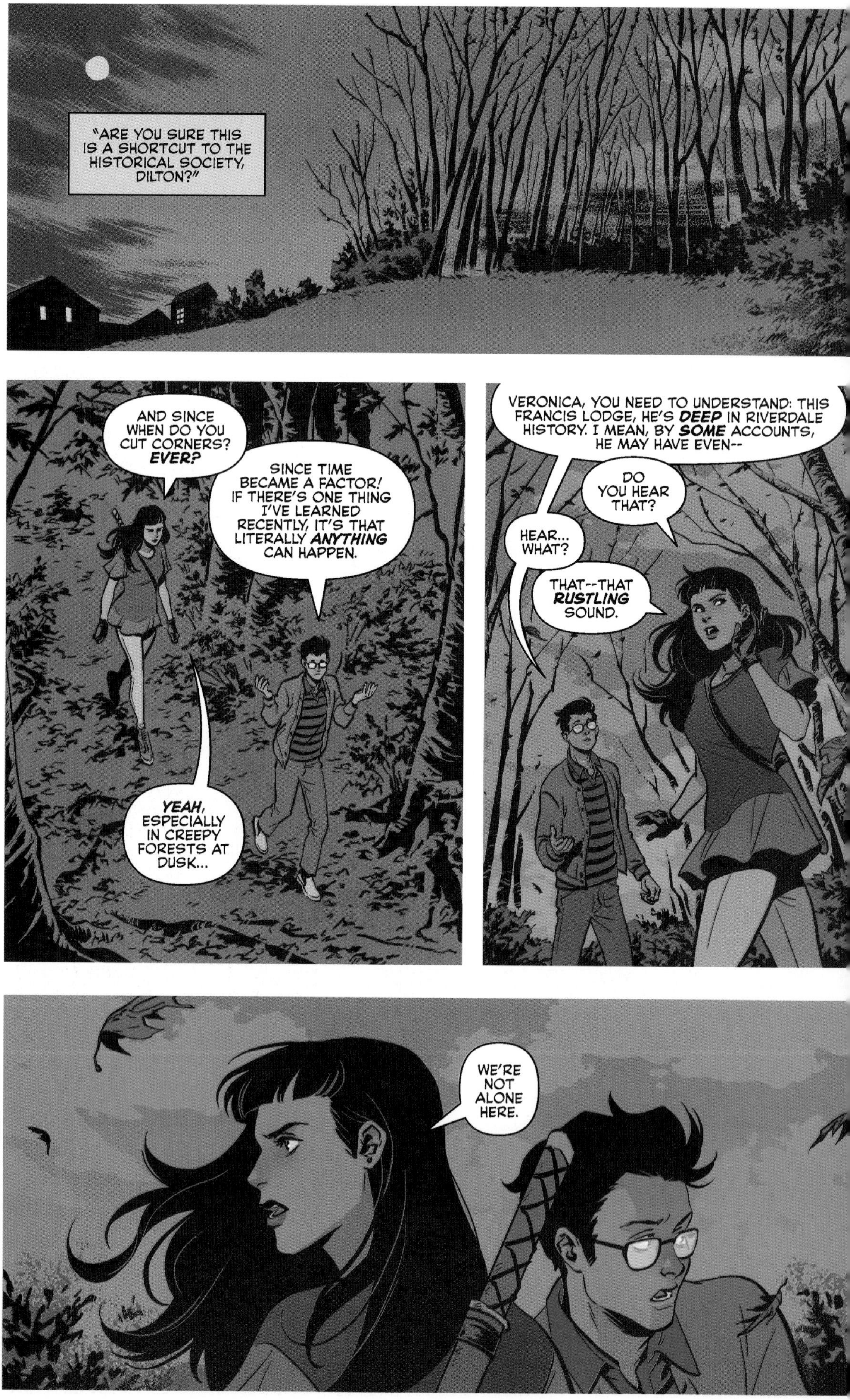
"ARE YOU SURE THIS IS A SHORTCUT TO THE HISTORICAL SOCIETY, DILTON?"
AND SINCE WHEN DO YOU CUT CORNERS? EVER?
SINCE TIME BECAME A FACTOR! IF THERE'S ONE THING I'VE LEARNED RECENTLY, IT'S THAT LITERALLY ANYTHING CAN HAPPEN.
YEAH, ESPECIALLY IN CREEPY FORESTS AT DUSK...
VERONICA, YOU NEED TO UNDERSTAND: THIS FRANCIS LODGE, HE'S DEEP IN RIVERDALE HISTORY. I MEAN, BY SOME ACCOUNTS, HE MAY HAVE EVEN--
DO YOU HEAR THAT?
HEAR... WHAT?
THAT--THAT RUSTLING SOUND.
WE'RE NOT ALONE HERE.

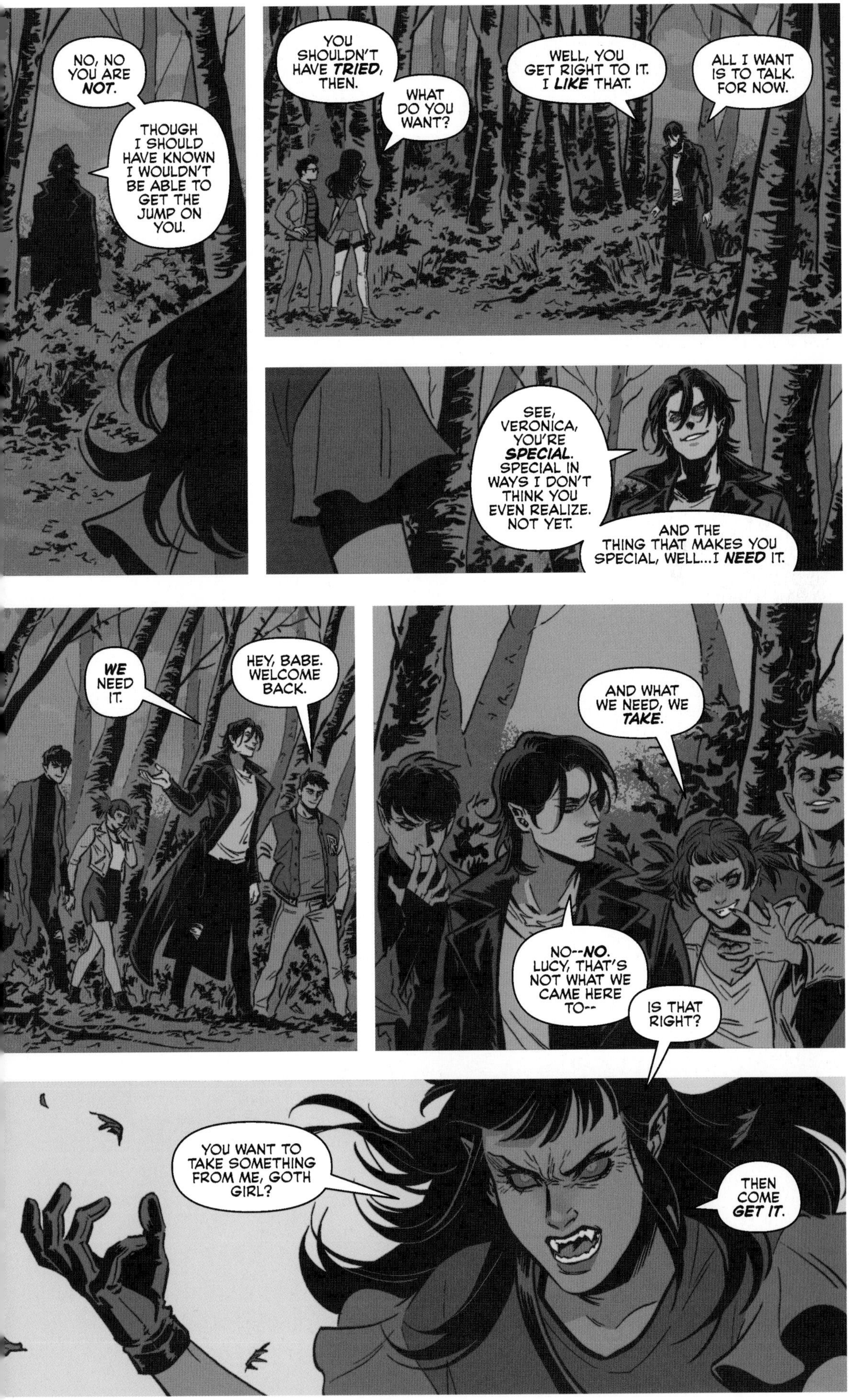
NO, NO YOU ARE NOT.
THOUGH I SHOULD HAVE KNOWN I WOULDN'T BE ABLE TO GET THE JUMP ON YOU.
YOU SHOULDN'T HAVE TRIED, THEN.
WHAT DO YOU WANT?
WELL, YOU GET RIGHT TO IT. I LIKE THAT.
ALL I WANT IS TO TALK. FOR NOW.
SEE, VERONICA, YOU'RE SPECIAL. SPECIAL IN WAYS I DON'T THINK YOU EVEN REALIZE. NOT YET.
AND THE THING THAT MAKES YOU SPECIAL, WELL...I NEED IT.
WE NEED IT.
HEY, BABE. WELCOME BACK.
AND WHAT WE NEED, WE TAKE.
NO--NO. LUCY, THAT'S NOT WHAT WE CAME HERE TO--
IS THAT RIGHT?
YOU WANT TO TAKE SOMETHING FROM ME, GOTH GIRL?
THEN COME GET IT.

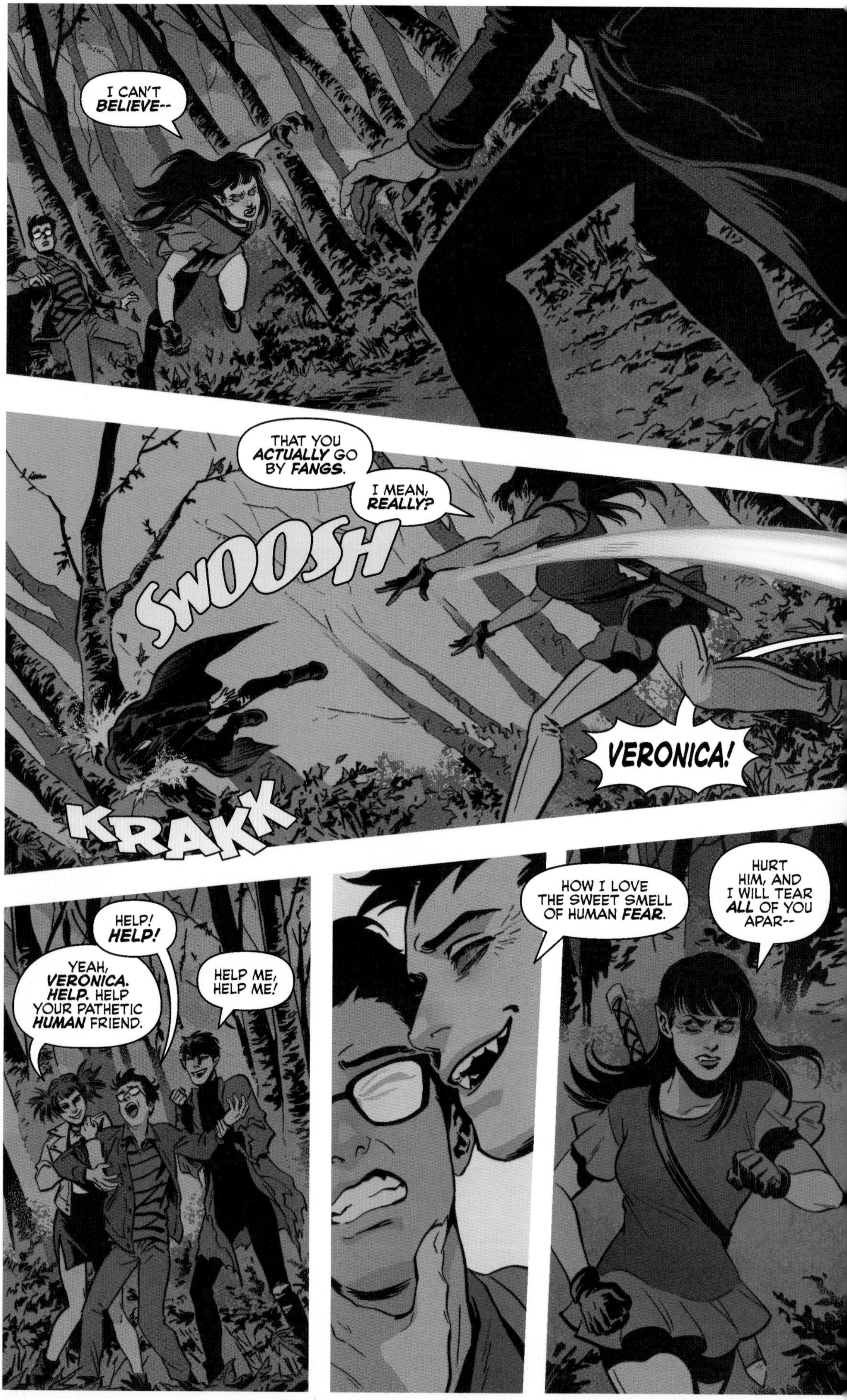
I CAN'T BELIEVE--
THAT YOU ACTUALLY GO BY FANGS.
I MEAN, REALLY?
SWOOSH
VERONICA!
KRAKK
HELP! HELP!
YEAH, VERONICA. HELP. HELP YOUR PATHETIC HUMAN FRIEND.
HELP ME, HELP ME!
HOW I LOVE THE SWEET SMELL OF HUMAN FEAR.
HURT HIM, AND I WILL TEAR ALL OF YOU APAR--

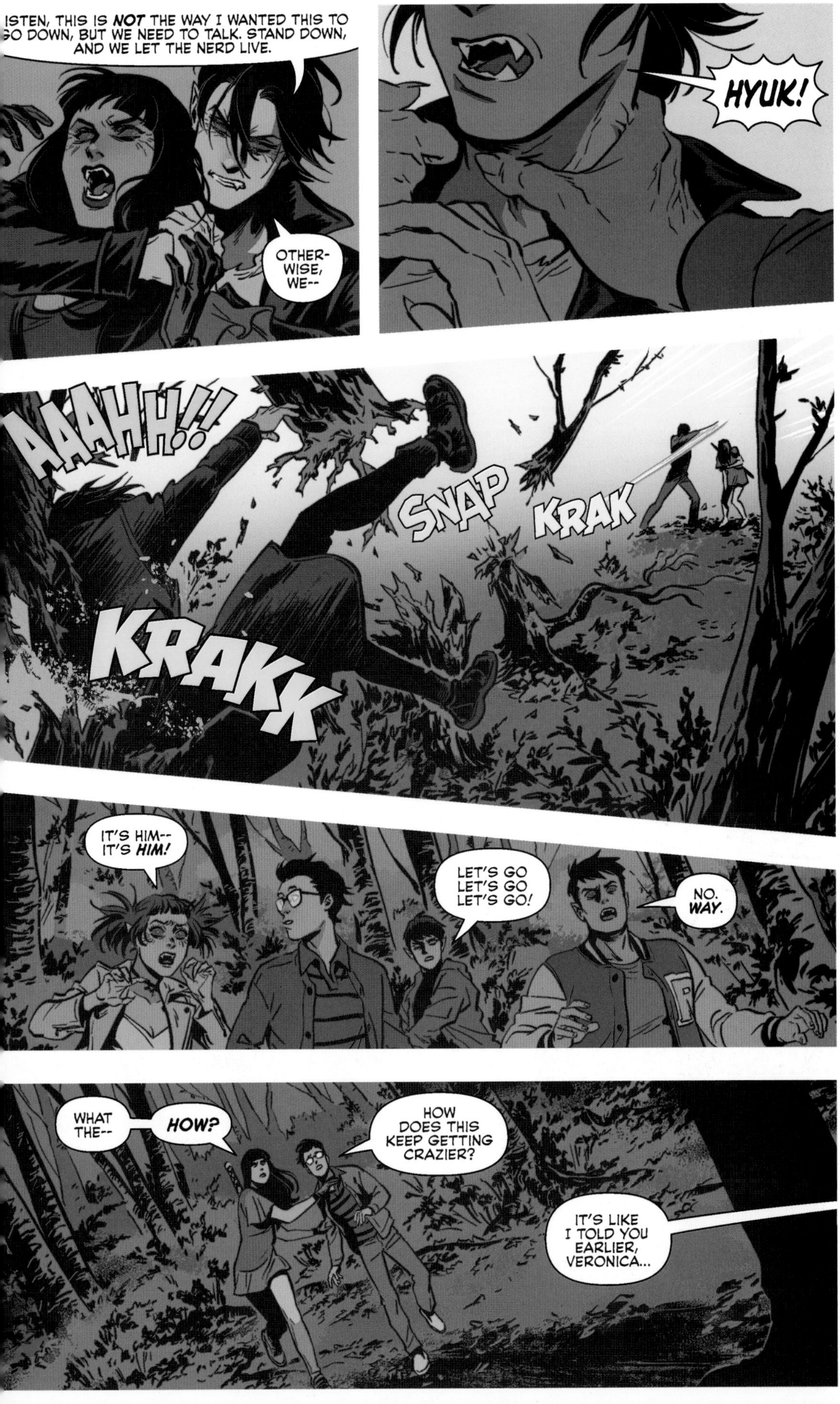
ISTEN, THIS IS NOT THE WAY I WANTED THIS TO GO DOWN, BUT WE NEED TO TALK. STAND DOWN, AND WE LET THE NERD LIVE.
OTHER-WISE, WE--
HYUK!
AAAHH!!
SNAP
KRAK
KRAKK
IT'S HIM-- IT'S HIM!
LET'S GO LET'S GO LET'S GO!
NO. WAY.
WHAT THE--
HOW?
HOW DOES THIS KEEP GETTING CRAZIER?
IT'S LIKE I TOLD YOU EARLIER, VERONICA...

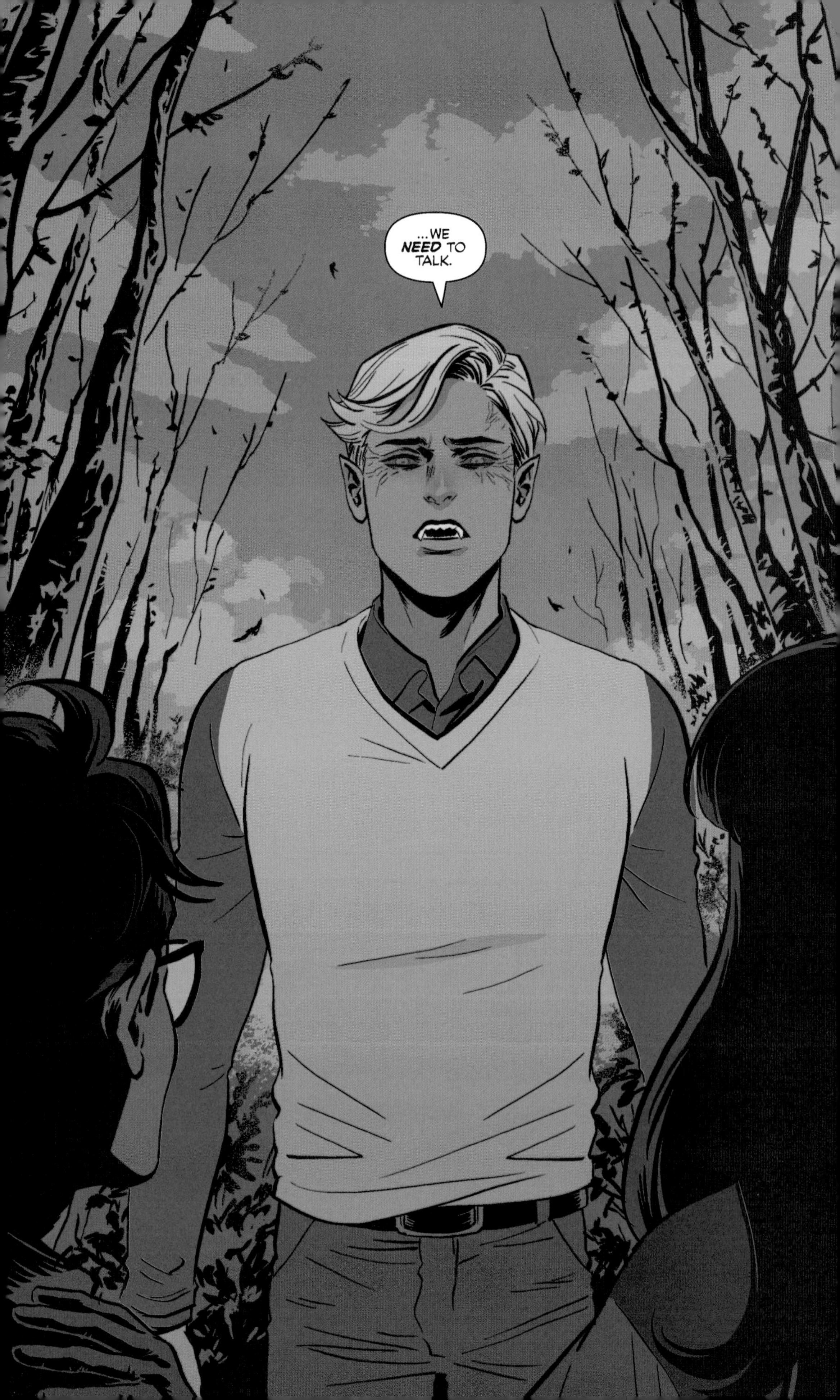
...WE *NEED* TO TALK.

TO BE CONTINUED

CHAPTER TWO

COVER ART BY **AUDREY MOK**

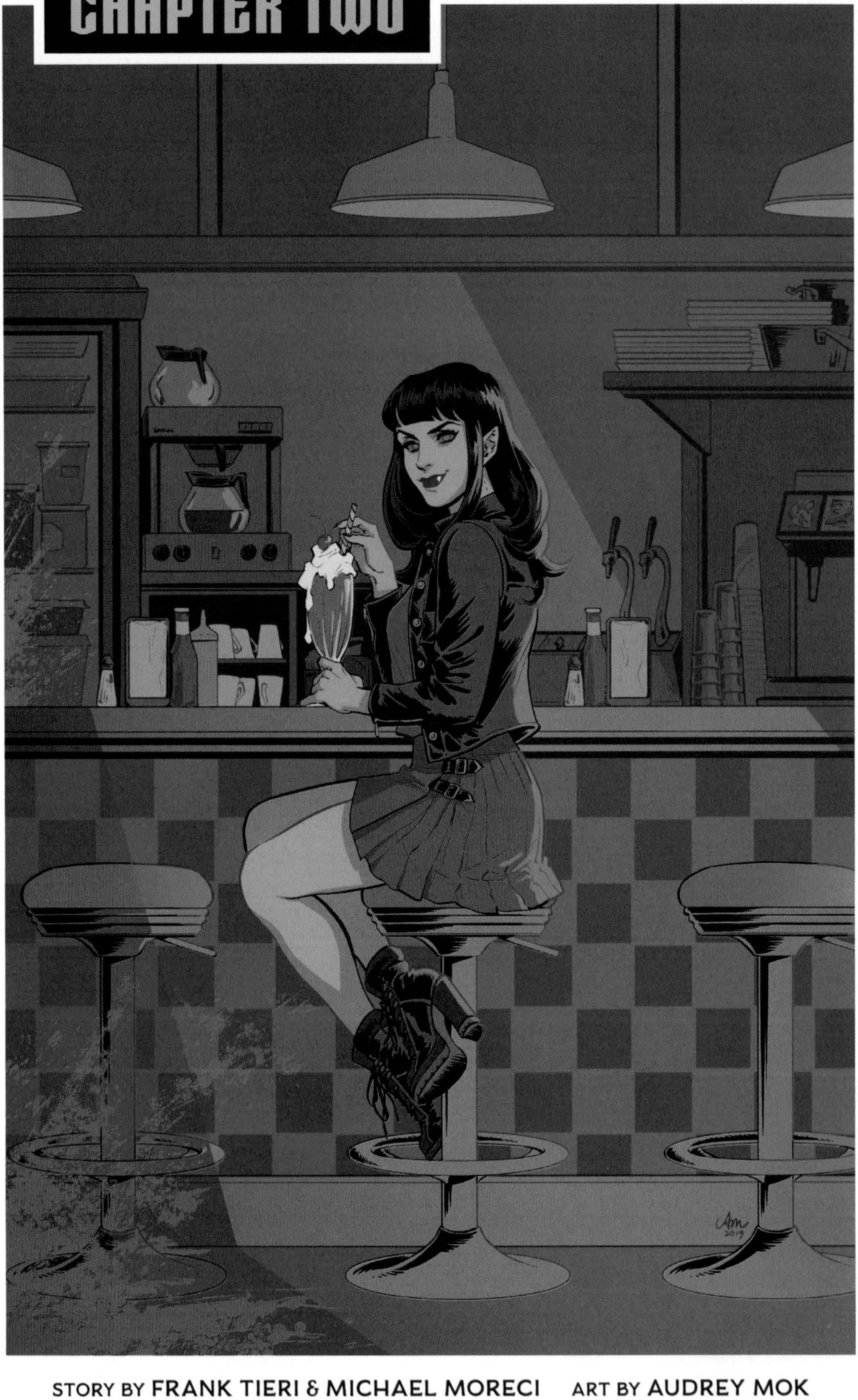

STORY BY **FRANK TIERI & MICHAEL MORECI** ART BY **AUDREY MOK**
COLORING BY **LEE LOUGHRIDGE** LETTERING BY **JACK MORELLI**

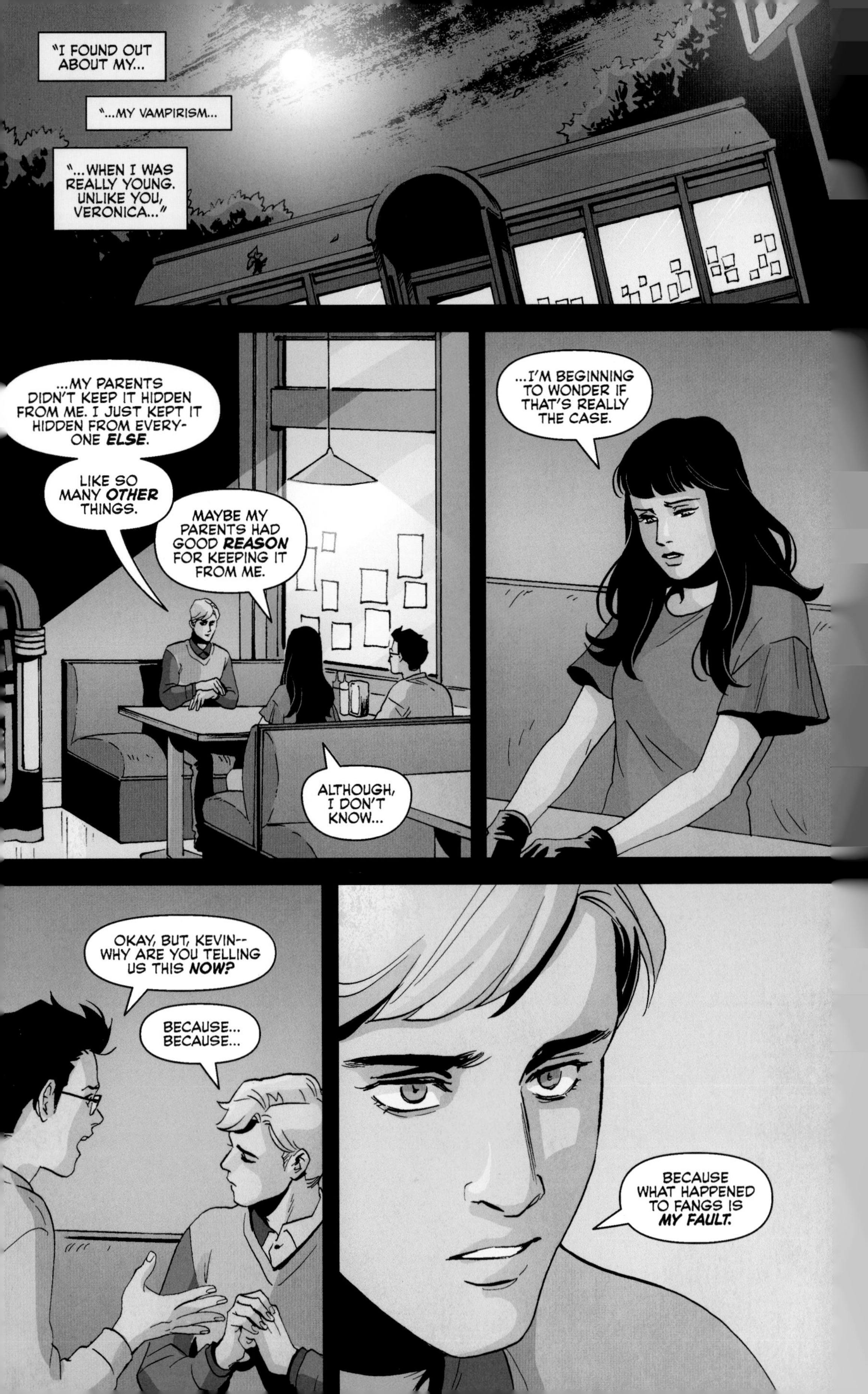
"I FOUND OUT ABOUT MY...
"...MY VAMPIRISM...
"...WHEN I WAS REALLY YOUNG. UNLIKE YOU, VERONICA..."
...MY PARENTS DIDN'T KEEP IT HIDDEN FROM ME. I JUST KEPT IT HIDDEN FROM EVERY-ONE *ELSE*.
LIKE SO MANY *OTHER* THINGS.
MAYBE MY PARENTS HAD GOOD *REASON* FOR KEEPING IT FROM ME.
ALTHOUGH, I DON'T KNOW...
...I'M BEGINNING TO WONDER IF THAT'S REALLY THE CASE.
OKAY, BUT, KEVIN-- WHY ARE YOU TELLING US THIS *NOW?*
BECAUSE... BECAUSE...
BECAUSE WHAT HAPPENED TO FANGS IS *MY FAULT.*

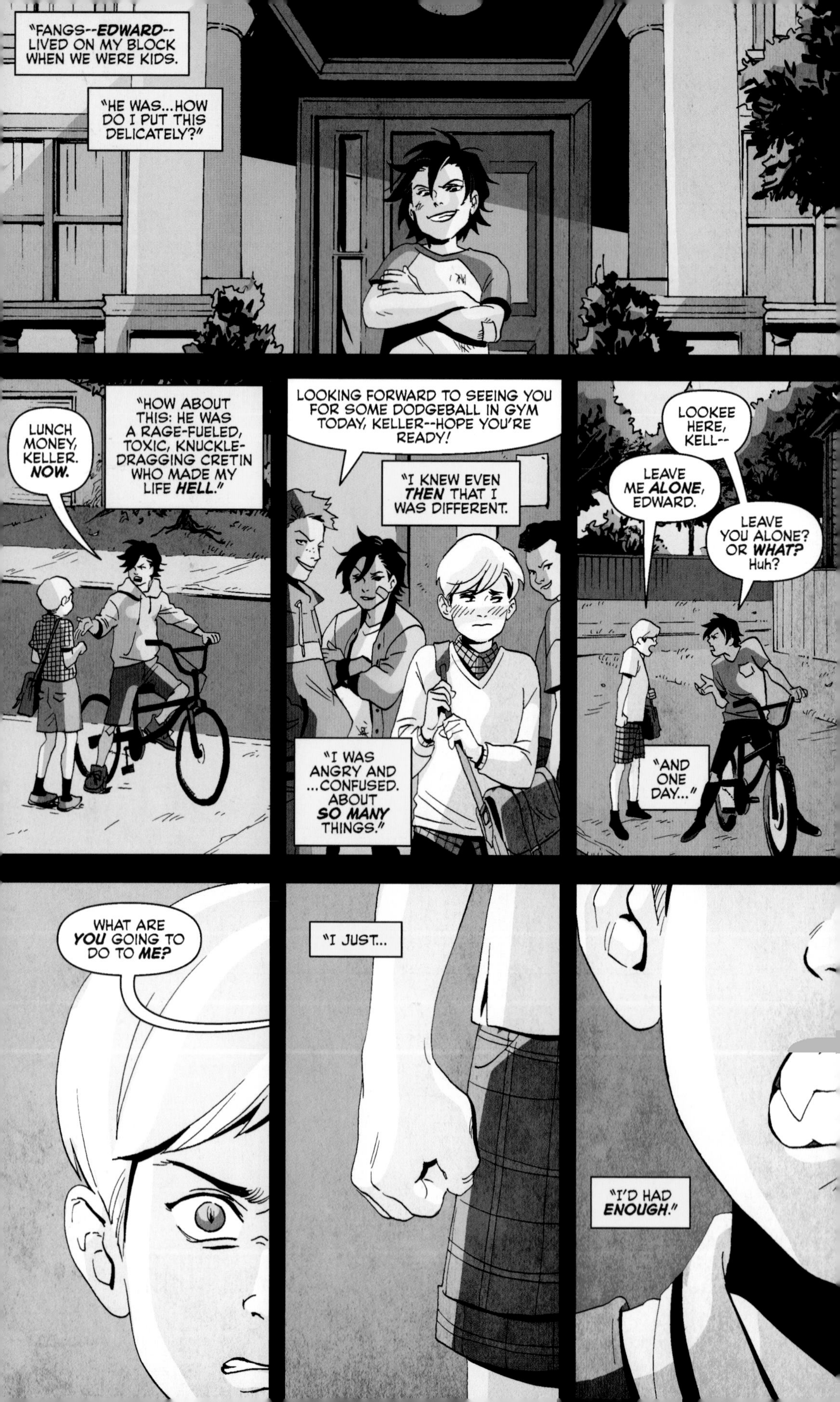

"FANGS--EDWARD--LIVED ON MY BLOCK WHEN WE WERE KIDS.
"HE WAS...HOW DO I PUT THIS DELICATELY?"
LUNCH MONEY, KELLER. NOW.
"HOW ABOUT THIS: HE WAS A RAGE-FUELED, TOXIC, KNUCKLE-DRAGGING CRETIN WHO MADE MY LIFE HELL."
LOOKING FORWARD TO SEEING YOU FOR SOME DODGEBALL IN GYM TODAY, KELLER--HOPE YOU'RE READY!
"I KNEW EVEN THEN THAT I WAS DIFFERENT.
"I WAS ANGRY AND ...CONFUSED. ABOUT SO MANY THINGS."
LOOKEE HERE, KELL--
LEAVE ME ALONE, EDWARD.
LEAVE YOU ALONE? OR WHAT? Huh?
"AND ONE DAY..."
WHAT ARE YOU GOING TO DO TO ME?
"I JUST...
"I'D HAD ENOUGH."

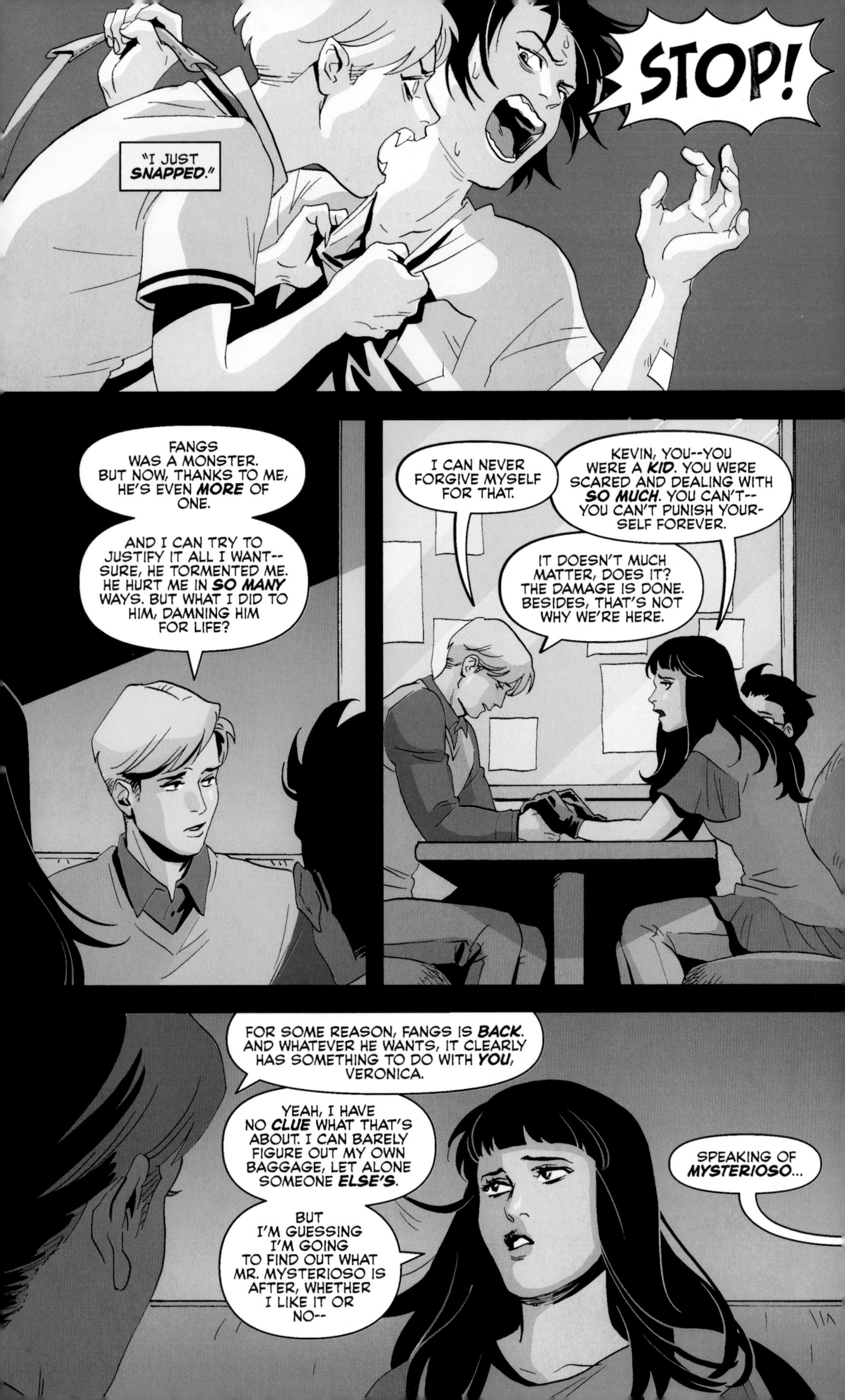
STOP!
"I JUST SNAPPED."
FANGS WAS A MONSTER. BUT NOW, THANKS TO ME, HE'S EVEN MORE OF ONE.
AND I CAN TRY TO JUSTIFY IT ALL I WANT-- SURE, HE TORMENTED ME. HE HURT ME IN SO MANY WAYS. BUT WHAT I DID TO HIM, DAMNING HIM FOR LIFE?
I CAN NEVER FORGIVE MYSELF FOR THAT.
KEVIN, YOU--YOU WERE A KID. YOU WERE SCARED AND DEALING WITH SO MUCH. YOU CAN'T-- YOU CAN'T PUNISH YOURSELF FOREVER.
IT DOESN'T MUCH MATTER, DOES IT? THE DAMAGE IS DONE. BESIDES, THAT'S NOT WHY WE'RE HERE.
FOR SOME REASON, FANGS IS BACK. AND WHATEVER HE WANTS, IT CLEARLY HAS SOMETHING TO DO WITH YOU, VERONICA.
YEAH, I HAVE NO CLUE WHAT THAT'S ABOUT. I CAN BARELY FIGURE OUT MY OWN BAGGAGE, LET ALONE SOMEONE ELSE'S.
BUT I'M GUESSING I'M GOING TO FIND OUT WHAT MR. MYSTERIOSO IS AFTER, WHETHER I LIKE IT OR NO--
SPEAKING OF MYSTERIOSO...

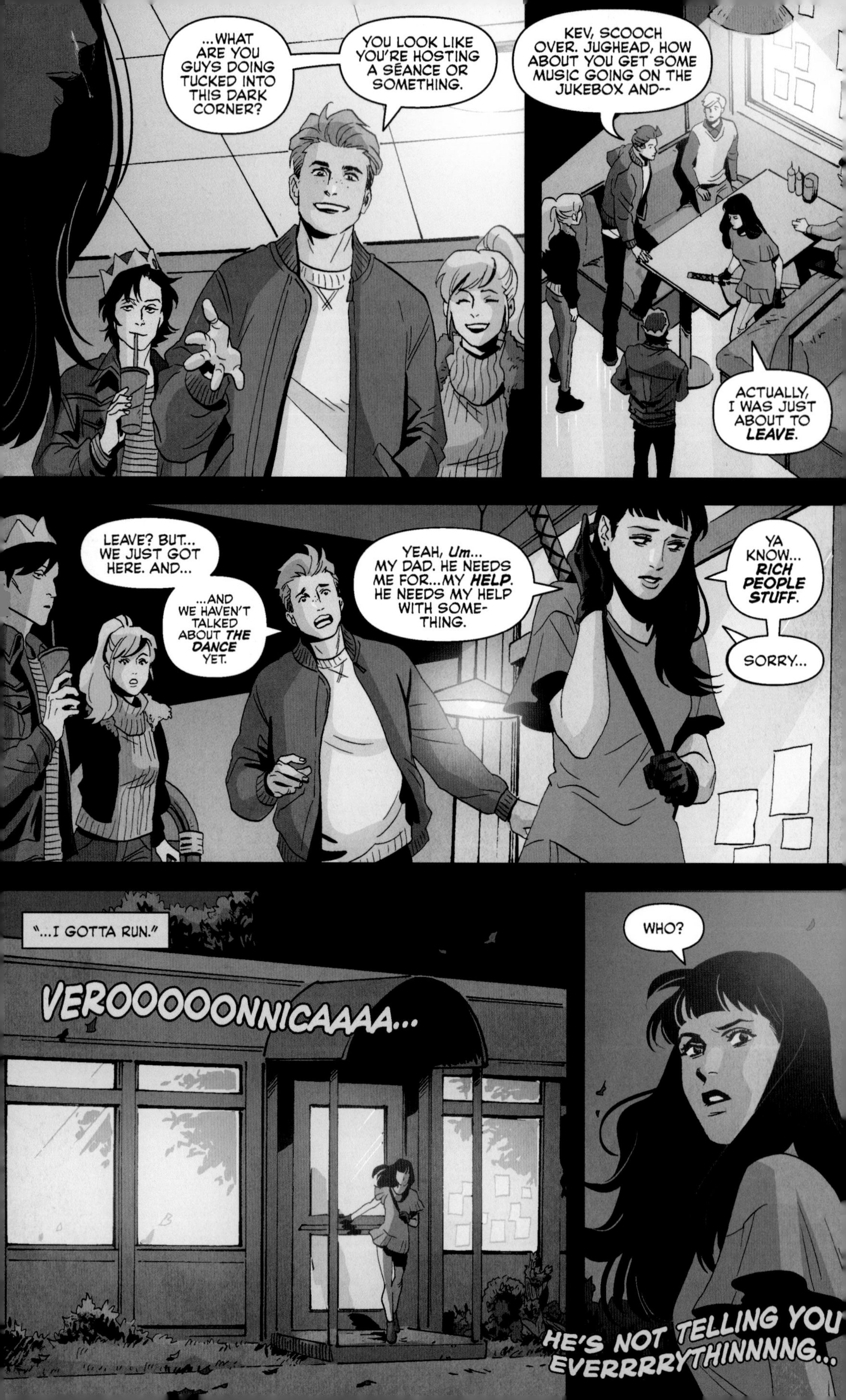
...WHAT ARE YOU GUYS DOING TUCKED INTO THIS DARK CORNER?
YOU LOOK LIKE YOU'RE HOSTING A SÉANCE OR SOMETHING.
KEV, SCOOCH OVER. JUGHEAD, HOW ABOUT YOU GET SOME MUSIC GOING ON THE JUKEBOX AND--
ACTUALLY, I WAS JUST ABOUT TO LEAVE.
LEAVE? BUT... WE JUST GOT HERE. AND...
...AND WE HAVEN'T TALKED ABOUT THE DANCE YET.
YEAH, Um... MY DAD. HE NEEDS ME FOR...MY HELP. HE NEEDS MY HELP WITH SOME-THING.
YA KNOW... RICH PEOPLE STUFF.
SORRY...
"...I GOTTA RUN."
VEROOOOONNICAAAA...
WHO?
HE'S NOT TELLING YOU EVERRRRYTHINNNNG...

BUT NOW PLEASE HEAR ME OUT...

YOU KNOW, I LEFT MY FAMILY WHEN I WAS A KID BECAUSE IT WAS THE ONLY WAY FOR ME NOT TO *DEVOUR THEM.* SO, YOU CAN SAY I'VE BEEN *AROUND.* AND YOU WANT TO KNOW ONE THING I'VE LEARNED?

NOT REALLY.

PEOPLE WHO *RESPECT* YOU...

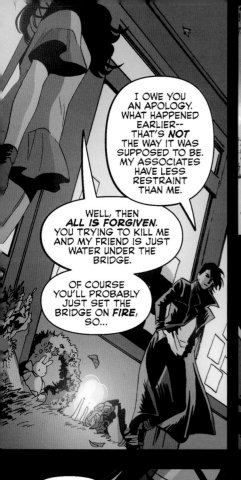

I OWE YOU AN APOLOGY. WHAT HAPPENED EARLIER-- THAT'S *NOT* THE WAY IT WAS SUPPOSED TO BE. MY ASSOCIATES HAVE LESS RESTRAINT THAN ME.

WELL, THEN *ALL IS FORGIVEN.* YOU TRYING TO KILL ME AND MY FRIEND IS JUST WATER UNDER THE BRIDGE.

OF COURSE YOU'LL PROBABLY JUST SET THE BRIDGE ON *FIRE,* SO...

...THEY TELL YOU THE *TRUTH.* THE *WHOLE* TRUTH.

I GET THE FEELING NOT MANY PEOPLE RESPECT YOU, RONNIE. BUT--

YOU DON'T *KNOW ME.*

BUT. THEY *SHOULD.*

AND I'M GUESSING YOU WOULD, RIGHT?

YOU'LL SEE.

DING

YOU'LL SEE...

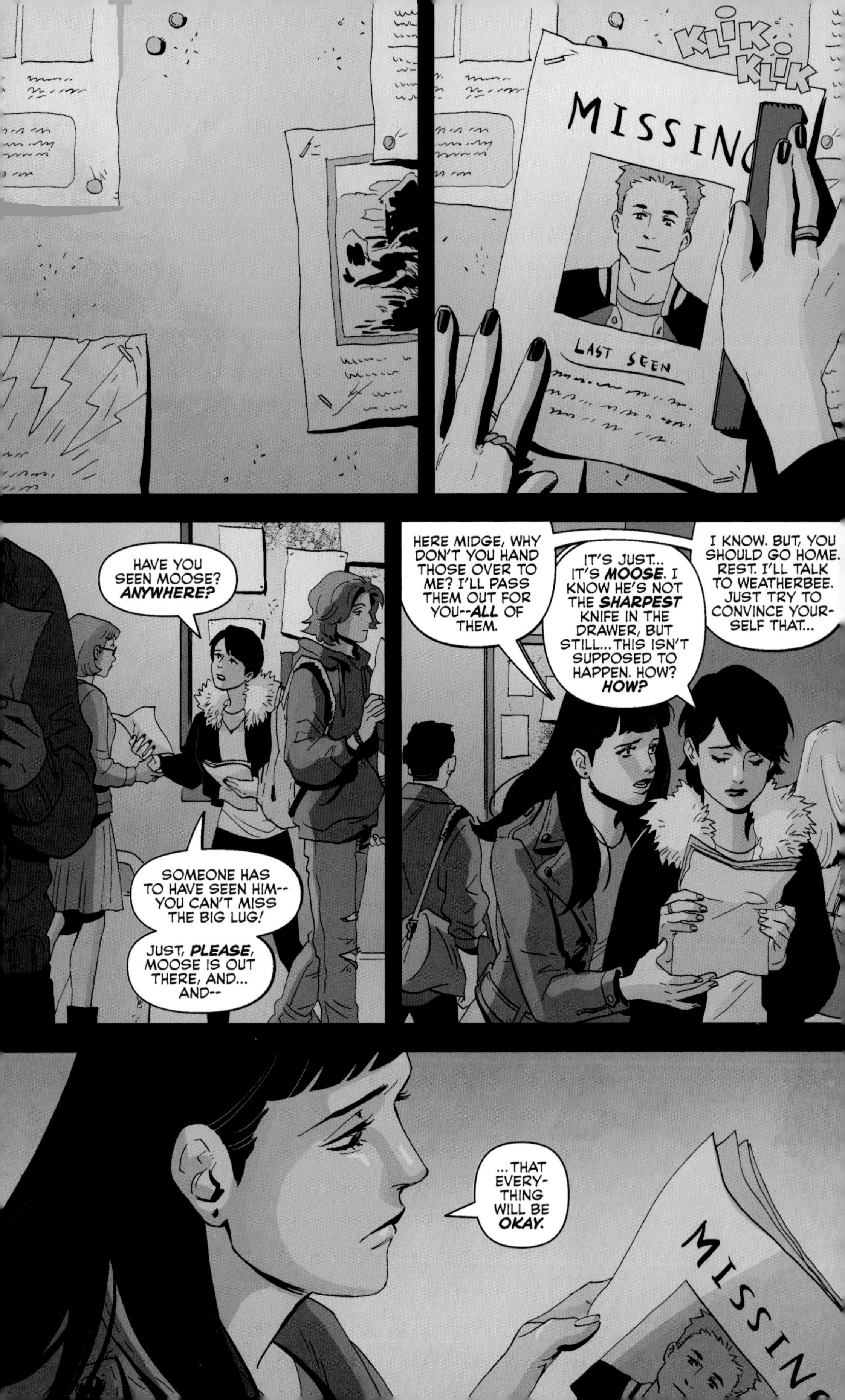
KLIK KLIK
MISSING
LAST SEEN
HAVE YOU SEEN MOOSE? ANYWHERE?
SOMEONE HAS TO HAVE SEEN HIM-- YOU CAN'T MISS THE BIG LUG!
JUST, PLEASE, MOOSE IS OUT THERE, AND... AND--
HERE MIDGE, WHY DON'T YOU HAND THOSE OVER TO ME? I'LL PASS THEM OUT FOR YOU--ALL OF THEM.
IT'S JUST... IT'S MOOSE. I KNOW HE'S NOT THE SHARPEST KNIFE IN THE DRAWER, BUT STILL... THIS ISN'T SUPPOSED TO HAPPEN. HOW? HOW?
I KNOW. BUT, YOU SHOULD GO HOME. REST. I'LL TALK TO WEATHERBEE. JUST TRY TO CONVINCE YOURSELF THAT...
...THAT EVERYTHING WILL BE OKAY.
MISSIN

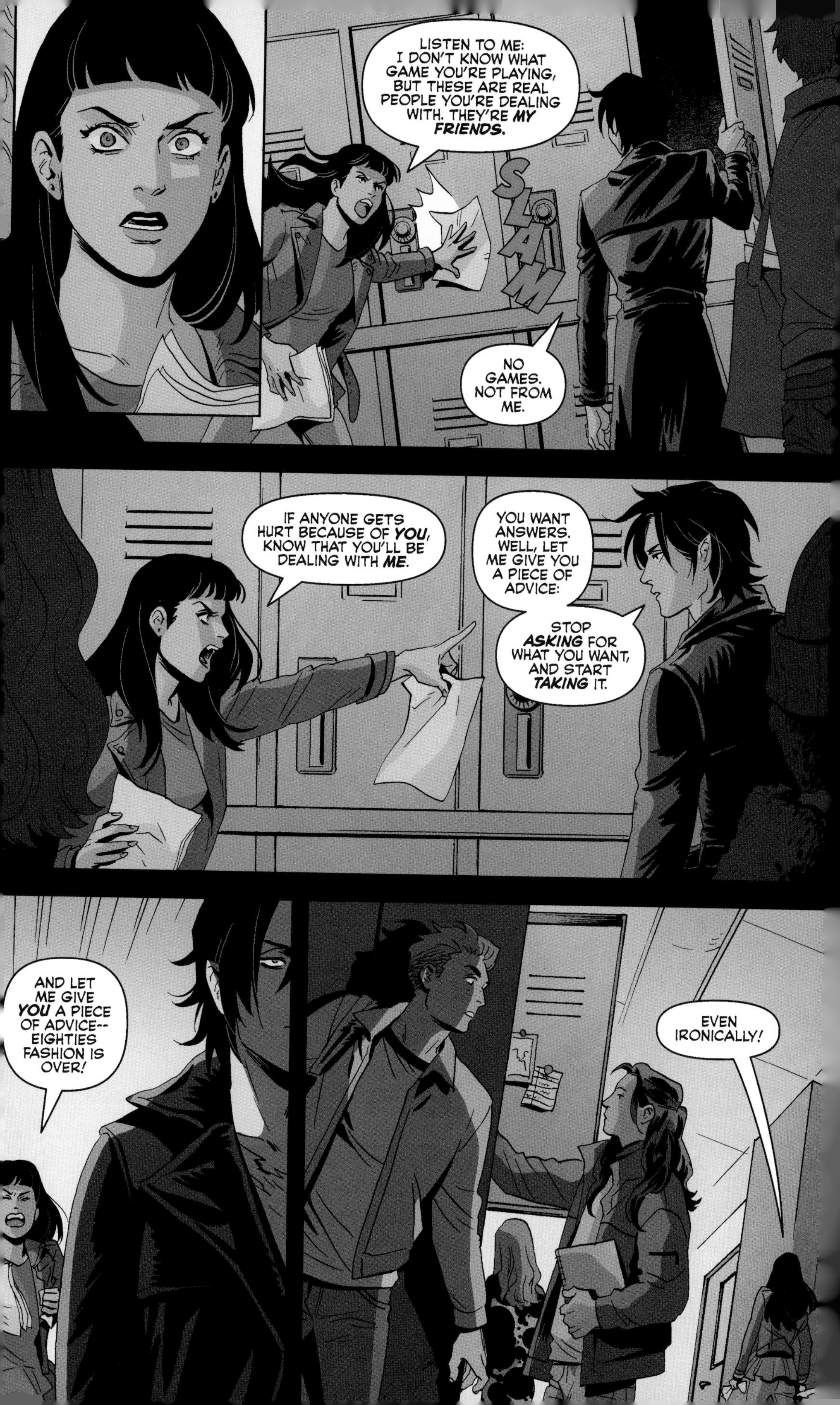
LISTEN TO ME: I DON'T KNOW WHAT GAME YOU'RE PLAYING, BUT THESE ARE REAL PEOPLE YOU'RE DEALING WITH. THEY'RE *MY FRIENDS.*
SLAM
NO GAMES. NOT FROM ME.
IF ANYONE GETS HURT BECAUSE OF *YOU*, KNOW THAT YOU'LL BE DEALING WITH *ME*.
YOU WANT ANSWERS. WELL, LET ME GIVE YOU A PIECE OF ADVICE:
STOP *ASKING* FOR WHAT YOU WANT, AND START *TAKING* IT.
AND LET ME GIVE *YOU* A PIECE OF ADVICE-- EIGHTIES FASHION IS OVER!
EVEN IRONICALLY!

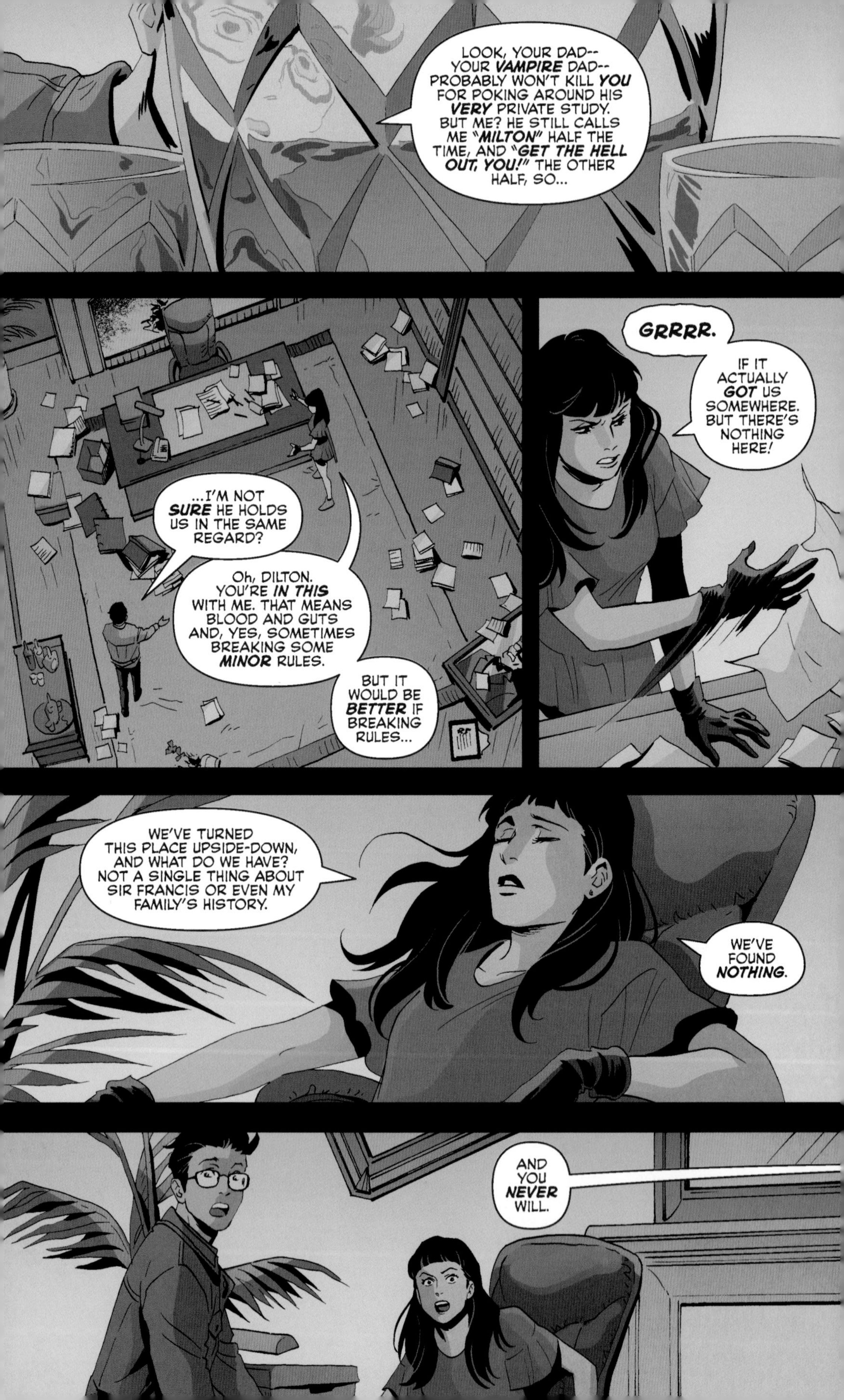
LOOK, YOUR DAD-- YOUR VAMPIRE DAD-- PROBABLY WON'T KILL YOU FOR POKING AROUND HIS VERY PRIVATE STUDY. BUT ME? HE STILL CALLS ME "MILTON" HALF THE TIME, AND "GET THE HELL OUT, YOU!" THE OTHER HALF, SO...
...I'M NOT SURE HE HOLDS US IN THE SAME REGARD?
Oh, DILTON. YOU'RE IN THIS WITH ME. THAT MEANS BLOOD AND GUTS AND, YES, SOMETIMES BREAKING SOME MINOR RULES.
BUT IT WOULD BE BETTER IF BREAKING RULES...
GRRRR.
IF IT ACTUALLY GOT US SOMEWHERE. BUT THERE'S NOTHING HERE!
WE'VE TURNED THIS PLACE UPSIDE-DOWN, AND WHAT DO WE HAVE? NOT A SINGLE THING ABOUT SIR FRANCIS OR EVEN MY FAMILY'S HISTORY.
WE'VE FOUND NOTHING.
AND YOU NEVER WILL.

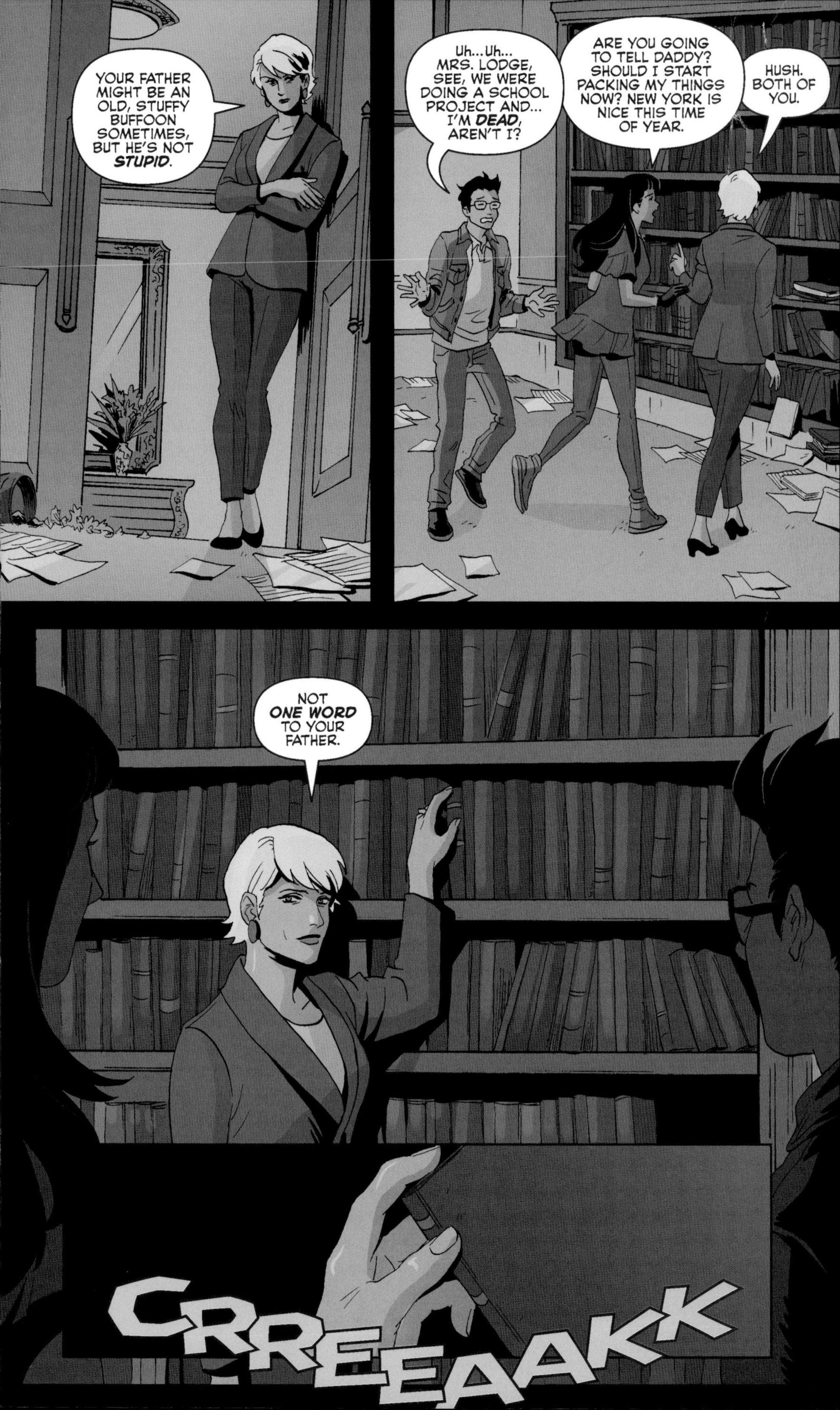
YOUR FATHER MIGHT BE AN OLD, STUFFY BUFFOON SOMETIMES, BUT HE'S NOT *STUPID*.
Uh...Uh... MRS. LODGE, SEE, WE WERE DOING A SCHOOL PROJECT AND... I'M *DEAD*, AREN'T I?
ARE YOU GOING TO TELL DADDY? SHOULD I START PACKING MY THINGS NOW? NEW YORK IS NICE THIS TIME OF YEAR.
HUSH. BOTH OF YOU.
NOT *ONE WORD* TO YOUR FATHER.
CRREEAAKK

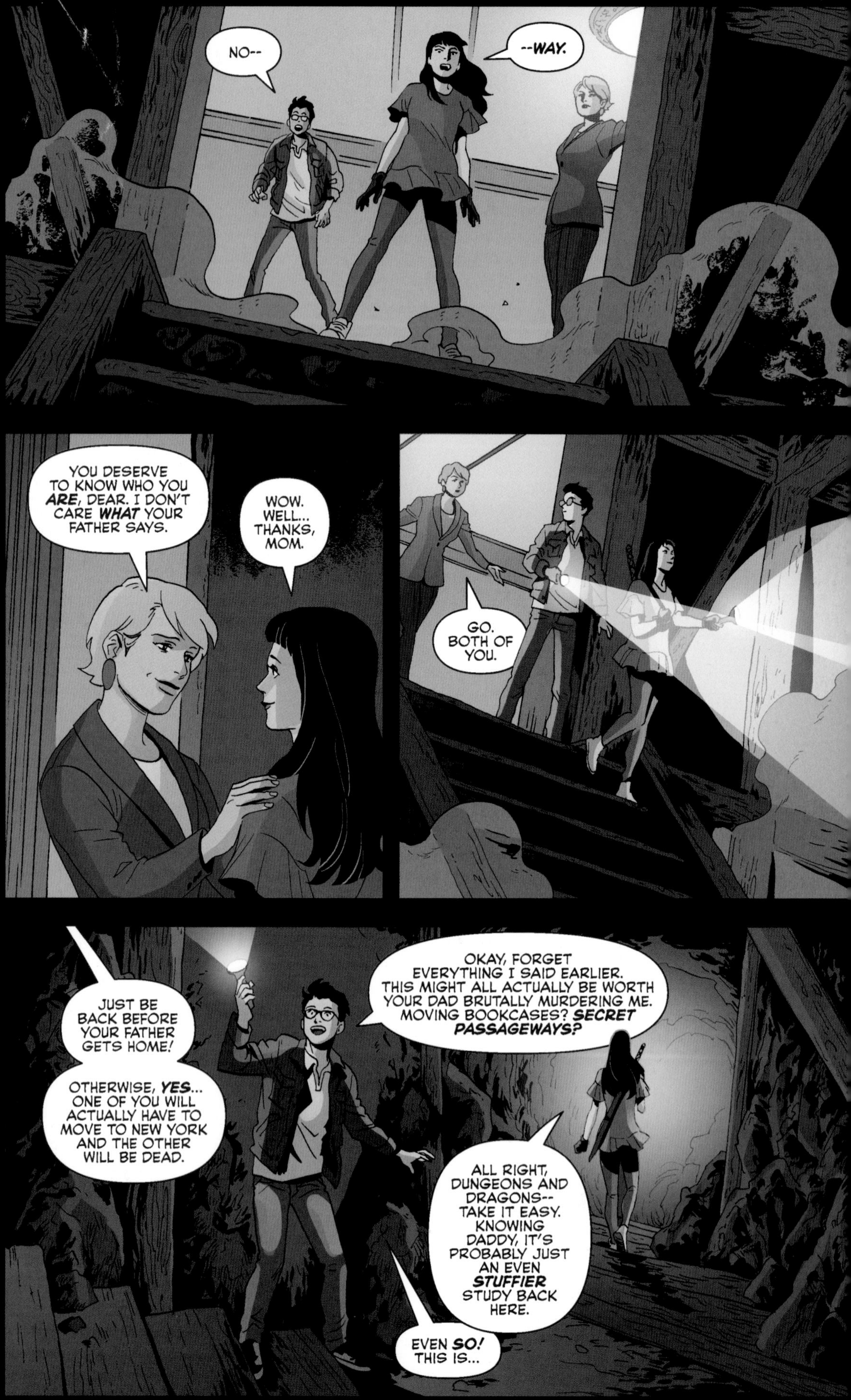
NO--
--WAY.
YOU DESERVE TO KNOW WHO YOU ARE, DEAR. I DON'T CARE WHAT YOUR FATHER SAYS.
WOW. WELL... THANKS, MOM.
GO. BOTH OF YOU.
JUST BE BACK BEFORE YOUR FATHER GETS HOME!
OTHERWISE, YES... ONE OF YOU WILL ACTUALLY HAVE TO MOVE TO NEW YORK AND THE OTHER WILL BE DEAD.
OKAY, FORGET EVERYTHING I SAID EARLIER. THIS MIGHT ALL ACTUALLY BE WORTH YOUR DAD BRUTALLY MURDERING ME. MOVING BOOKCASES? SECRET PASSAGEWAYS?
ALL RIGHT, DUNGEONS AND DRAGONS-- TAKE IT EASY. KNOWING DADDY, IT'S PROBABLY JUST AN EVEN STUFFIER STUDY BACK HERE.
EVEN SO! THIS IS...

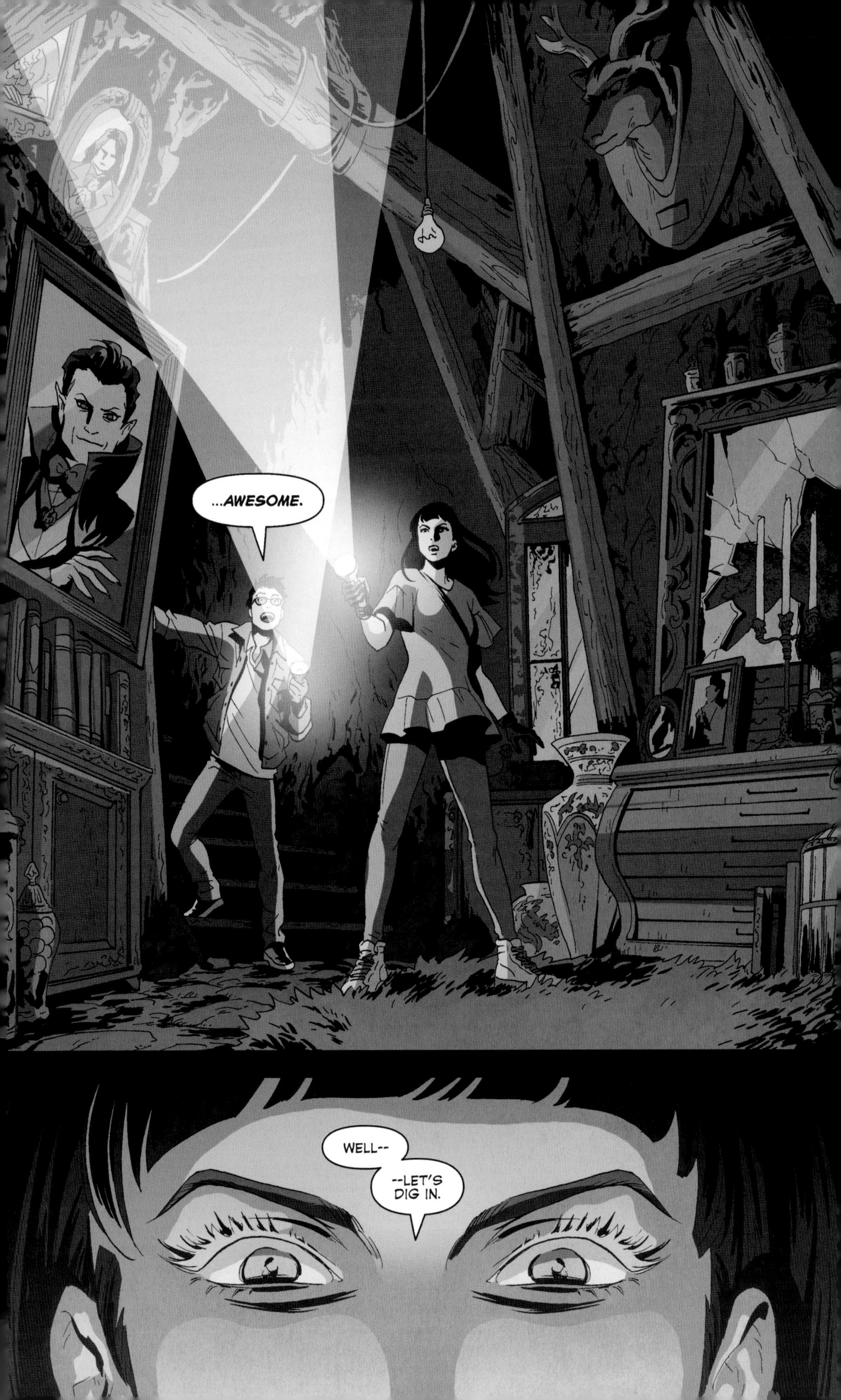

...AWESOME.
WELL--
--LET'S DIG IN.

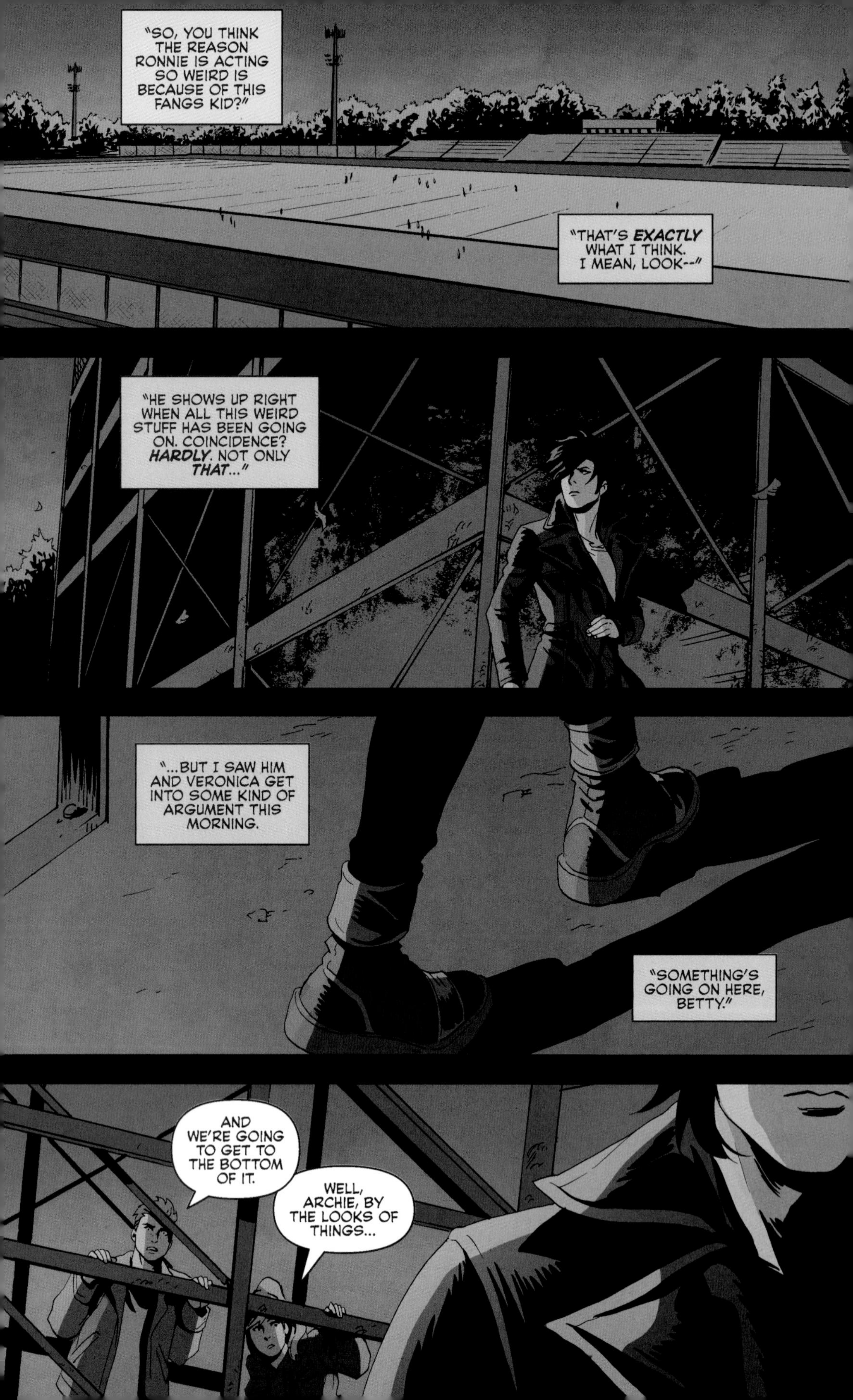
"SO, YOU THINK THE REASON RONNIE IS ACTING SO WEIRD IS BECAUSE OF THIS FANGS KID?"
"THAT'S *EXACTLY* WHAT I THINK. I MEAN, LOOK--"
"HE SHOWS UP RIGHT WHEN ALL THIS WEIRD STUFF HAS BEEN GOING ON. COINCIDENCE? *HARDLY*. NOT ONLY *THAT*..."
"...BUT I SAW HIM AND VERONICA GET INTO SOME KIND OF ARGUMENT THIS MORNING.
"SOMETHING'S GOING ON HERE, BETTY."
AND WE'RE GOING TO GET TO THE BOTTOM OF IT.
WELL, ARCHIE, BY THE LOOKS OF THINGS...

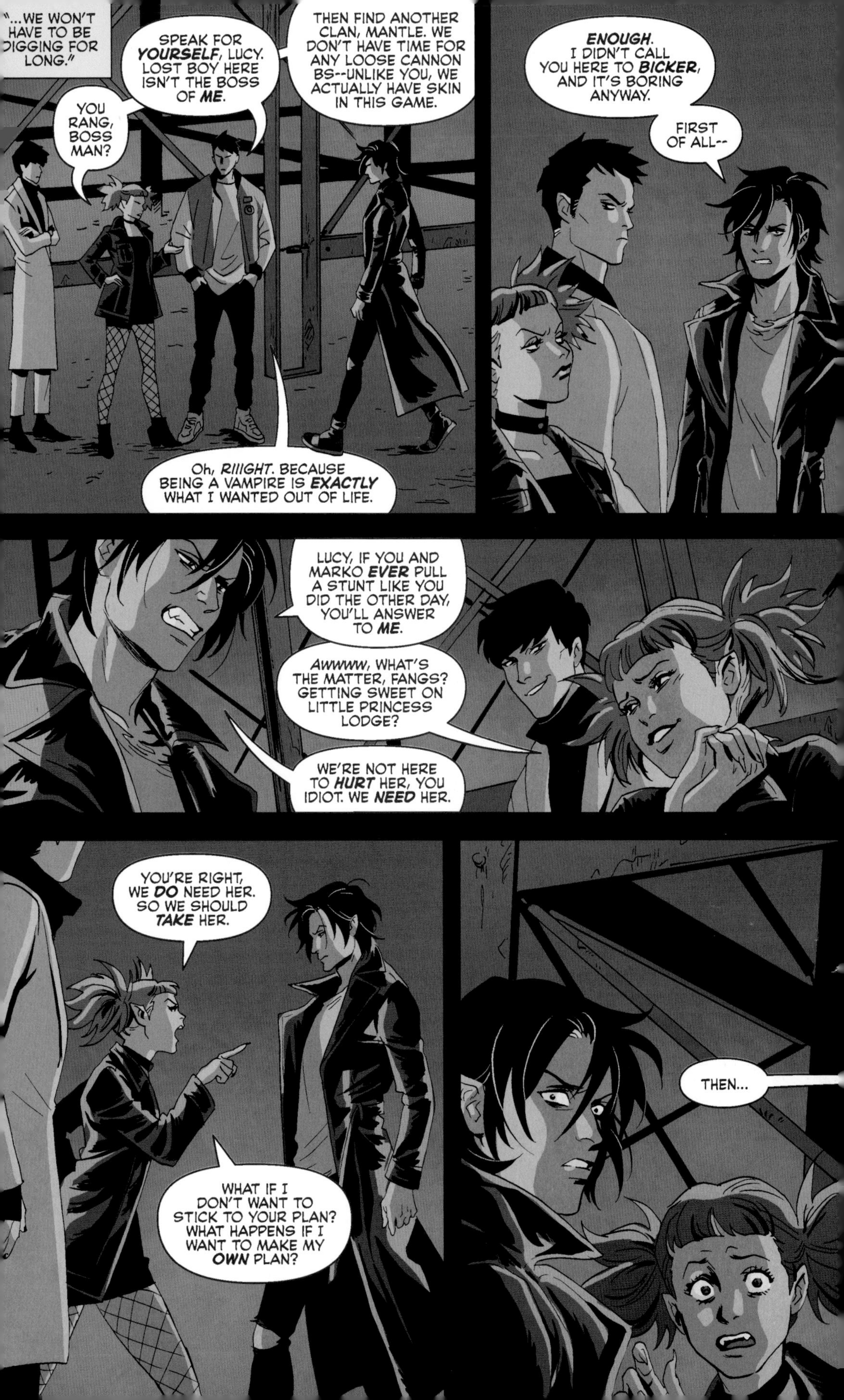
"...WE WON'T HAVE TO BE DIGGING FOR LONG."
YOU RANG, BOSS MAN?
SPEAK FOR YOURSELF, LUCY. LOST BOY HERE ISN'T THE BOSS OF ME.
THEN FIND ANOTHER CLAN, MANTLE. WE DON'T HAVE TIME FOR ANY LOOSE CANNON BS--UNLIKE YOU, WE ACTUALLY HAVE SKIN IN THIS GAME.
Oh, RIIIGHT. BECAUSE BEING A VAMPIRE IS EXACTLY WHAT I WANTED OUT OF LIFE.
ENOUGH. I DIDN'T CALL YOU HERE TO BICKER, AND IT'S BORING ANYWAY.
FIRST OF ALL--
LUCY, IF YOU AND MARKO EVER PULL A STUNT LIKE YOU DID THE OTHER DAY, YOU'LL ANSWER TO ME.
Awwww, WHAT'S THE MATTER, FANGS? GETTING SWEET ON LITTLE PRINCESS LODGE?
WE'RE NOT HERE TO HURT HER, YOU IDIOT. WE NEED HER.
YOU'RE RIGHT, WE DO NEED HER. SO WE SHOULD TAKE HER.
WHAT IF I DON'T WANT TO STICK TO YOUR PLAN? WHAT HAPPENS IF I WANT TO MAKE MY OWN PLAN?
THEN...

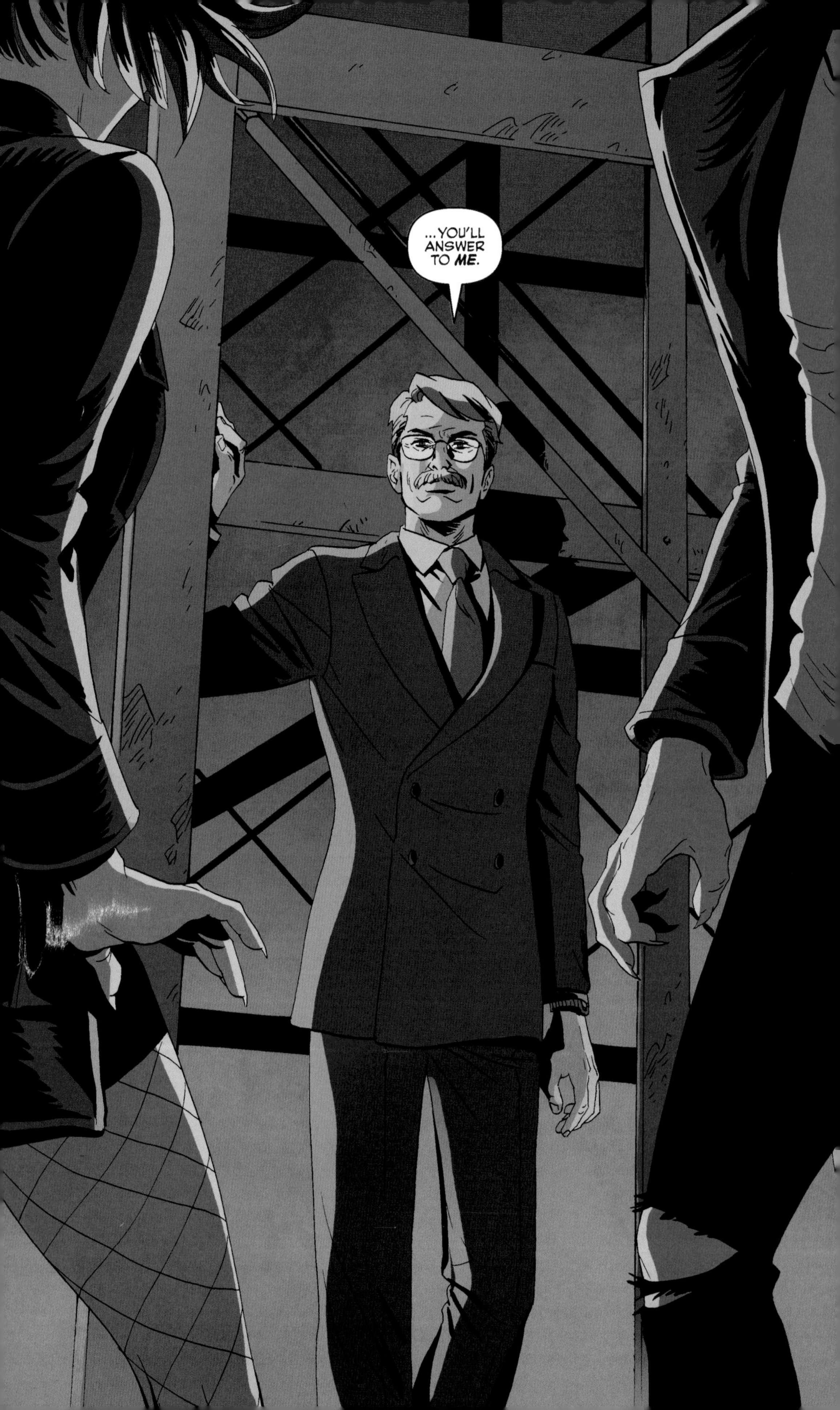
...YOU'LL ANSWER TO ME.

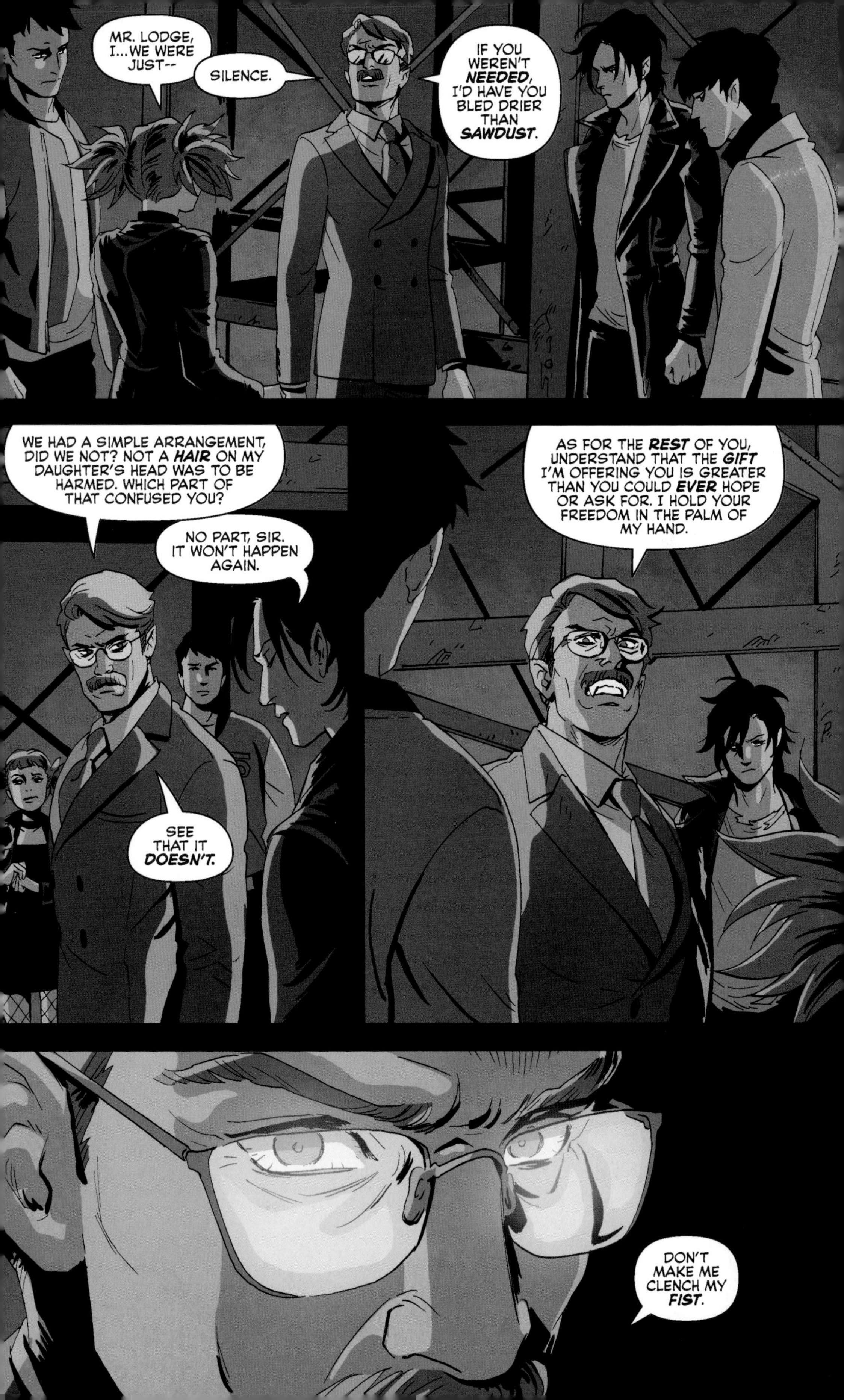
MR. LODGE, I...WE WERE JUST--
SILENCE.
IF YOU WEREN'T NEEDED, I'D HAVE YOU BLED DRIER THAN SAWDUST.
WE HAD A SIMPLE ARRANGEMENT, DID WE NOT? NOT A HAIR ON MY DAUGHTER'S HEAD WAS TO BE HARMED. WHICH PART OF THAT CONFUSED YOU?
NO PART, SIR. IT WON'T HAPPEN AGAIN.
SEE THAT IT DOESN'T.
AS FOR THE REST OF YOU, UNDERSTAND THAT THE GIFT I'M OFFERING YOU IS GREATER THAN YOU COULD EVER HOPE OR ASK FOR. I HOLD YOUR FREEDOM IN THE PALM OF MY HAND.
DON'T MAKE ME CLENCH MY FIST.

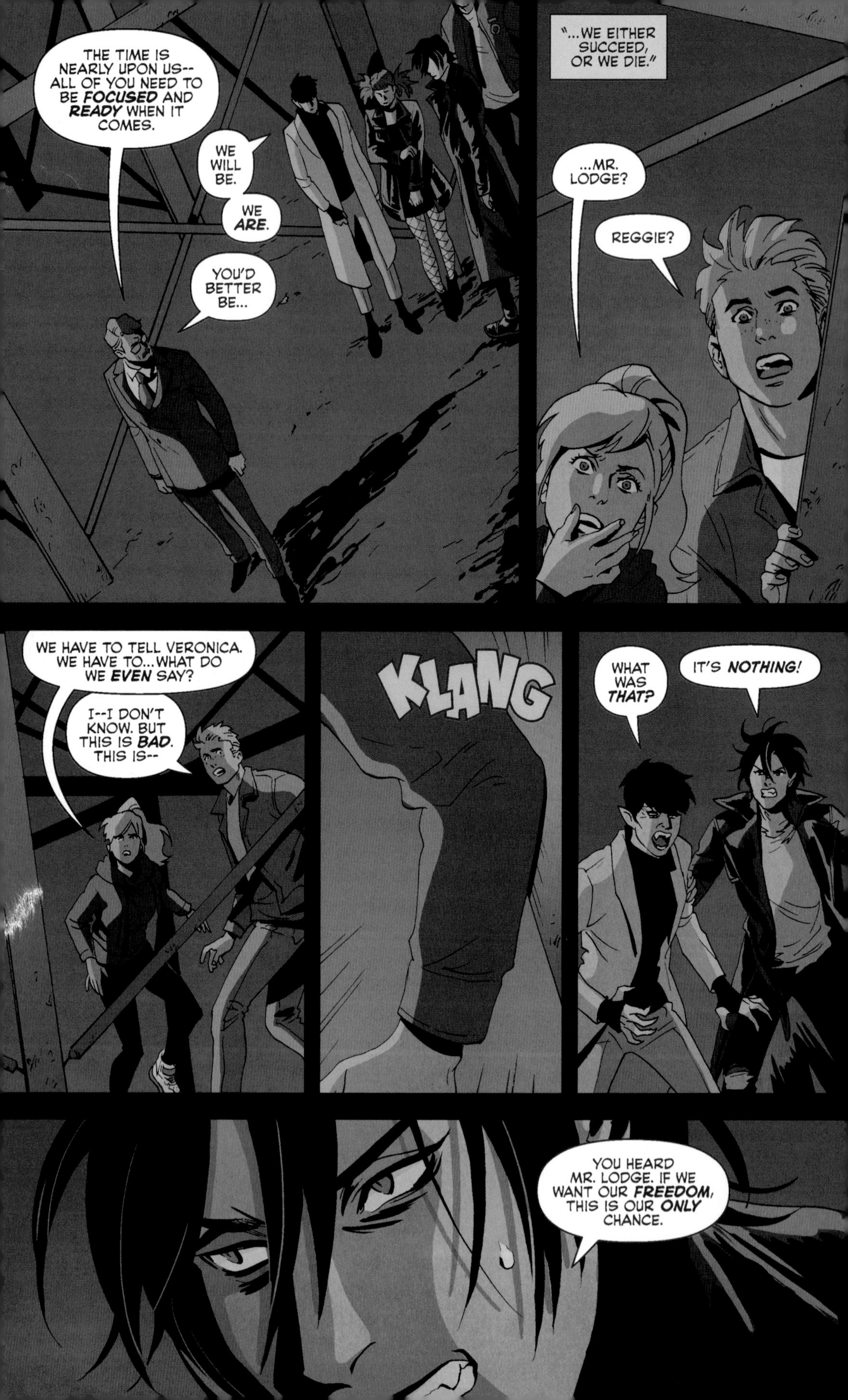
THE TIME IS NEARLY UPON US-- ALL OF YOU NEED TO BE FOCUSED AND READY WHEN IT COMES.
WE WILL BE.
WE ARE.
YOU'D BETTER BE...
"...WE EITHER SUCCEED, OR WE DIE."
...MR. LODGE?
REGGIE?
WE HAVE TO TELL VERONICA. WE HAVE TO...WHAT DO WE EVEN SAY?
I--I DON'T KNOW. BUT THIS IS BAD. THIS IS--
KLANG
WHAT WAS THAT?
IT'S NOTHING!
YOU HEARD MR. LODGE. IF WE WANT OUR FREEDOM, THIS IS OUR ONLY CHANCE.

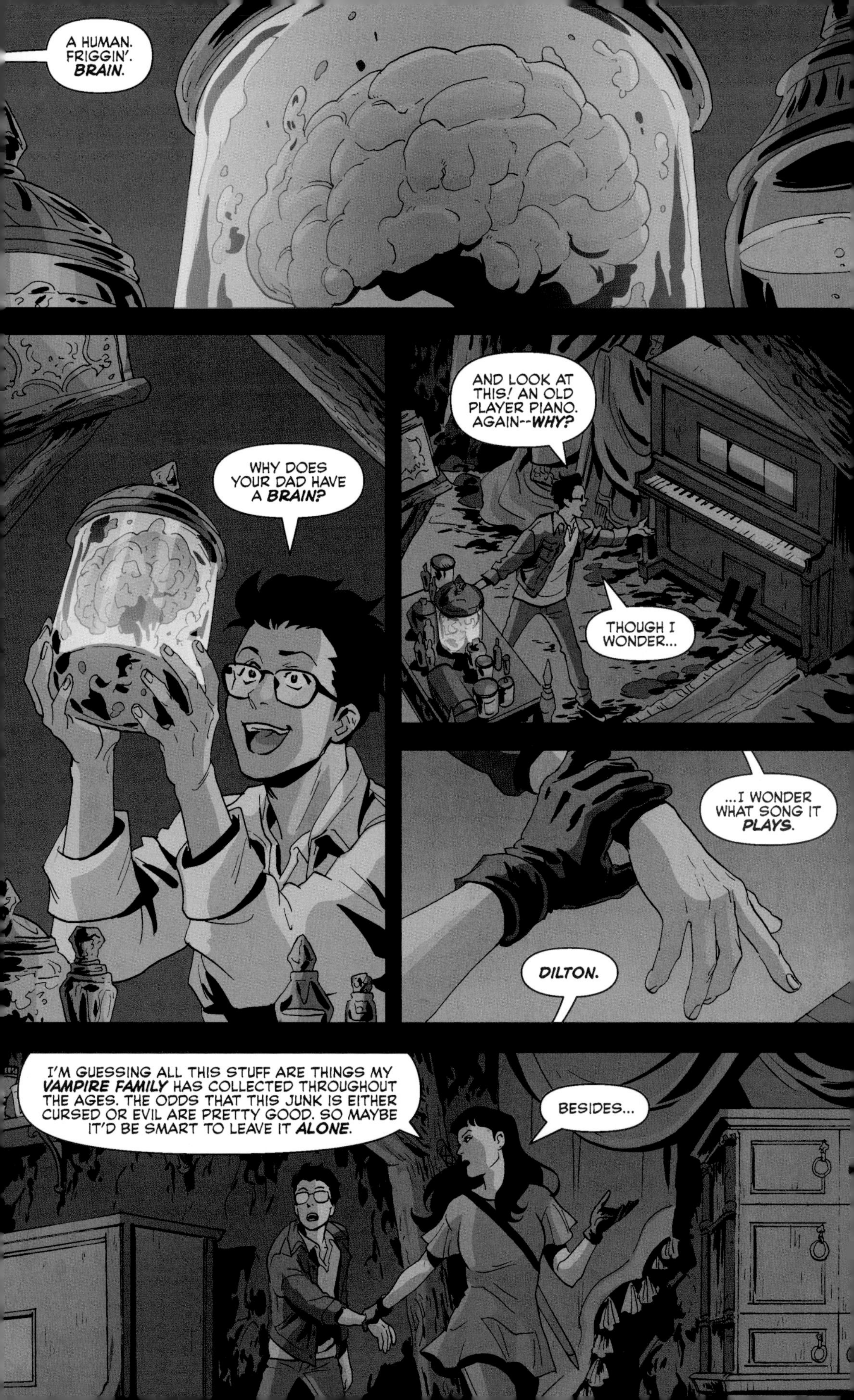
A HUMAN. FRIGGIN'. BRAIN.
WHY DOES YOUR DAD HAVE A BRAIN?
AND LOOK AT THIS! AN OLD PLAYER PIANO. AGAIN--WHY?
THOUGH I WONDER...
...I WONDER WHAT SONG IT PLAYS.
DILTON.
I'M GUESSING ALL THIS STUFF ARE THINGS MY VAMPIRE FAMILY HAS COLLECTED THROUGHOUT THE AGES. THE ODDS THAT THIS JUNK IS EITHER CURSED OR EVIL ARE PRETTY GOOD. SO MAYBE IT'D BE SMART TO LEAVE IT ALONE.
BESIDES...

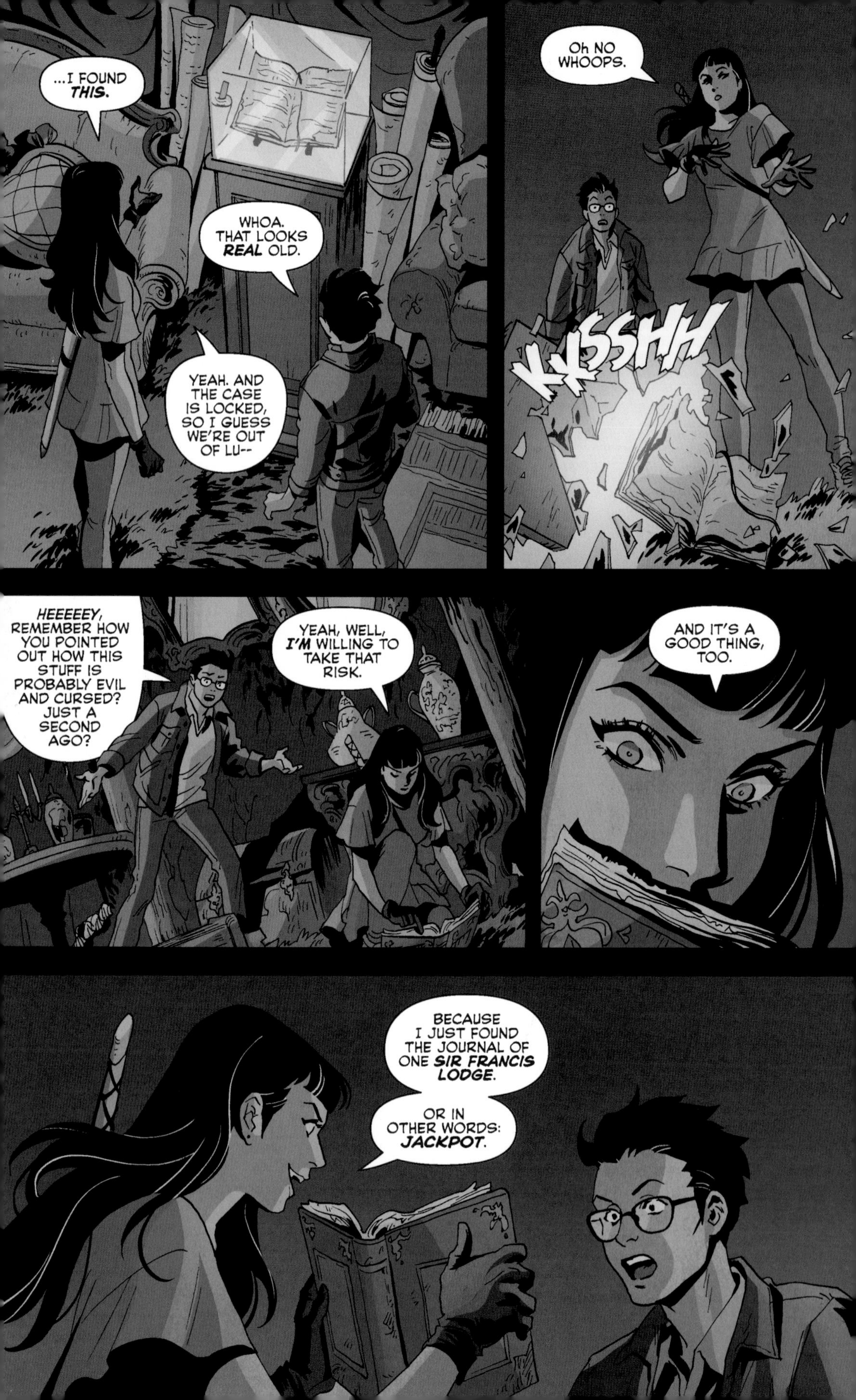
...I FOUND **THIS.**
WHOA. THAT LOOKS **REAL** OLD.
YEAH. AND THE CASE IS LOCKED, SO I GUESS WE'RE OUT OF LU--
Oh NO WHOOPS.
KSSHH
HEEEEEY, REMEMBER HOW YOU POINTED OUT HOW THIS STUFF IS PROBABLY EVIL AND CURSED? JUST A SECOND AGO?
YEAH, WELL, ***I'M*** WILLING TO TAKE THAT RISK.
AND IT'S A GOOD THING, TOO.
BECAUSE I JUST FOUND THE JOURNAL OF ONE ***SIR FRANCIS LODGE***.
OR IN OTHER WORDS: ***JACKPOT***.

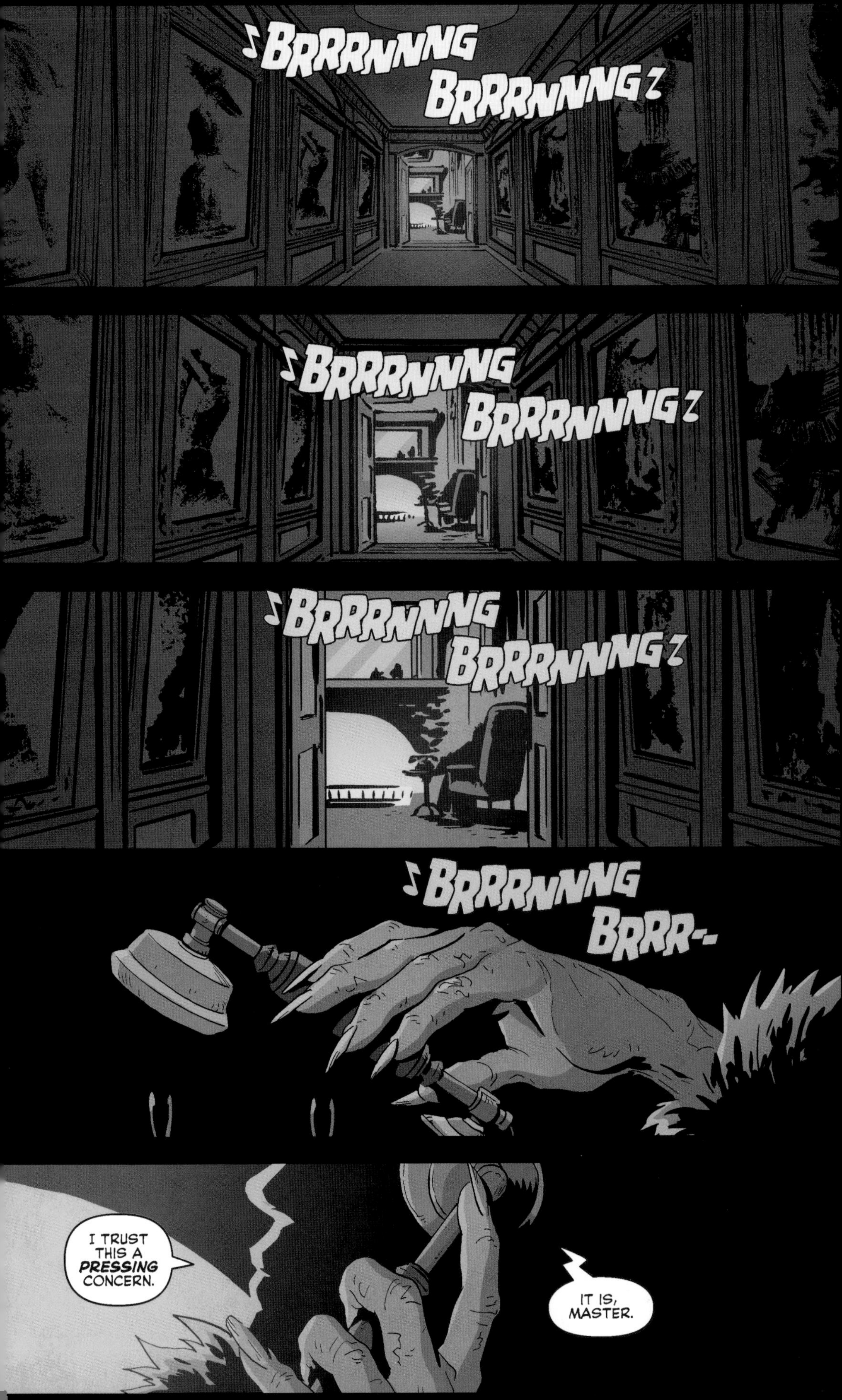
BRRRNNNG BRRRNNNG
BRRRNNNG BRRRNNNG
BRRRNNNG BRRRNNNG
BRRRNNNG BRRR--
I TRUST THIS A PRESSING CONCERN.
IT IS, MASTER.

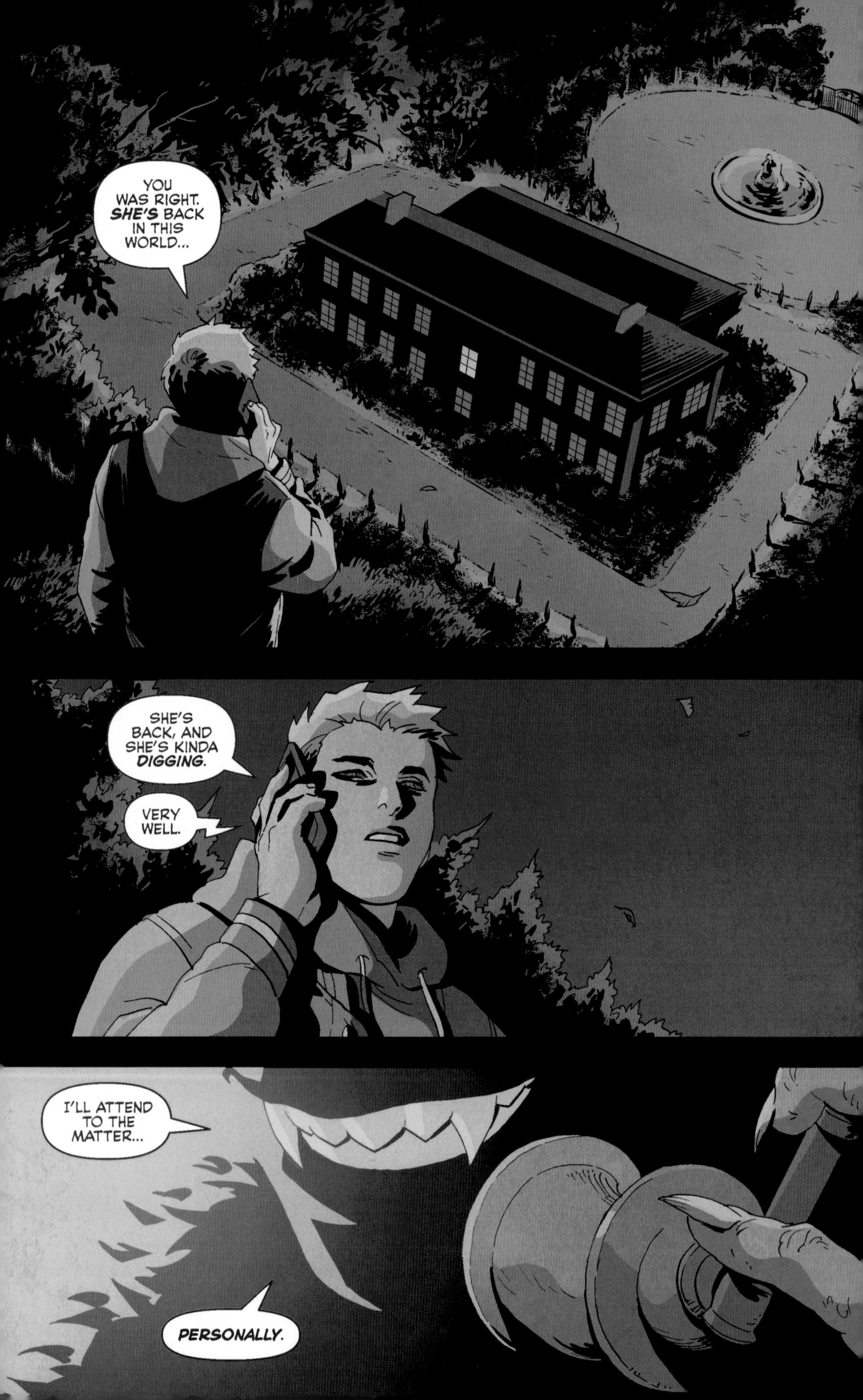
YOU WAS RIGHT. SHE'S BACK IN THIS WORLD...
SHE'S BACK, AND SHE'S KINDA DIGGING.
VERY WELL.
I'LL ATTEND TO THE MATTER...
PERSONALLY.

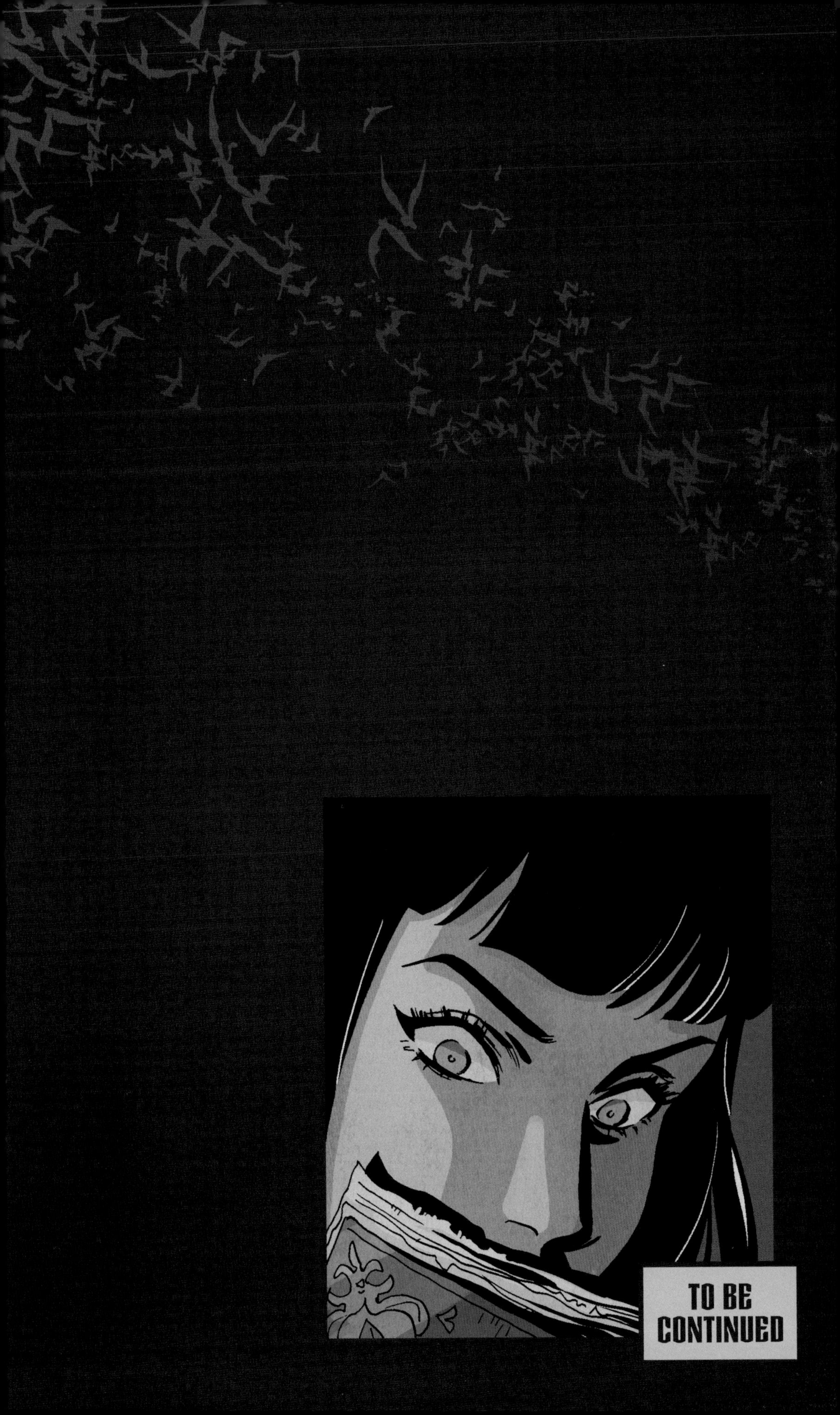
TO BE CONTINUED

CHAPTER THREE

COVER ART BY AUDREY MOK

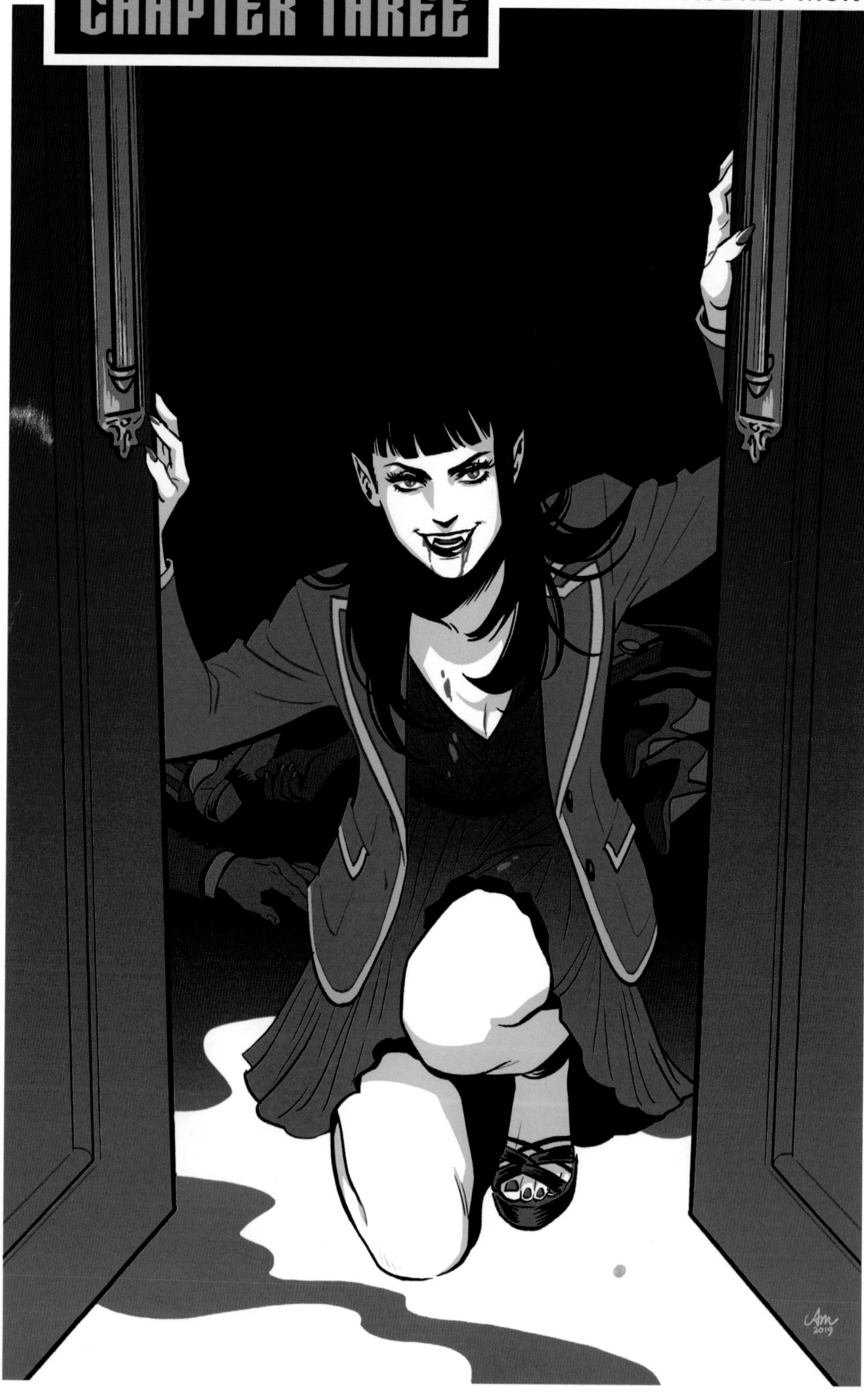

STORY BY FRANK TIERI & MICHAEL MORECI   ART BY AUDREY MOK
COLORING BY MATT HERMS   LETTERING BY JACK MORELLI

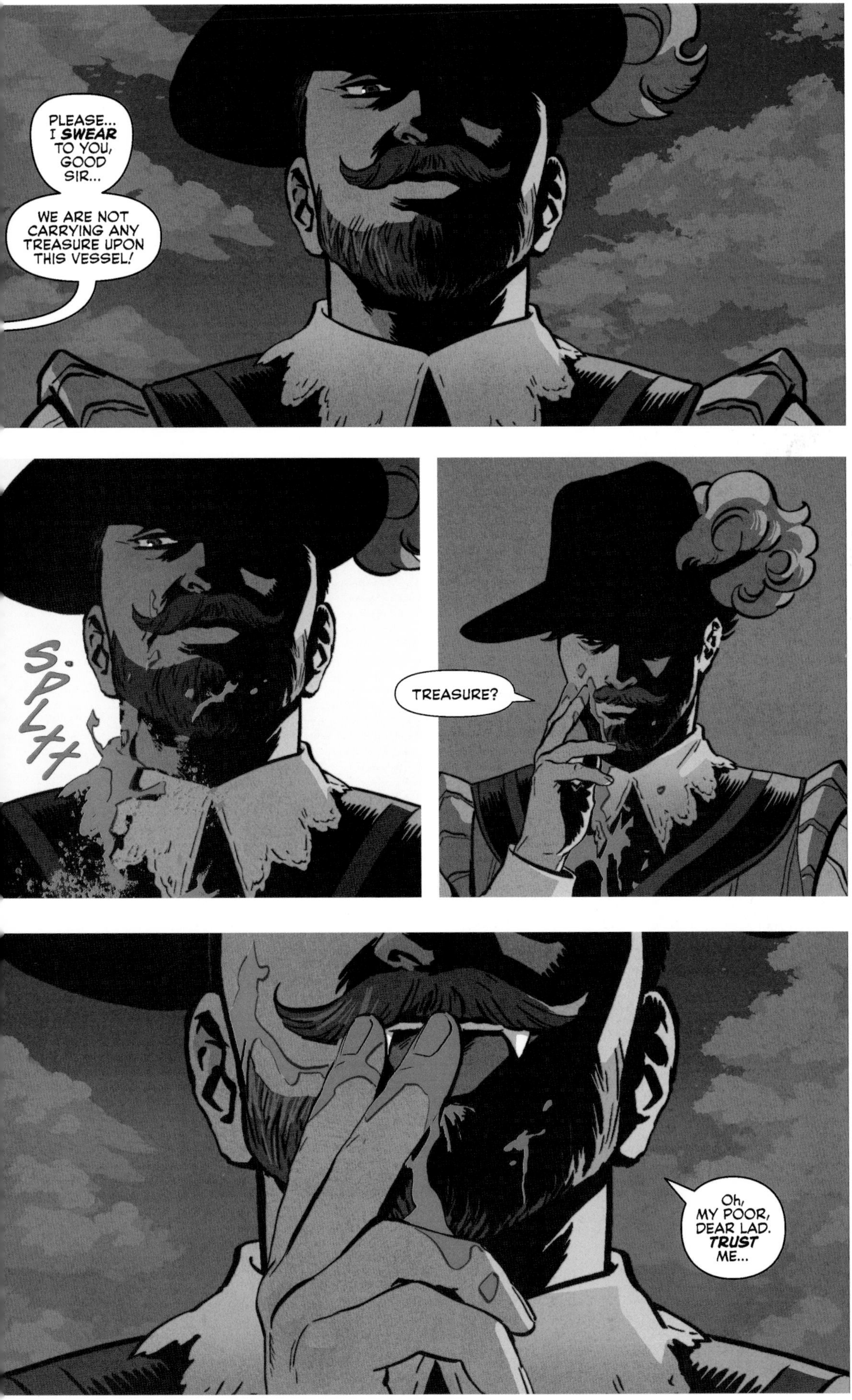
PLEASE... I SWEAR TO YOU, GOOD SIR...
WE ARE NOT CARRYING ANY TREASURE UPON THIS VESSEL!
SPLTT
TREASURE?
Oh, MY POOR, DEAR LAD. TRUST ME...

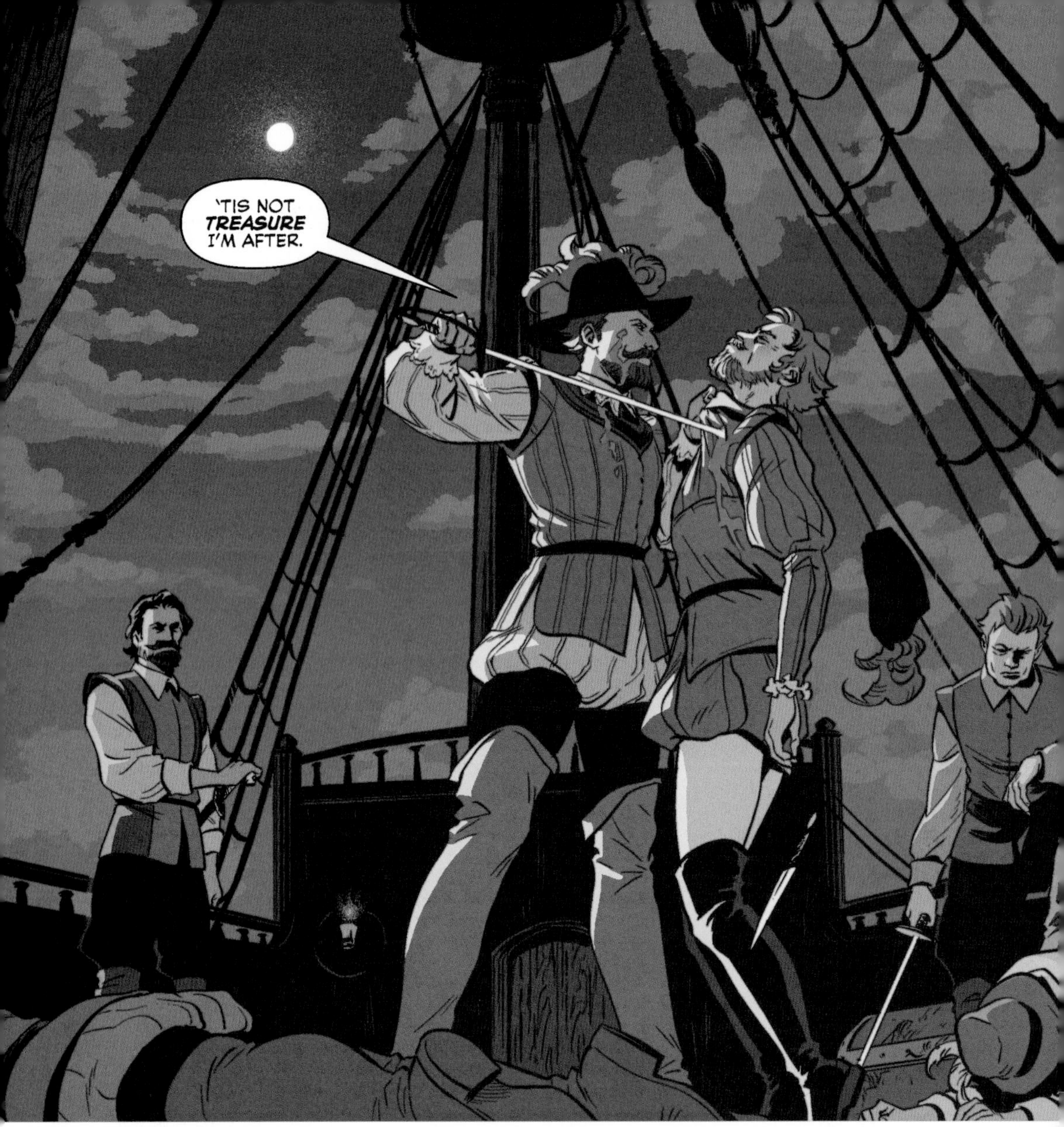
'TIS NOT **TREASURE** I'M AFTER.

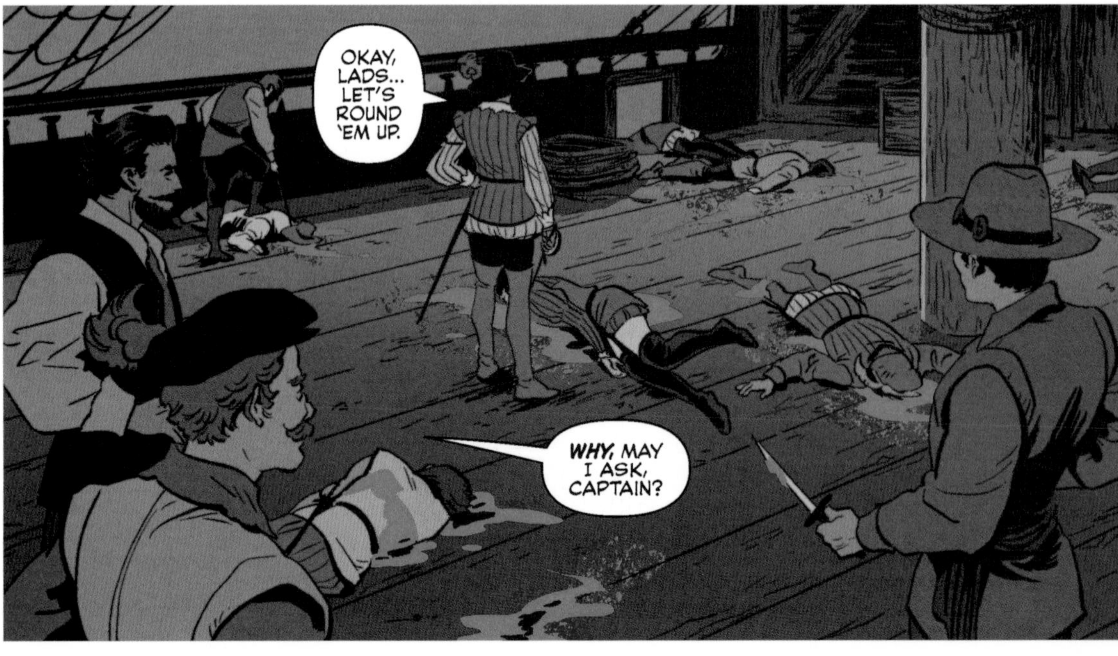
OKAY, LADS... LET'S ROUND 'EM UP.
WHY, MAY I ASK, CAPTAIN?

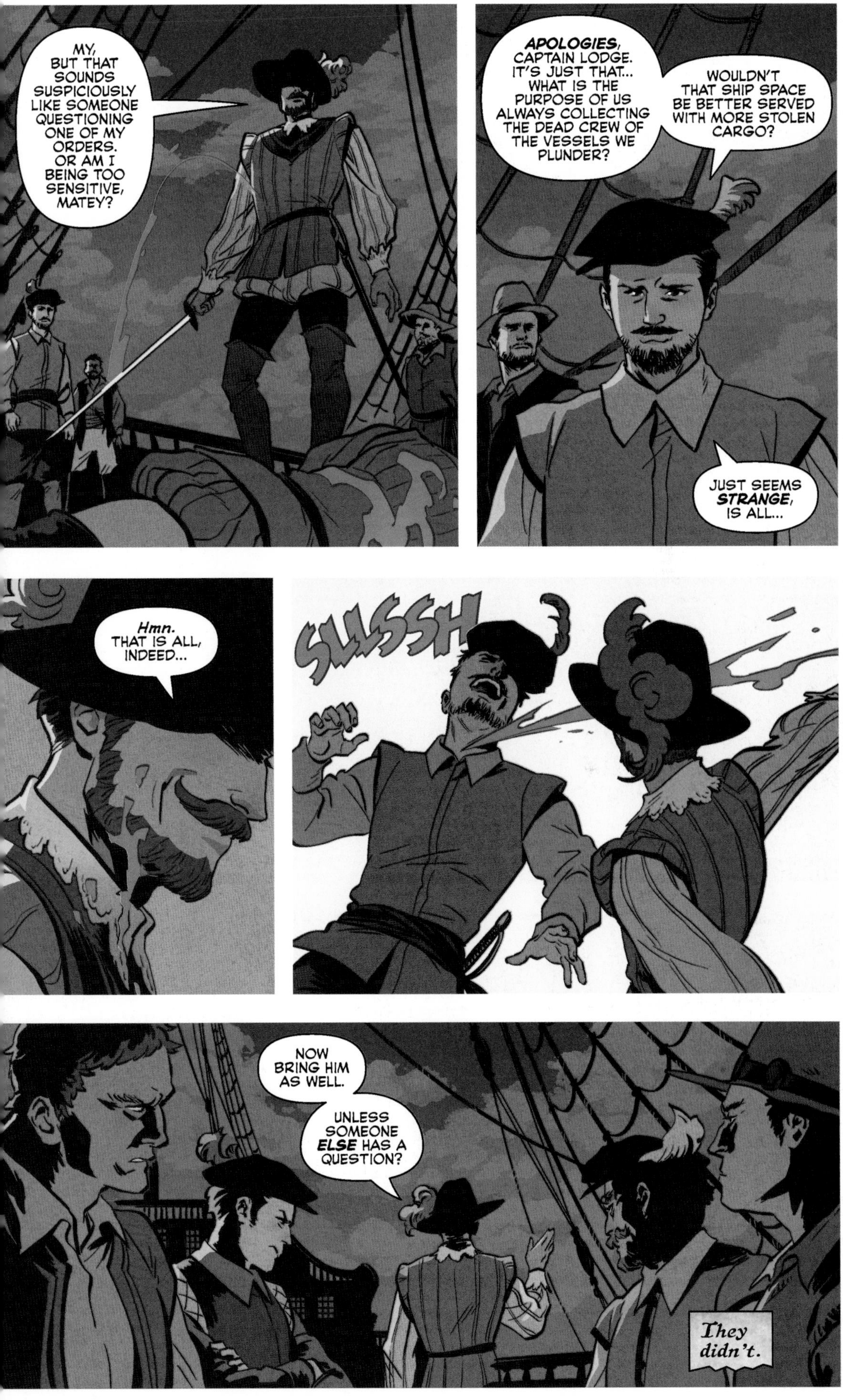
MY, BUT THAT SOUNDS SUSPICIOUSLY LIKE SOMEONE QUESTIONING ONE OF MY ORDERS. OR AM I BEING TOO SENSITIVE, MATEY?
APOLOGIES, CAPTAIN LODGE. IT'S JUST THAT... WHAT IS THE PURPOSE OF US ALWAYS COLLECTING THE DEAD CREW OF THE VESSELS WE PLUNDER?
WOULDN'T THAT SHIP SPACE BE BETTER SERVED WITH MORE STOLEN CARGO?
JUST SEEMS STRANGE, IS ALL...
Hmn. THAT IS ALL, INDEED...
SLISSH
NOW BRING HIM AS WELL.
UNLESS SOMEONE ELSE HAS A QUESTION?
They didn't.

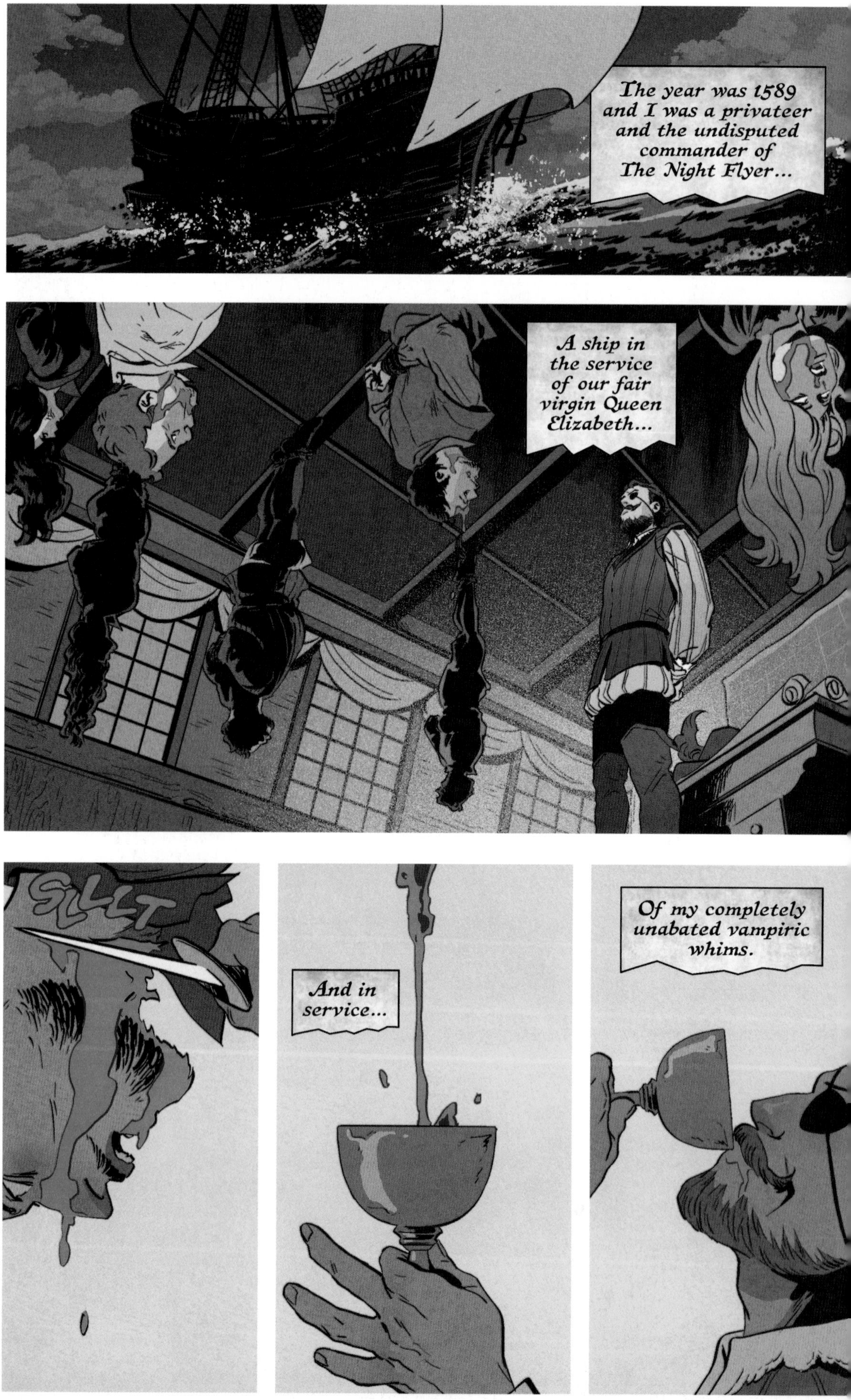
The year was 1589 and I was a privateer and the undisputed commander of The Night Flyer...
A ship in the service of our fair virgin Queen Elizabeth...
SLLT
And in service...
Of my completely unabated vampiric whims.

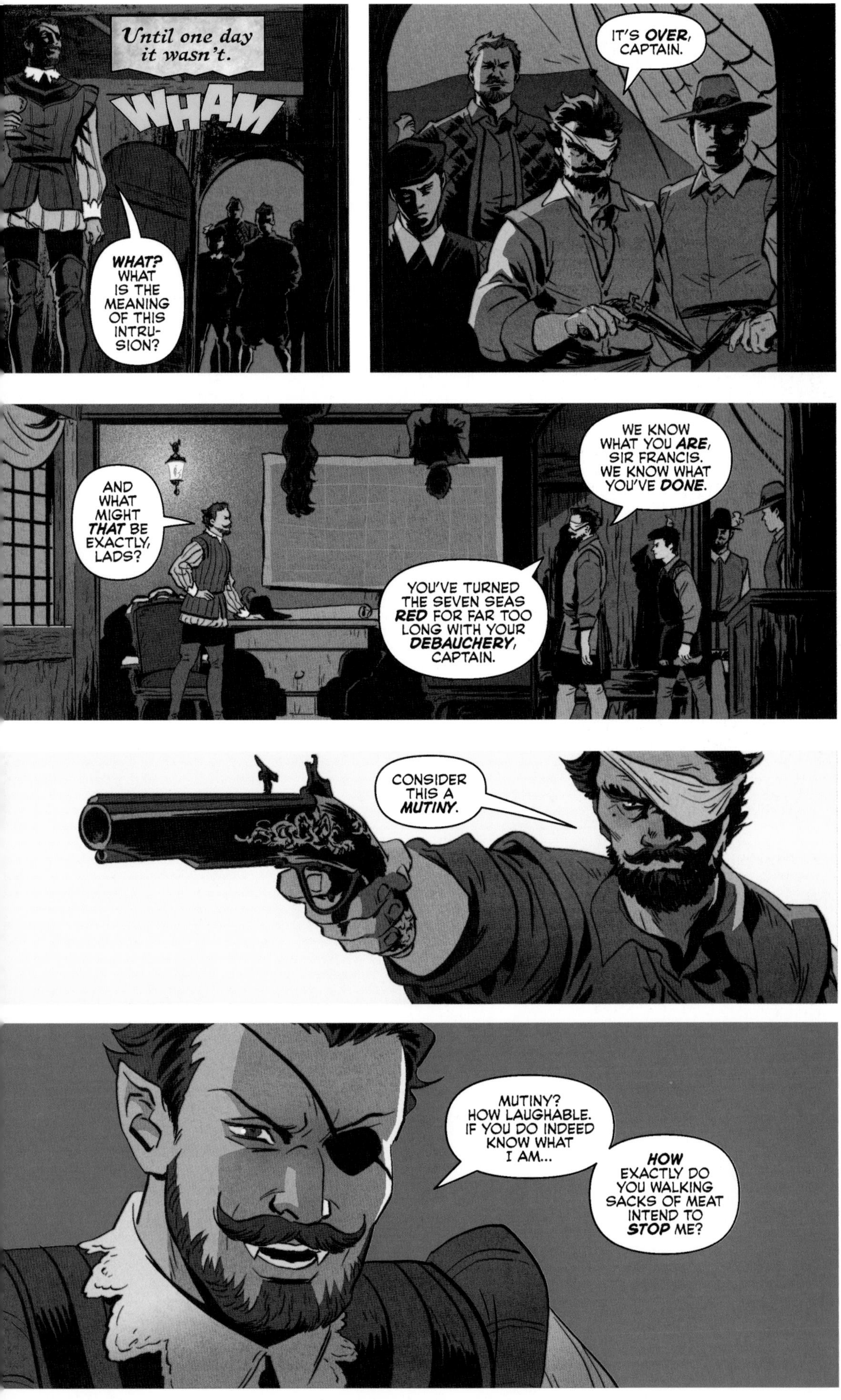
Until one day it wasn't.
WHAM
WHAT? WHAT IS THE MEANING OF THIS INTRUSION?
IT'S OVER, CAPTAIN.
AND WHAT MIGHT THAT BE EXACTLY, LADS?
WE KNOW WHAT YOU ARE, SIR FRANCIS. WE KNOW WHAT YOU'VE DONE.
YOU'VE TURNED THE SEVEN SEAS RED FOR FAR TOO LONG WITH YOUR DEBAUCHERY, CAPTAIN.
CONSIDER THIS A MUTINY.
MUTINY? HOW LAUGHABLE. IF YOU DO INDEED KNOW WHAT I AM...
HOW EXACTLY DO YOU WALKING SACKS OF MEAT INTEND TO STOP ME?

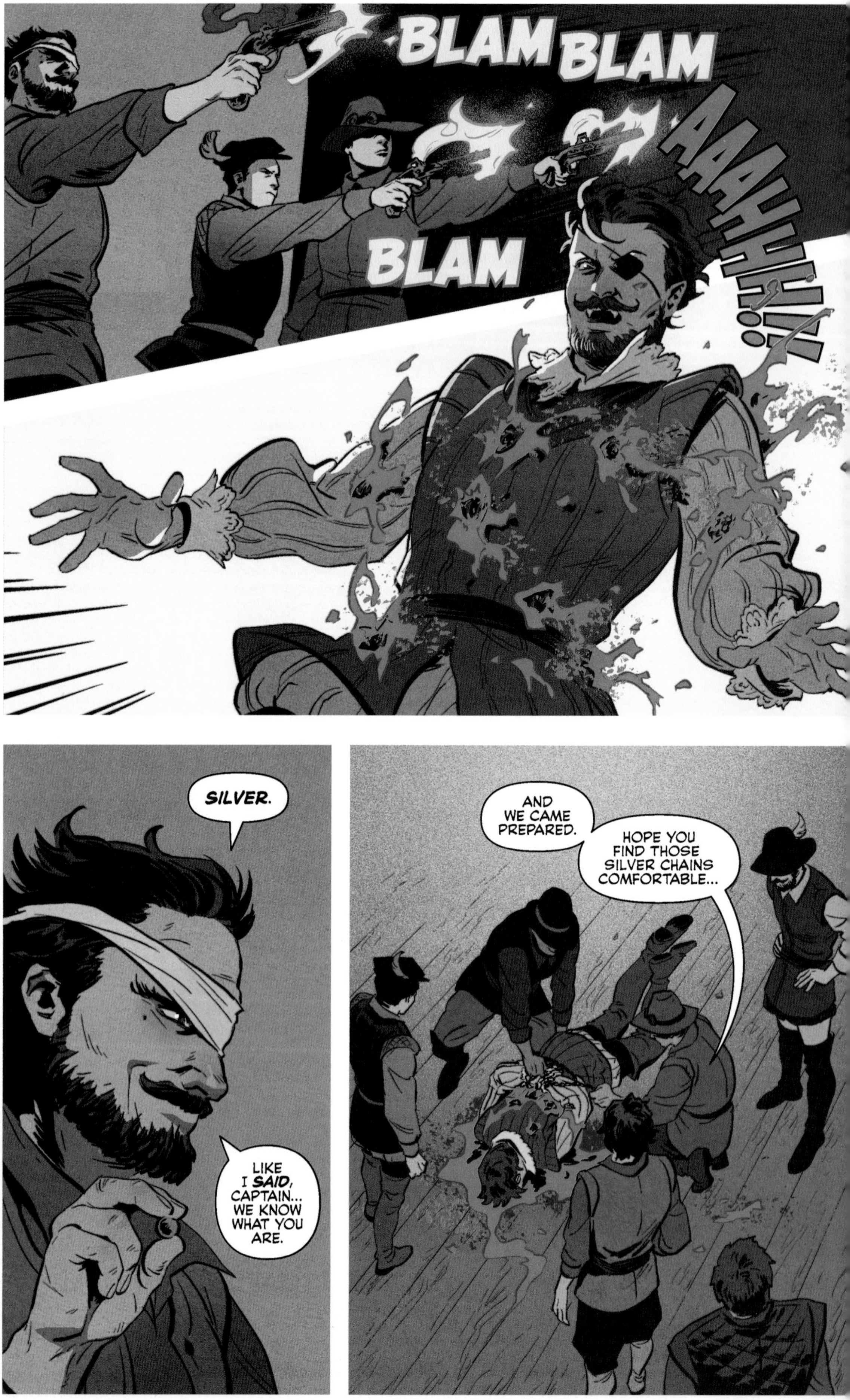

BLAM BLAM
BLAM
AAAHHH!!!
SILVER.
LIKE I SAID, CAPTAIN... WE KNOW WHAT YOU ARE.
AND WE CAME PREPARED.
HOPE YOU FIND THOSE SILVER CHAINS COMFORTABLE...

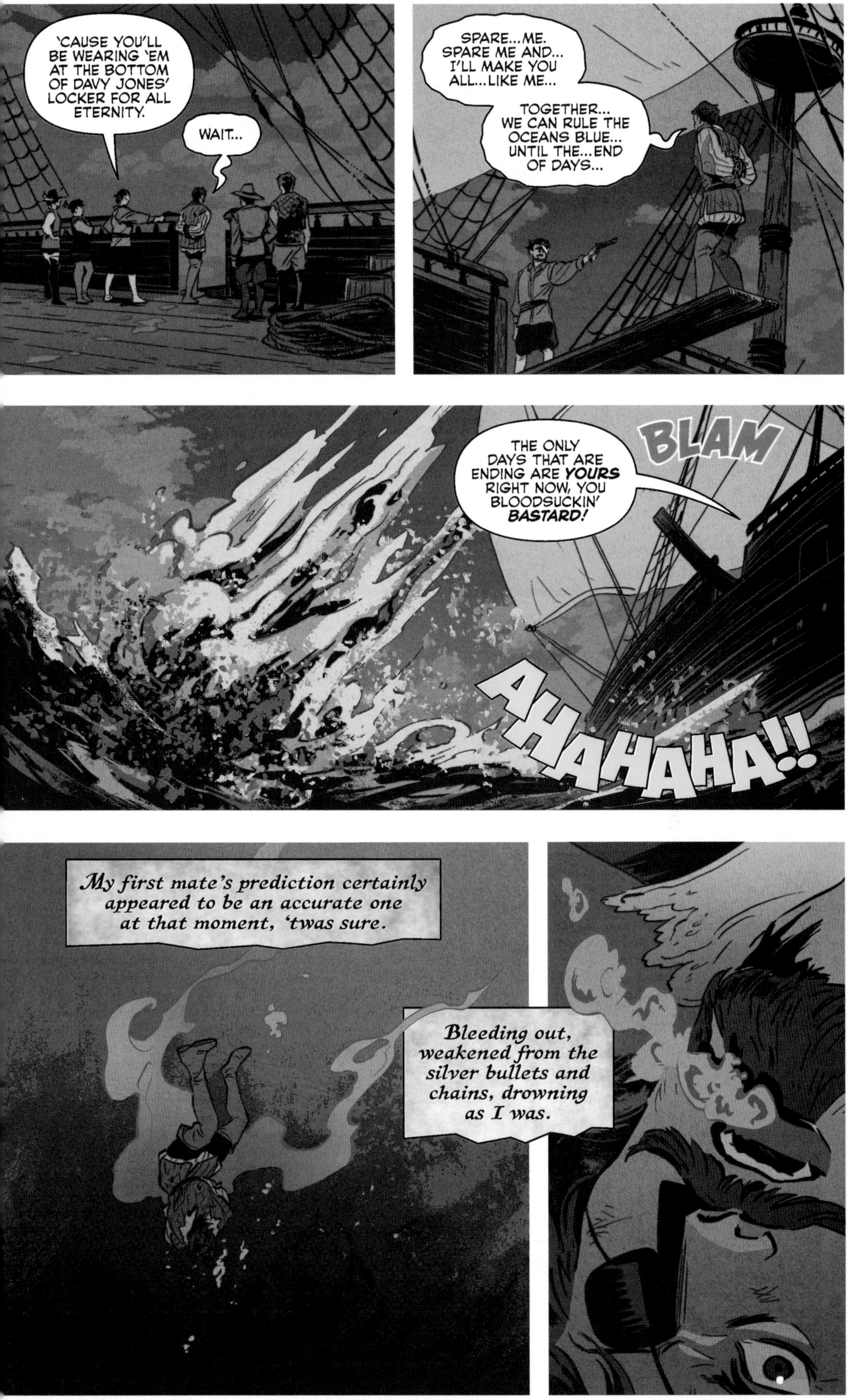
'CAUSE YOU'LL BE WEARING 'EM AT THE BOTTOM OF DAVY JONES' LOCKER FOR ALL ETERNITY.
WAIT...
SPARE...ME. SPARE ME AND... I'LL MAKE YOU ALL...LIKE ME...
TOGETHER... WE CAN RULE THE OCEANS BLUE... UNTIL THE...END OF DAYS...
THE ONLY DAYS THAT ARE ENDING ARE YOURS RIGHT NOW, YOU BLOODSUCKIN' BASTARD!
BLAM
AHAHAHA!!
My first mate's prediction certainly appeared to be an accurate one at that moment, 'twas sure.
Bleeding out, weakened from the silver bullets and chains, drowning as I was.

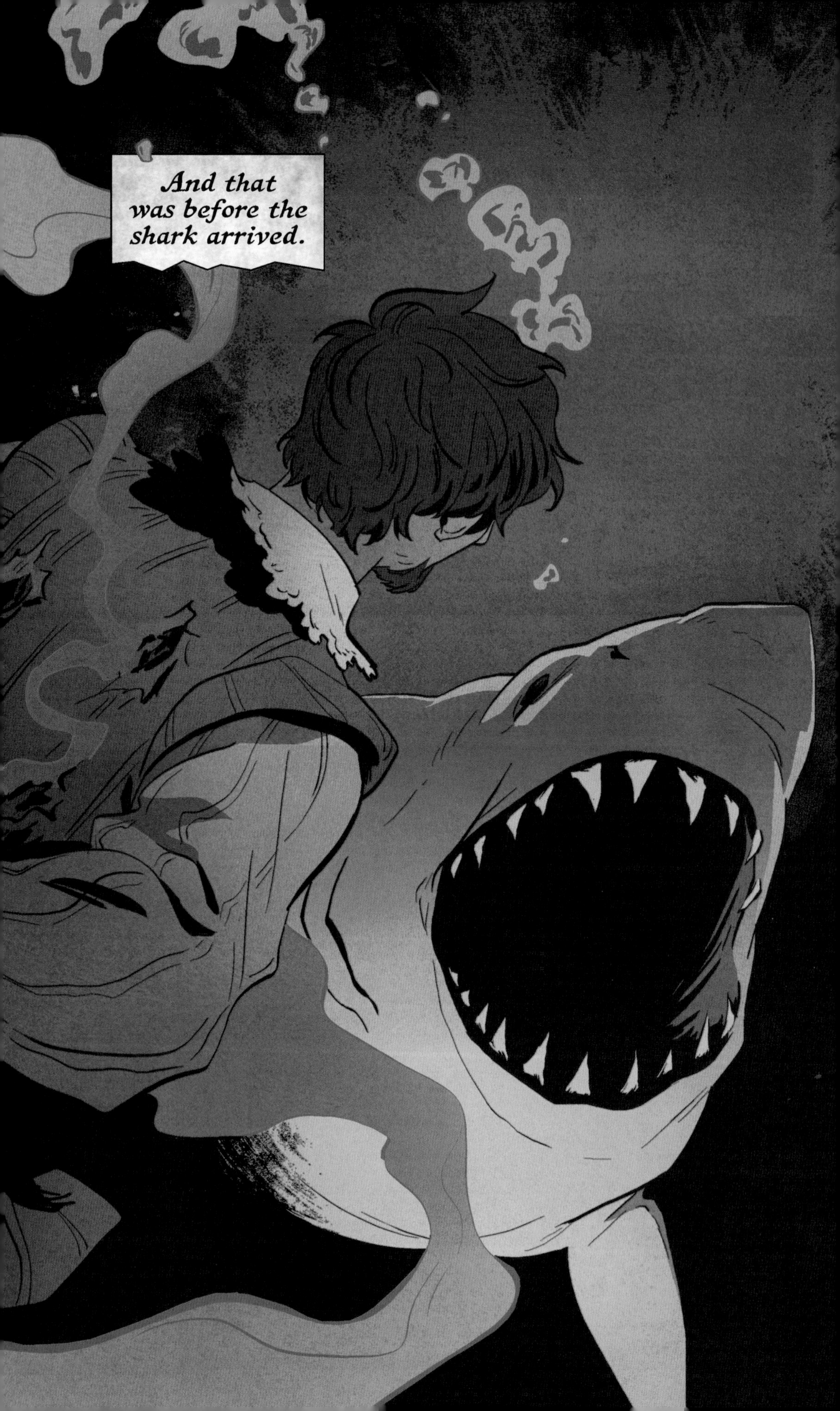
And that was before the shark arrived.

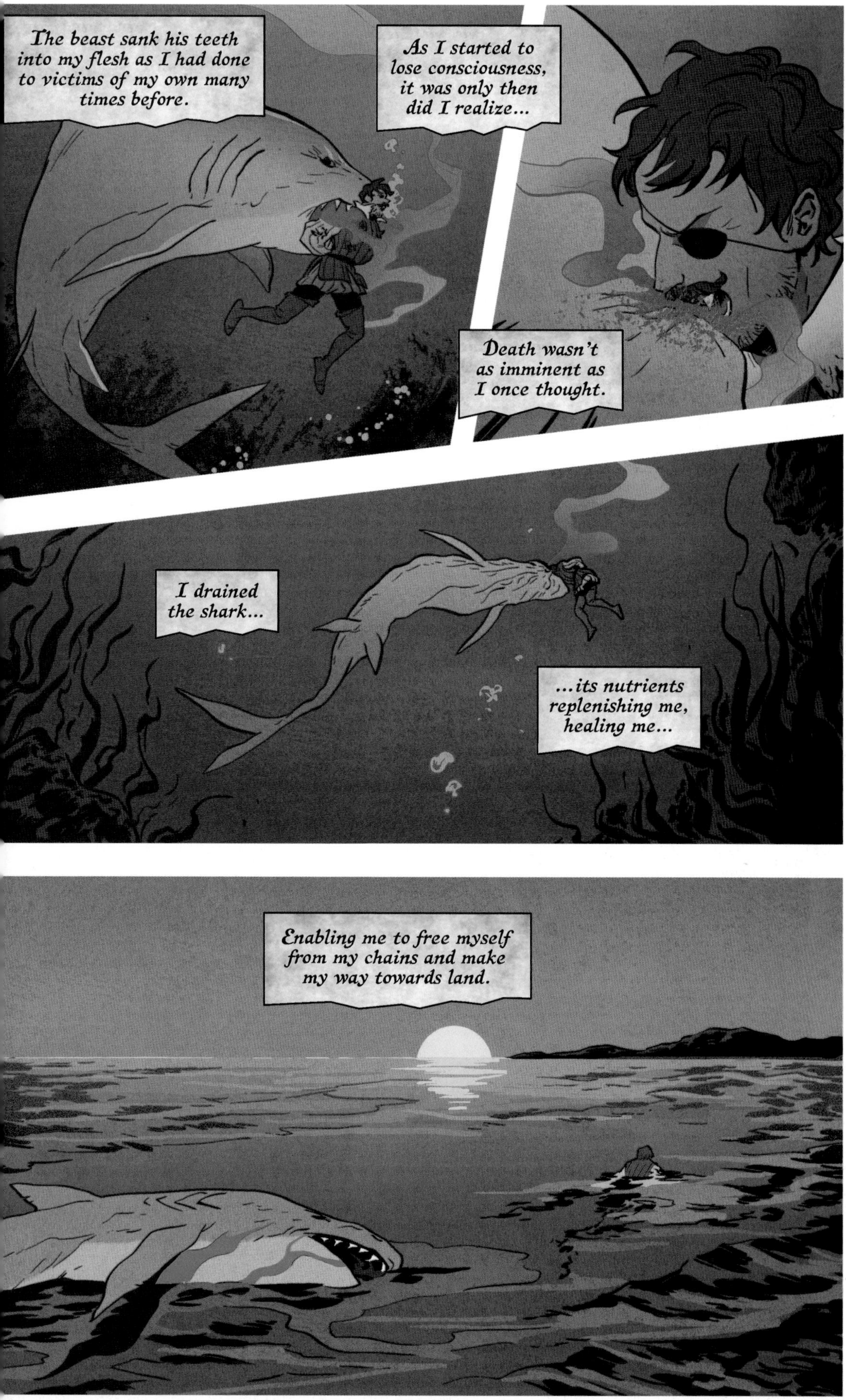
The beast sank his teeth into my flesh as I had done to victims of my own many times before.
As I started to lose consciousness, it was only then did I realize...
Death wasn't as imminent as I once thought.
I drained the shark...
...its nutrients replenishing me, healing me...
Enabling me to free myself from my chains and make my way towards land.

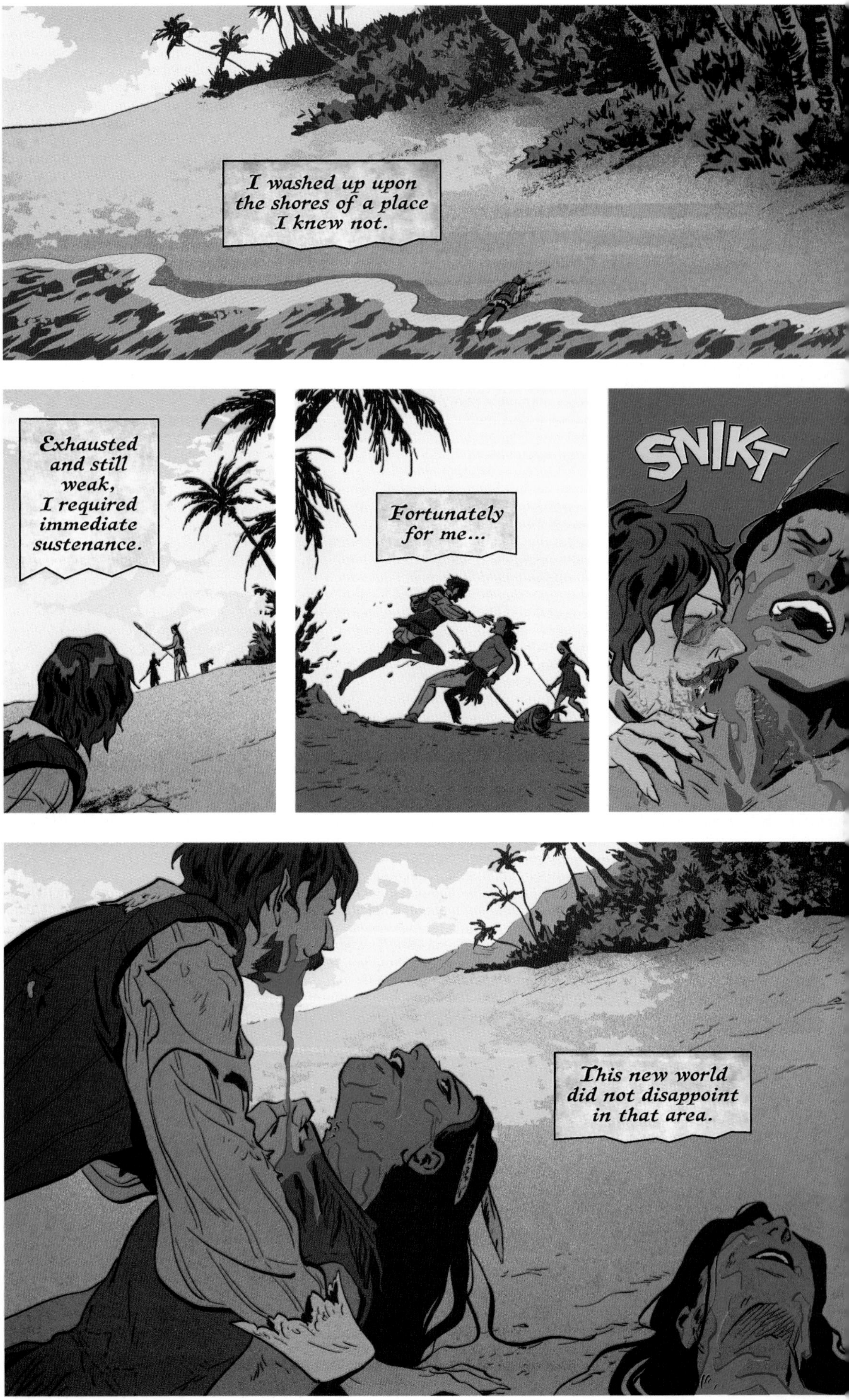

I washed up upon the shores of a place I knew not.
Exhausted and still weak, I required immediate sustenance.
Fortunately for me...
SNIKT
This new world did not disappoint in that area.

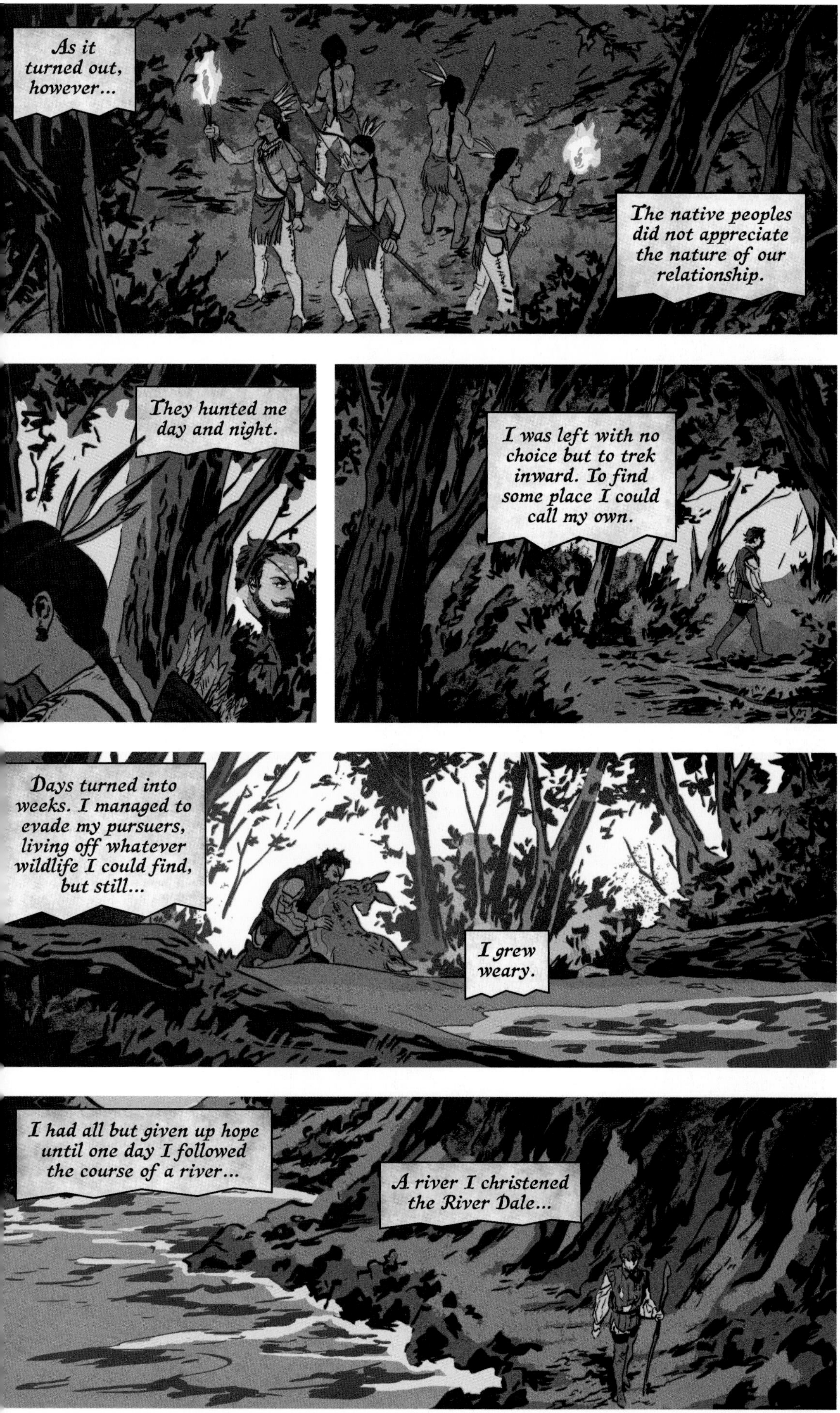
As it turned out, however...
The native peoples did not appreciate the nature of our relationship.
They hunted me day and night.
I was left with no choice but to trek inward. To find some place I could call my own.
Days turned into weeks. I managed to evade my pursuers, living off whatever wildlife I could find, but still...
I grew weary.
I had all but given up hope until one day I followed the course of a river...
A river I christened the River Dale...

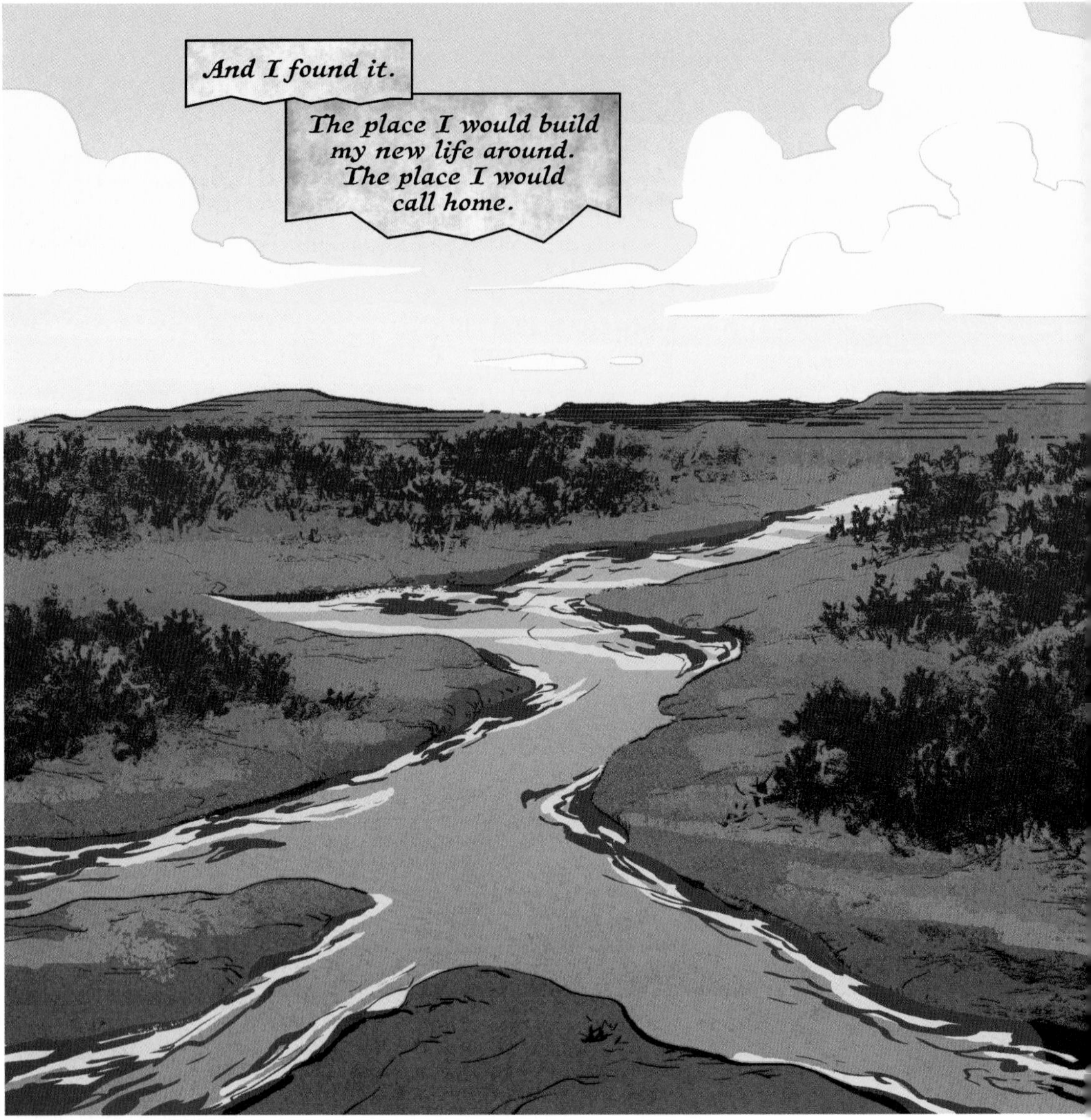
And I found it.
The place I would build my new life around. The place I would call home.

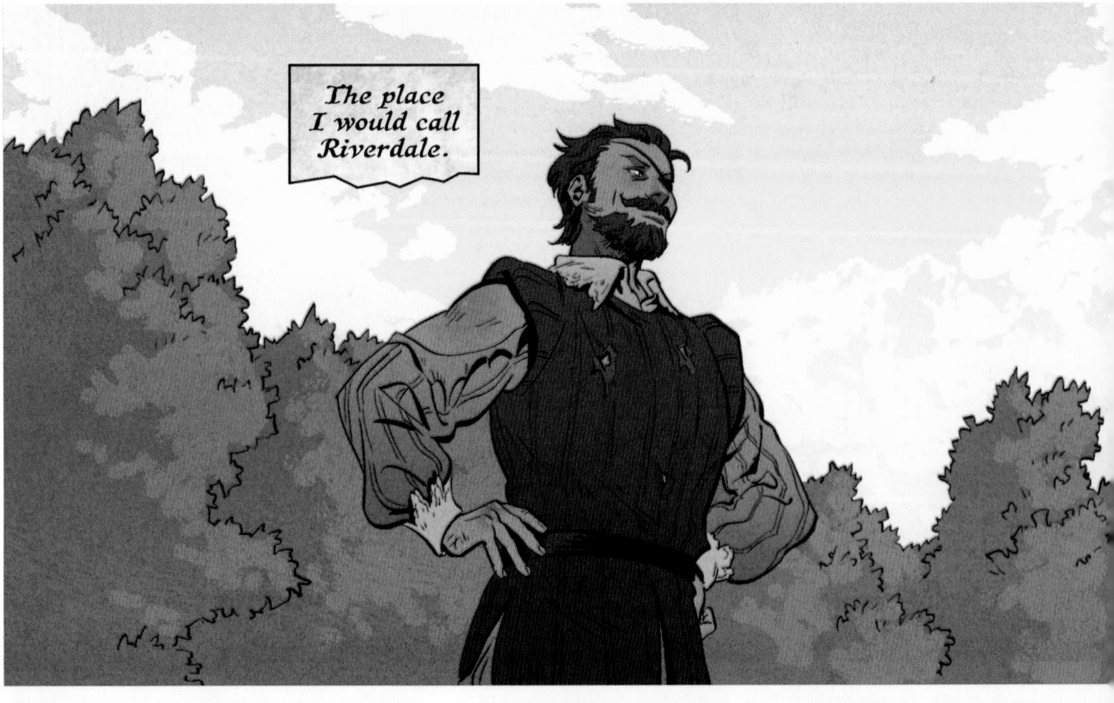
The place I would call Riverdale.

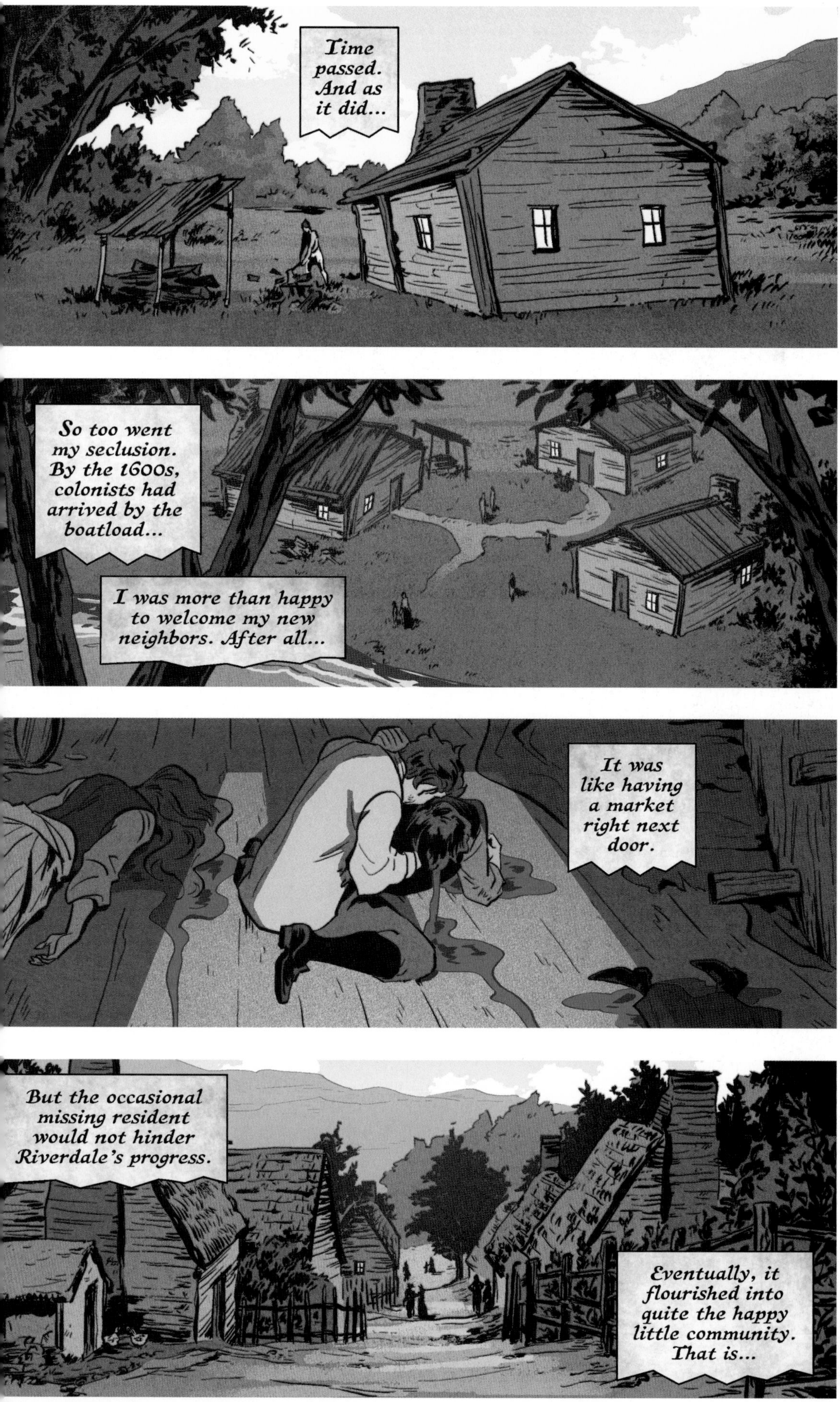
Time passed. And as it did...
So too went my seclusion. By the 1600s, colonists had arrived by the boatload...
I was more than happy to welcome my new neighbors. After all...
It was like having a market right next door.
But the occasional missing resident would not hinder Riverdale's progress.
Eventually, it flourished into quite the happy little community. That is...

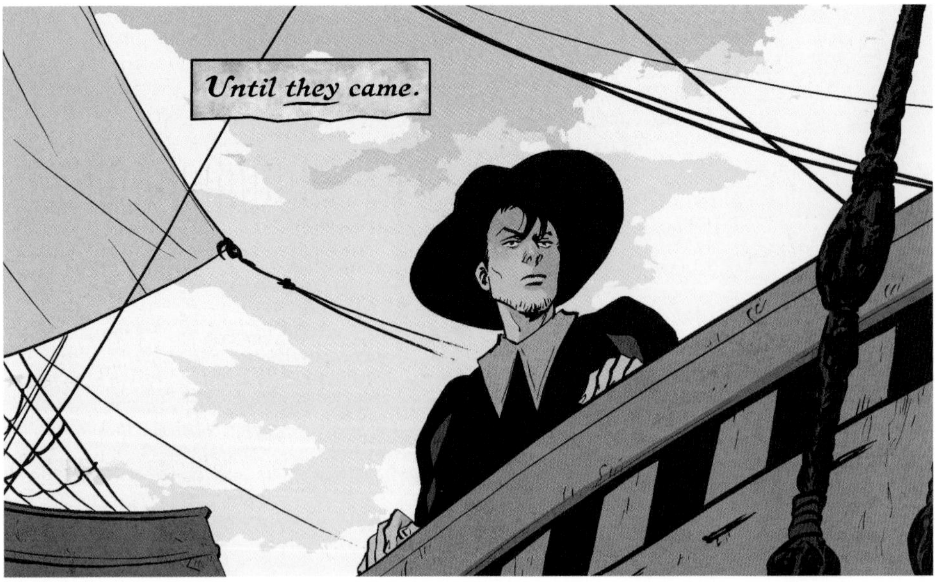
Until they came.

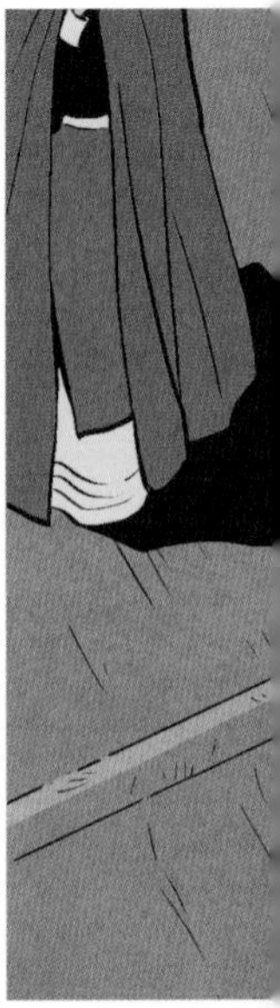

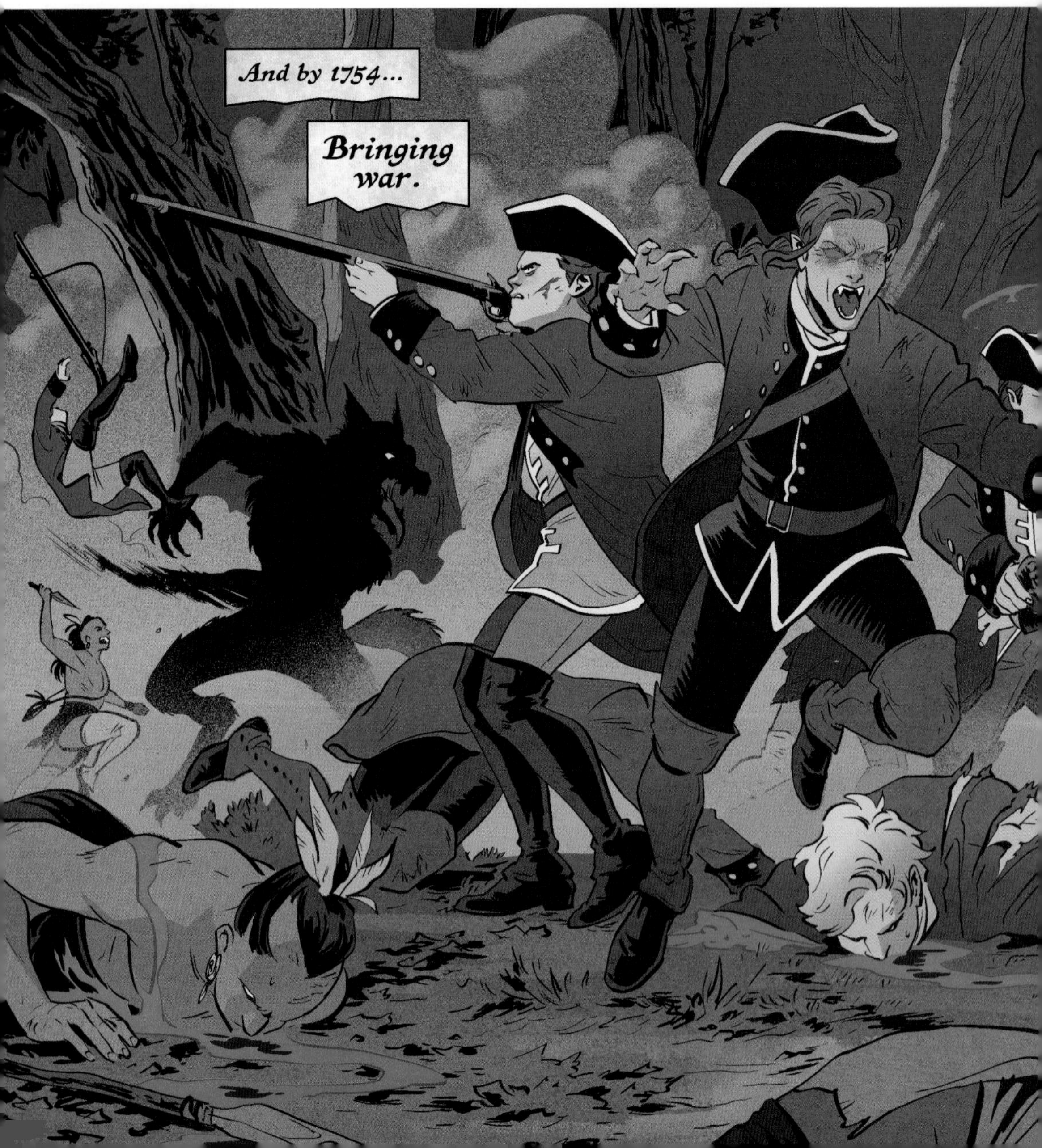
And by 1754...
Bringing war.

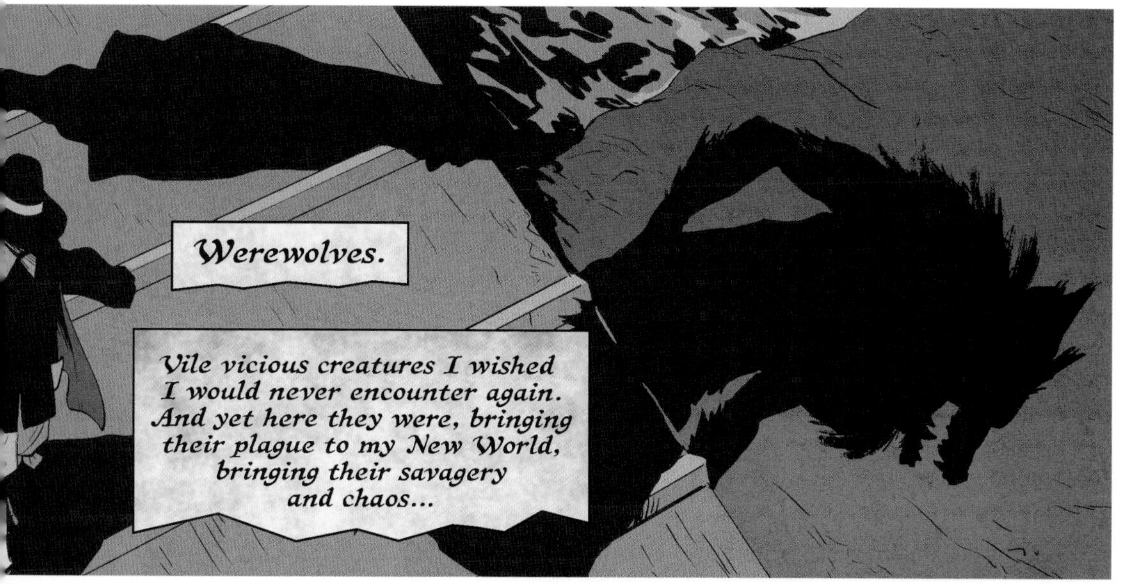
Werewolves.
Vile vicious creatures I wished I would never encounter again. And yet here they were, bringing their plague to my New World, bringing their savagery and chaos...

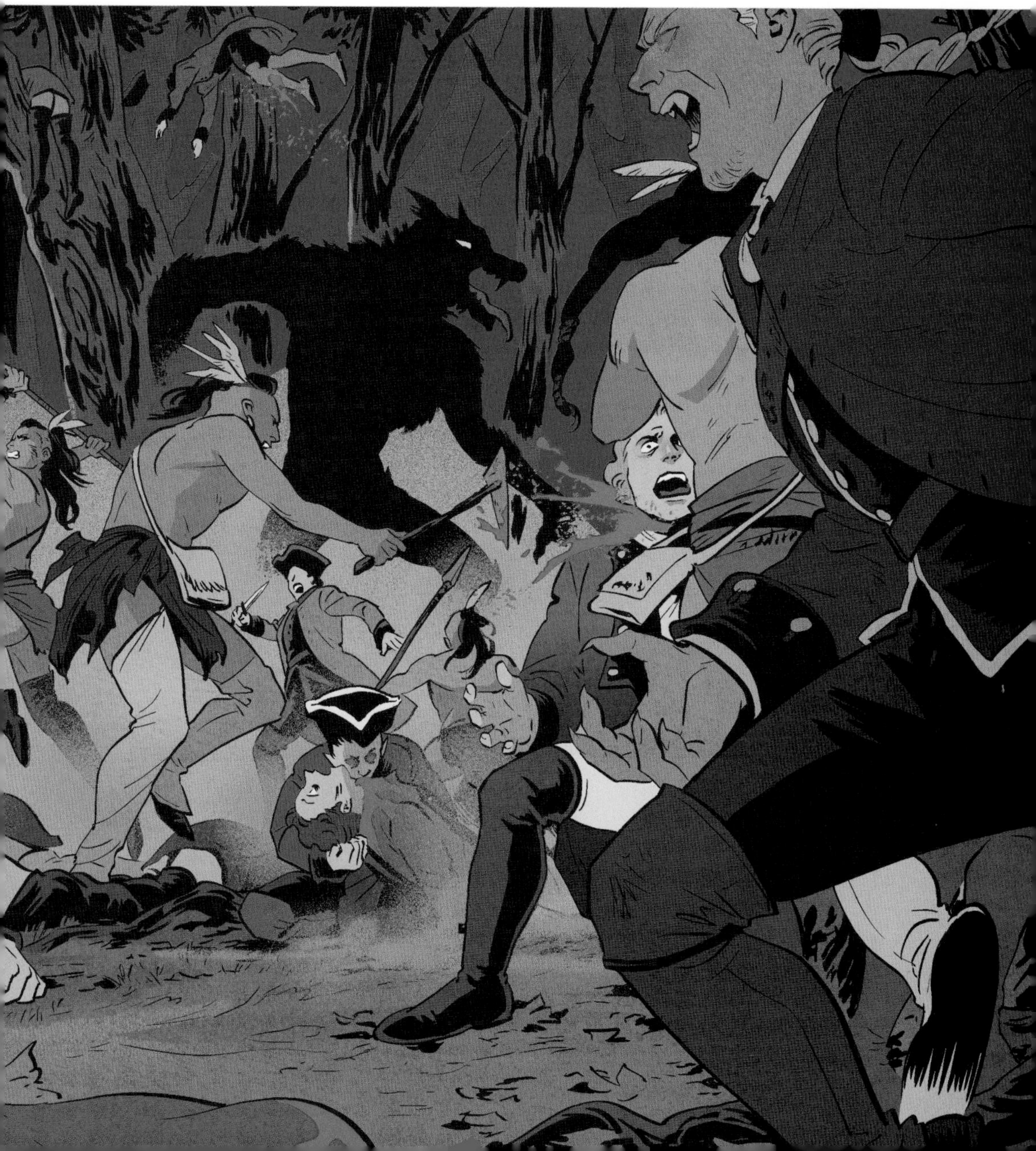

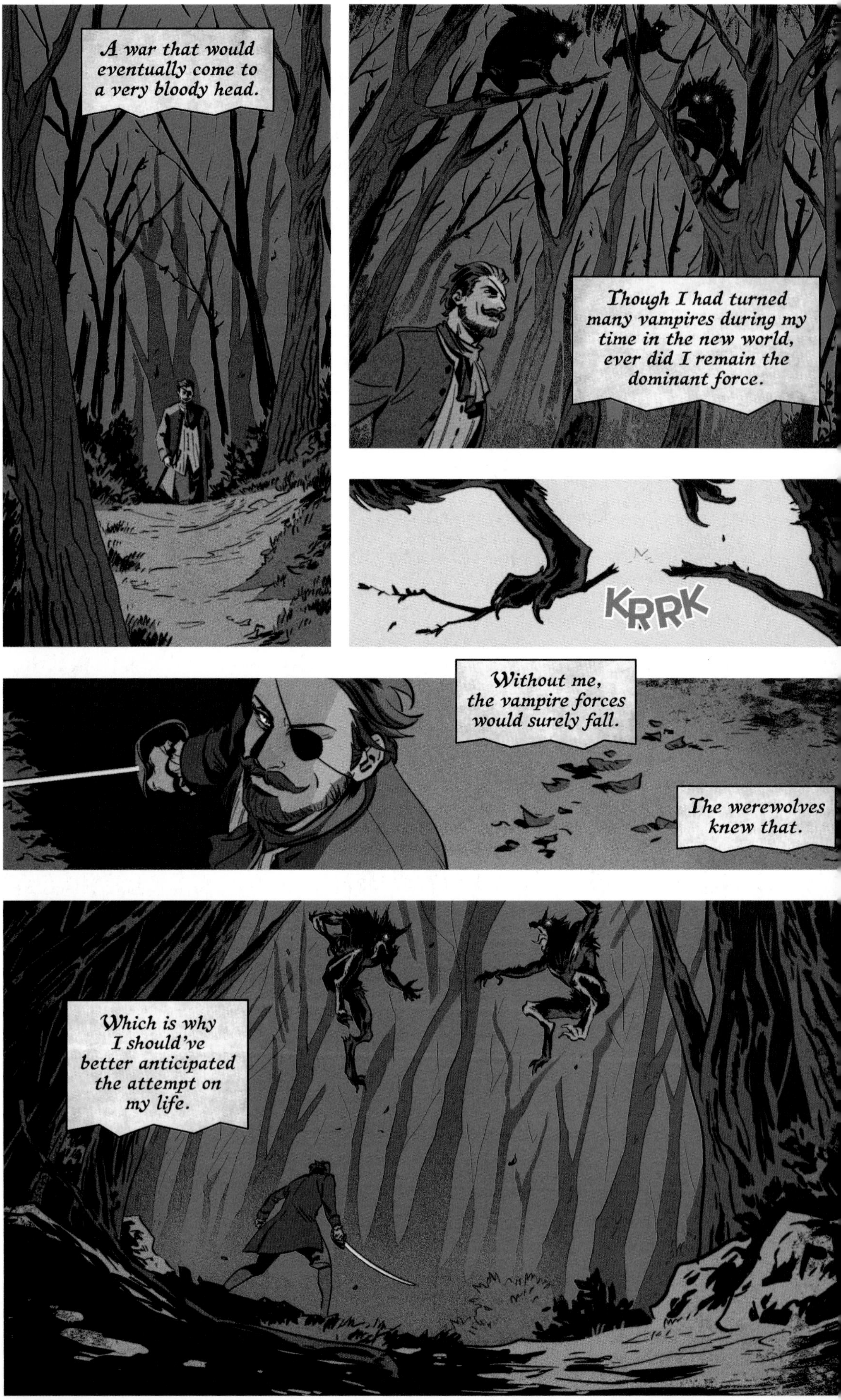
A war that would eventually come to a very bloody head.
Though I had turned many vampires during my time in the new world, ever did I remain the dominant force.
KRRK
Without me, the vampire forces would surely fall.
The werewolves knew that.
Which is why I should've better anticipated the attempt on my life.

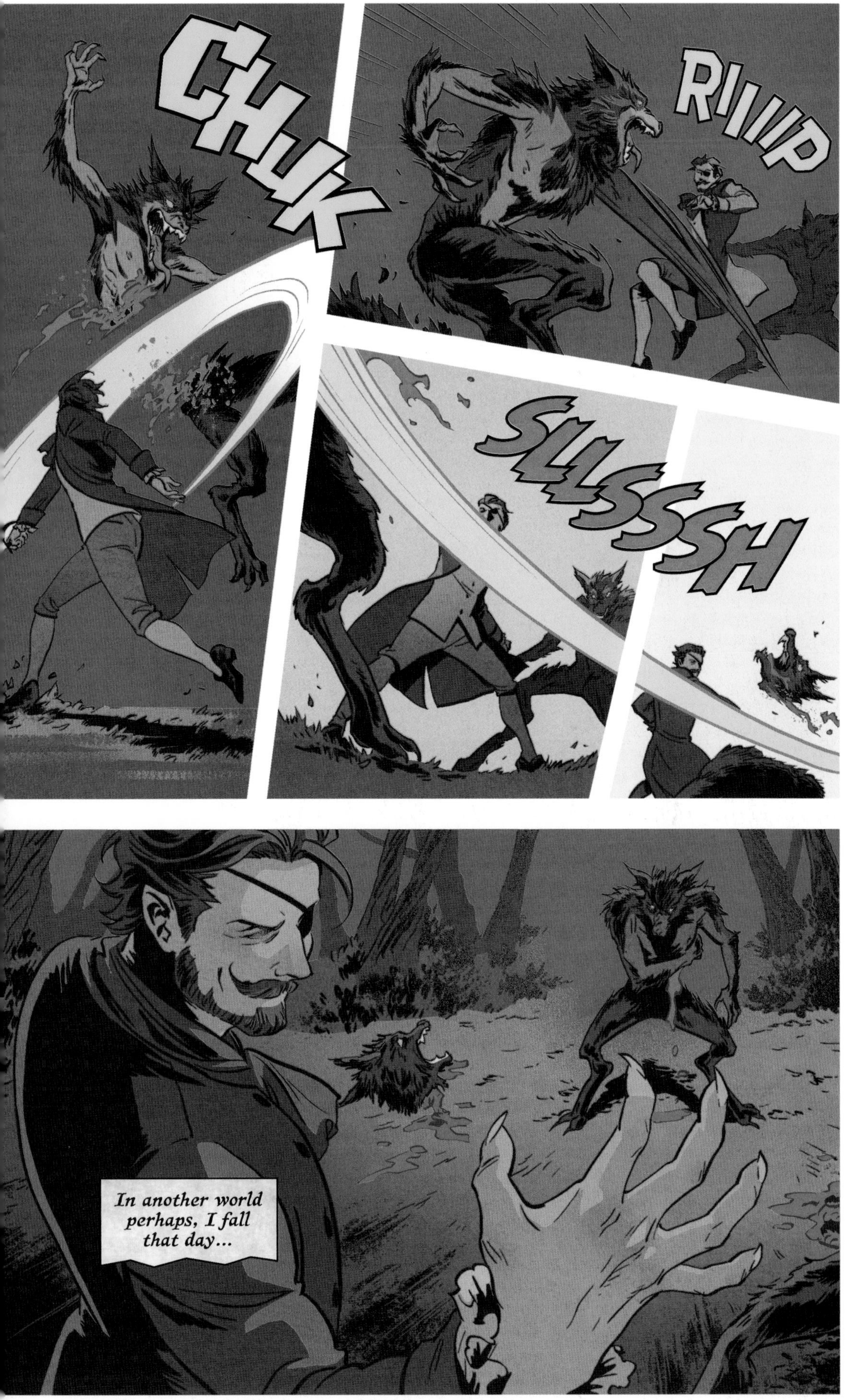
CHUK
RIIIP
SLLSSSH
In another world perhaps, I fall that day...

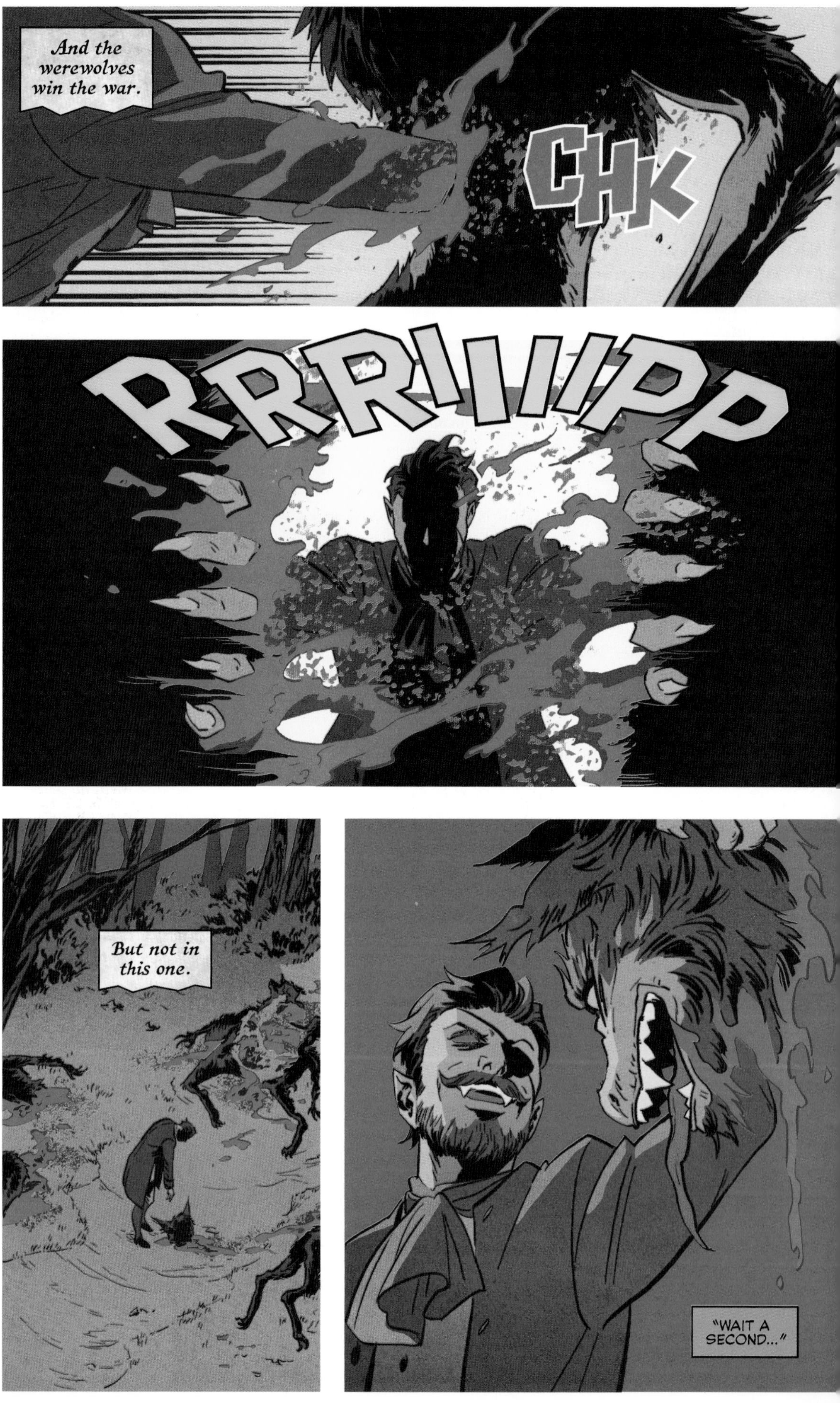
And the werewolves win the war.
CHK
RRRIIIIPP
But not in this one.
"WAIT A SECOND..."

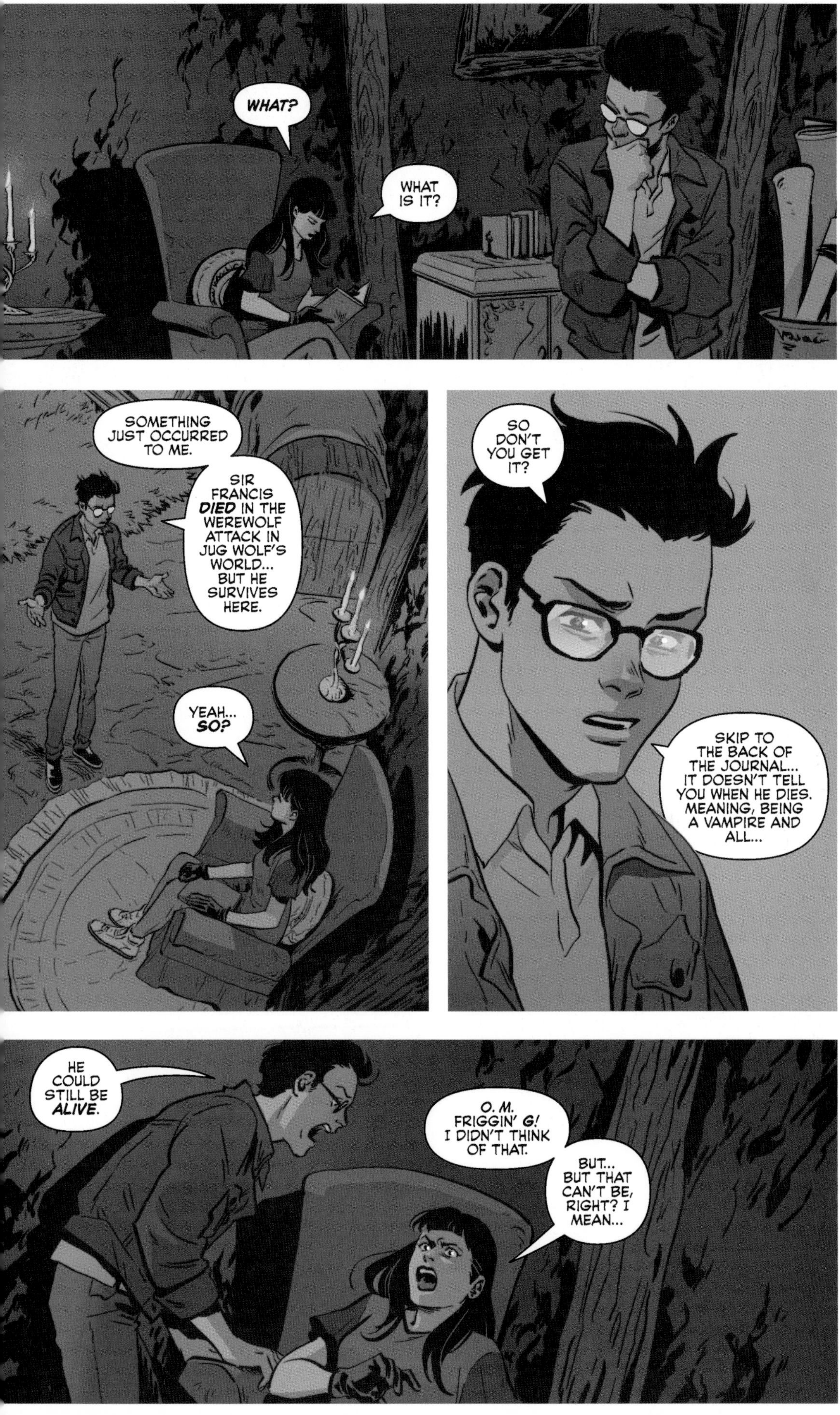
WHAT?
WHAT IS IT?
SOMETHING JUST OCCURRED TO ME.
SIR FRANCIS DIED IN THE WEREWOLF ATTACK IN JUG WOLF'S WORLD... BUT HE SURVIVES HERE.
YEAH... SO?
SO DON'T YOU GET IT?
SKIP TO THE BACK OF THE JOURNAL... IT DOESN'T TELL YOU WHEN HE DIES. MEANING, BEING A VAMPIRE AND ALL...
HE COULD STILL BE ALIVE.
O. M. FRIGGIN' G! I DIDN'T THINK OF THAT.
BUT... BUT THAT CAN'T BE, RIGHT? I MEAN...

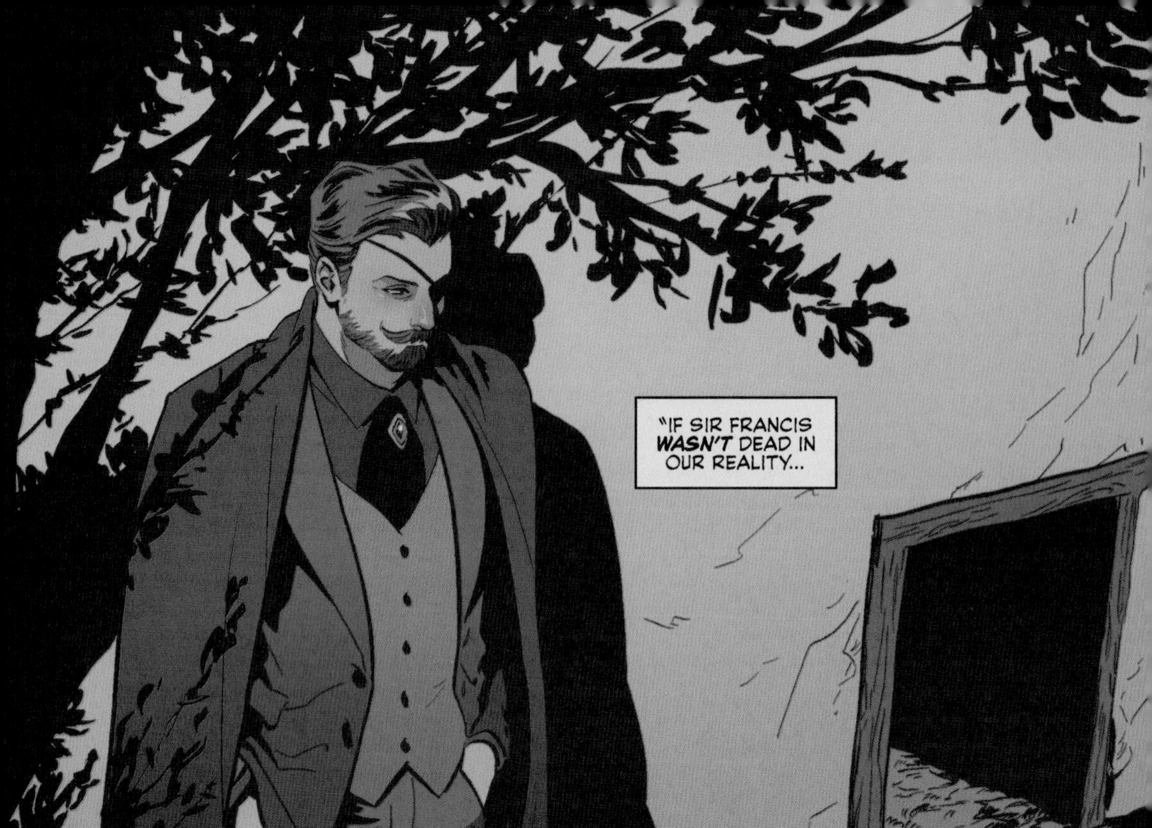
"IF SIR FRANCIS WASN'T DEAD IN OUR REALITY...

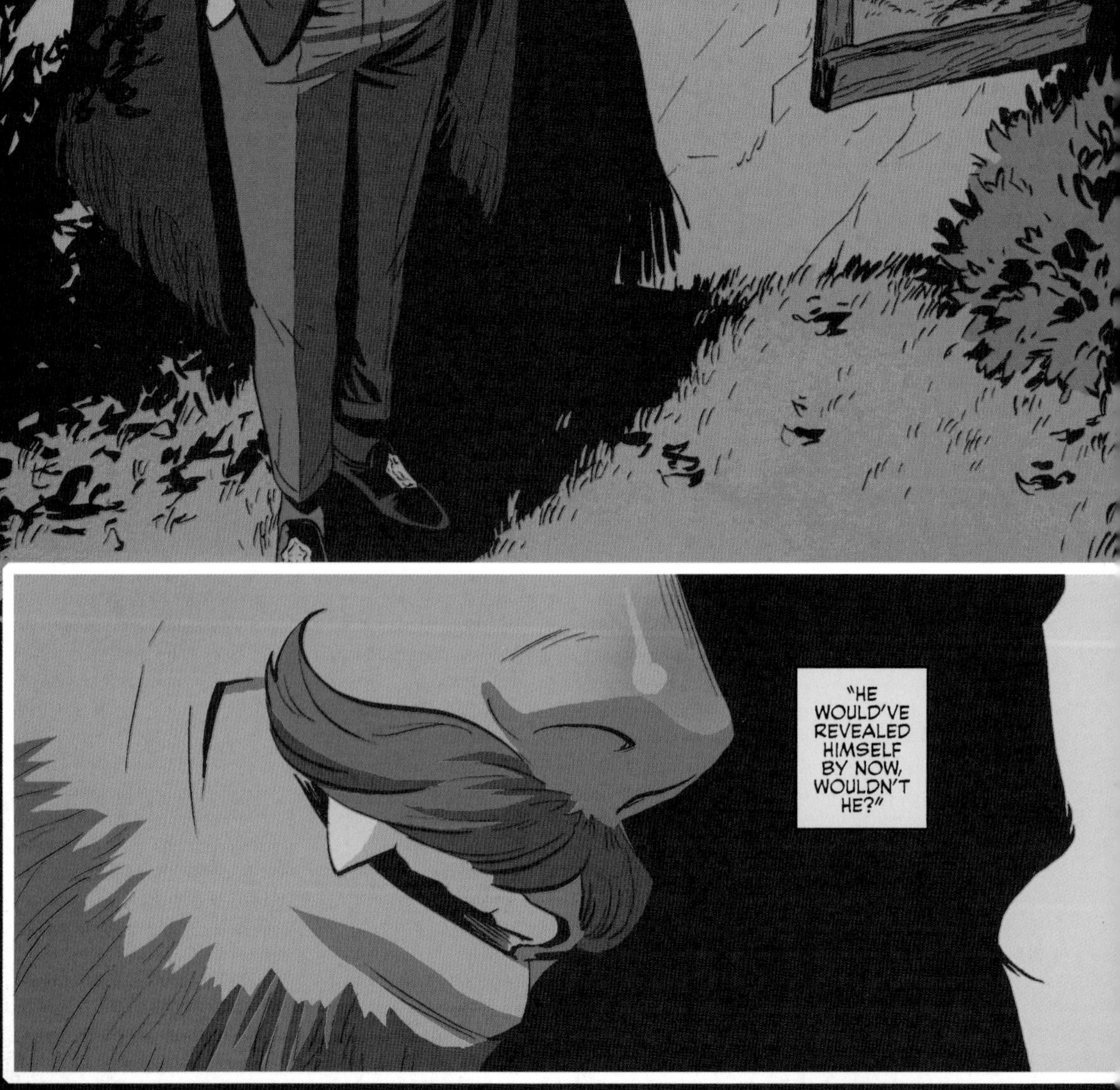
"HE WOULD'VE REVEALED HIMSELF BY NOW, WOULDN'T HE?"

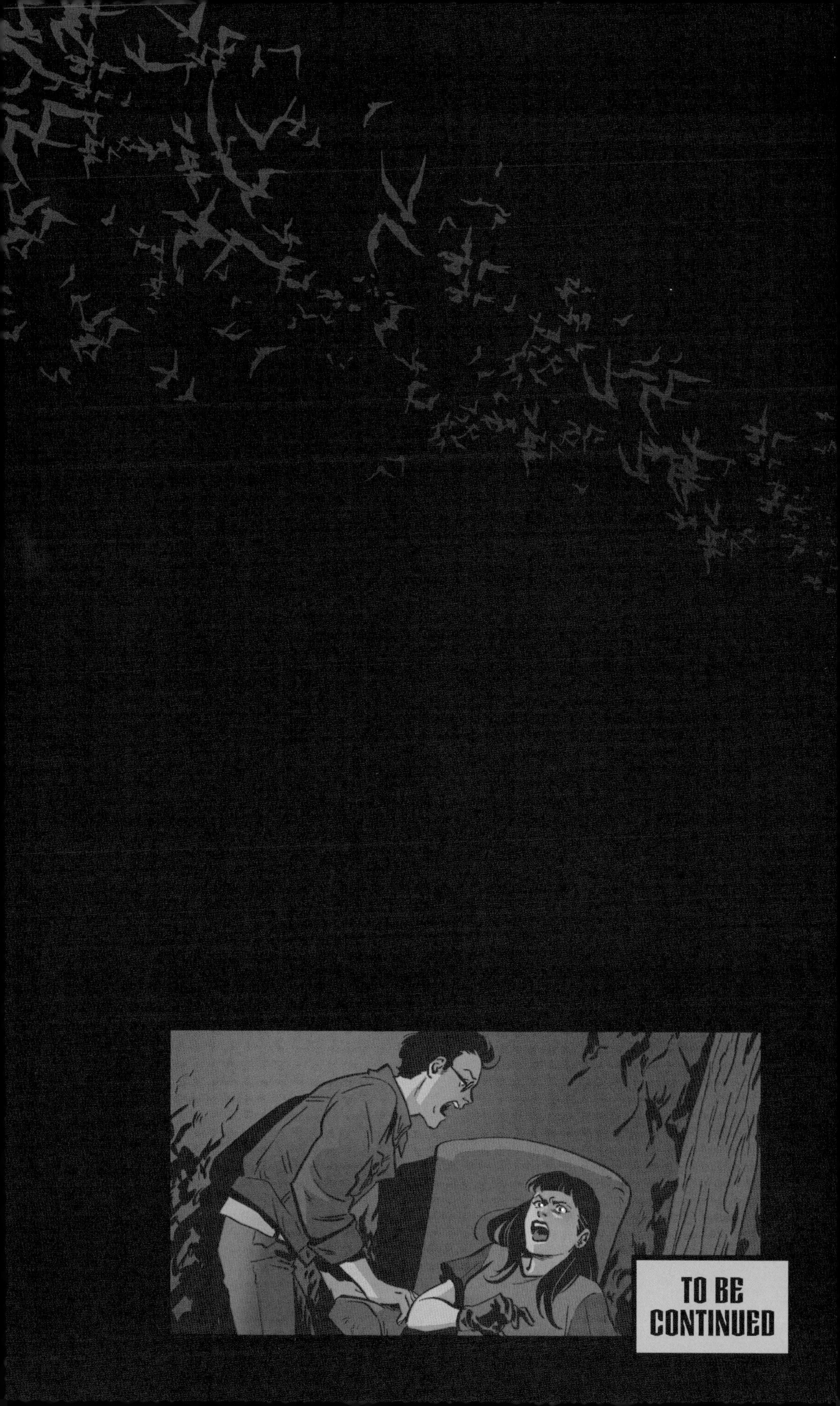
TO BE CONTINUED

CHAPTER FOUR

COVER ART BY **AUDREY MOK**

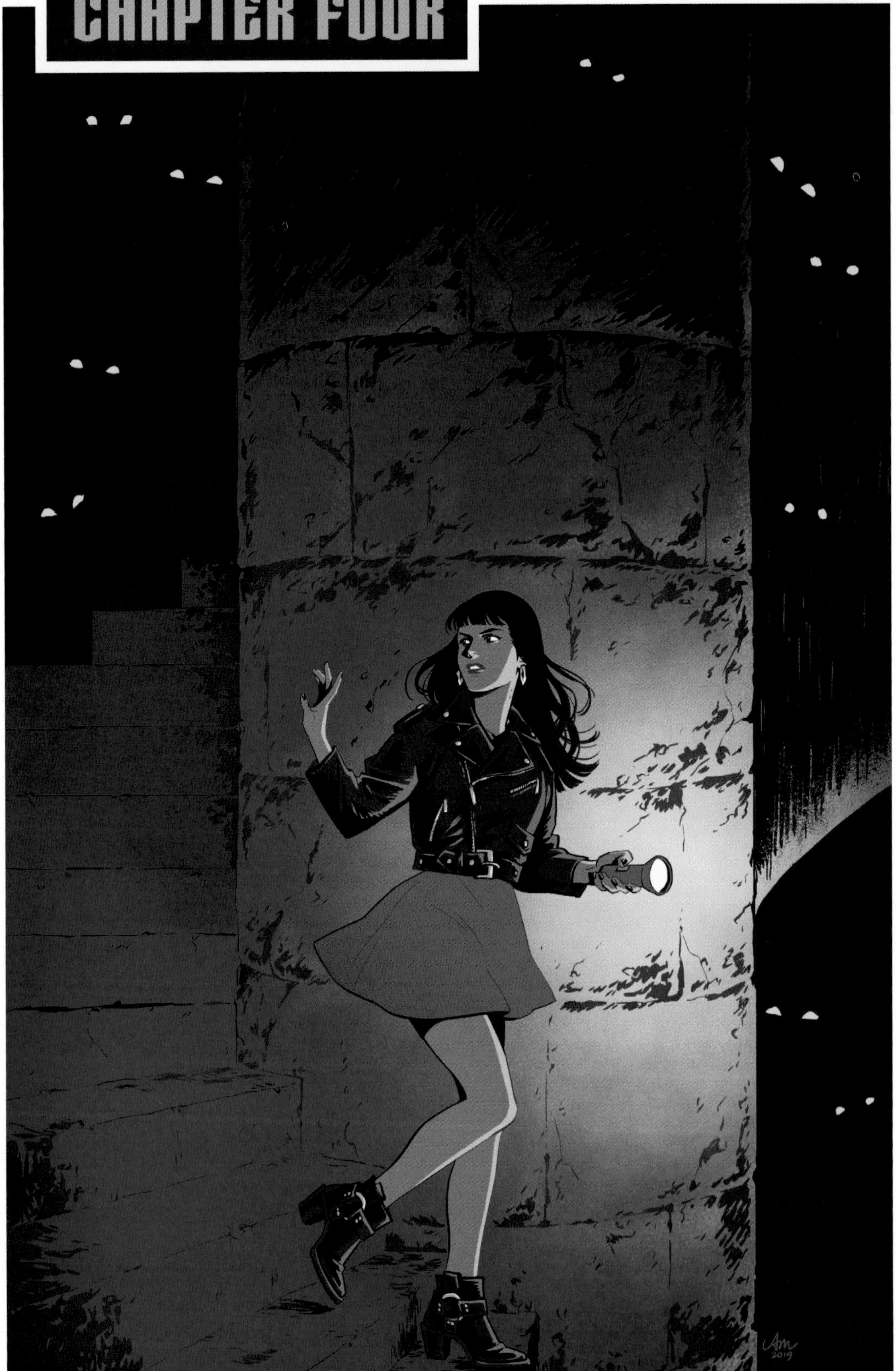

STORY BY **FRANK TIERI & MICHAEL MORECI**

ART BY **AUDREY MOK** (1-15) **& JOE EISMA** (16-25) LETTERING BY **JACK MORELLI**

COLORING BY **MATT HERMS & RYAN JAMPOLE** (16-25 RENDERING)

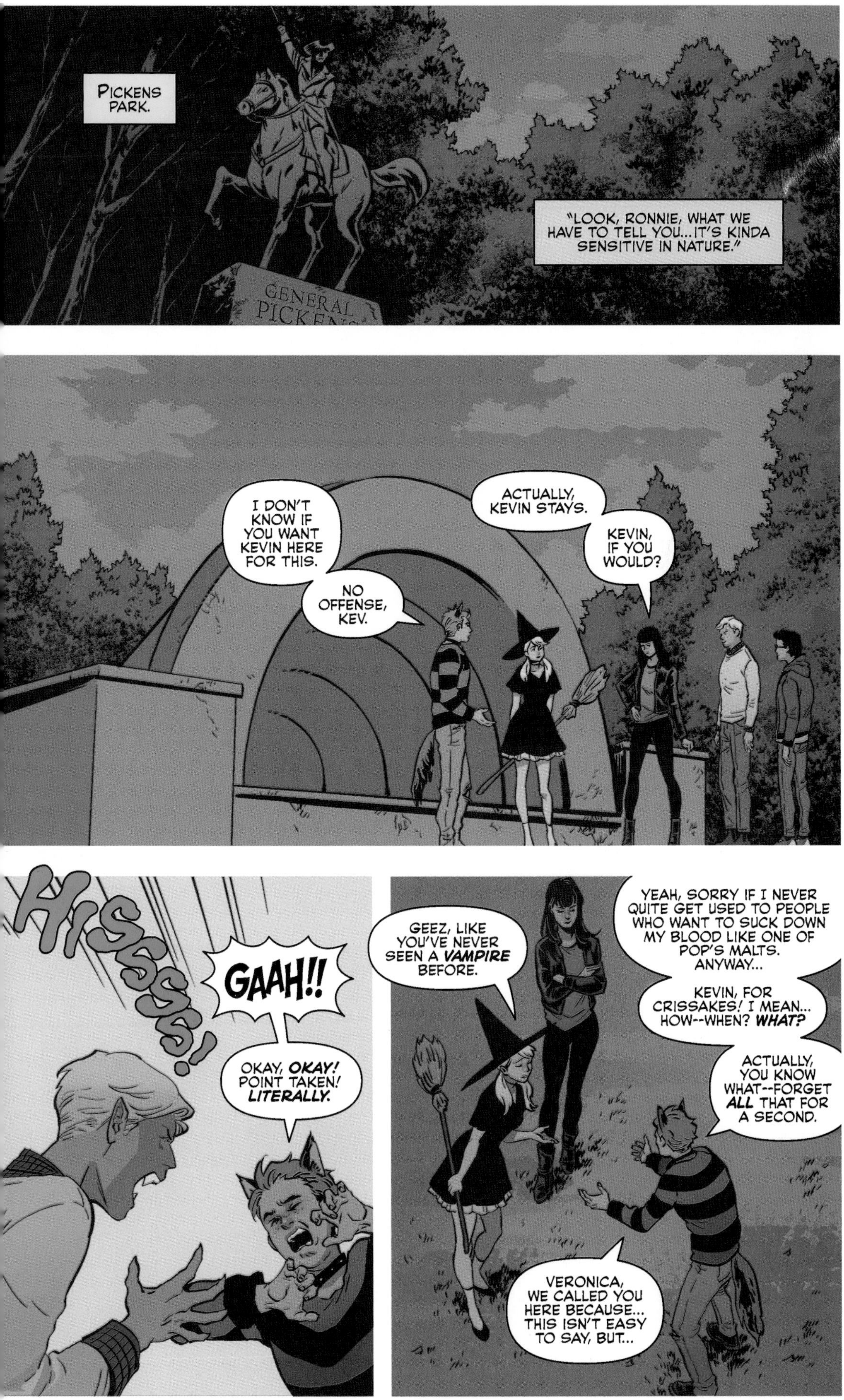

PICKENS PARK.
"LOOK, RONNIE, WHAT WE HAVE TO TELL YOU...IT'S KINDA SENSITIVE IN NATURE."
GENERAL PICKENS
I DON'T KNOW IF YOU WANT KEVIN HERE FOR THIS.
NO OFFENSE, KEV.
ACTUALLY, KEVIN STAYS.
KEVIN, IF YOU WOULD?
HISSSS!
GAAH!!
OKAY, OKAY! POINT TAKEN! LITERALLY.
GEEZ, LIKE YOU'VE NEVER SEEN A VAMPIRE BEFORE.
YEAH, SORRY IF I NEVER QUITE GET USED TO PEOPLE WHO WANT TO SUCK DOWN MY BLOOD LIKE ONE OF POP'S MALTS. ANYWAY...
KEVIN, FOR CRISSAKES! I MEAN... HOW--WHEN? WHAT?
ACTUALLY, YOU KNOW WHAT--FORGET ALL THAT FOR A SECOND.
VERONICA, WE CALLED YOU HERE BECAUSE... THIS ISN'T EASY TO SAY, BUT...

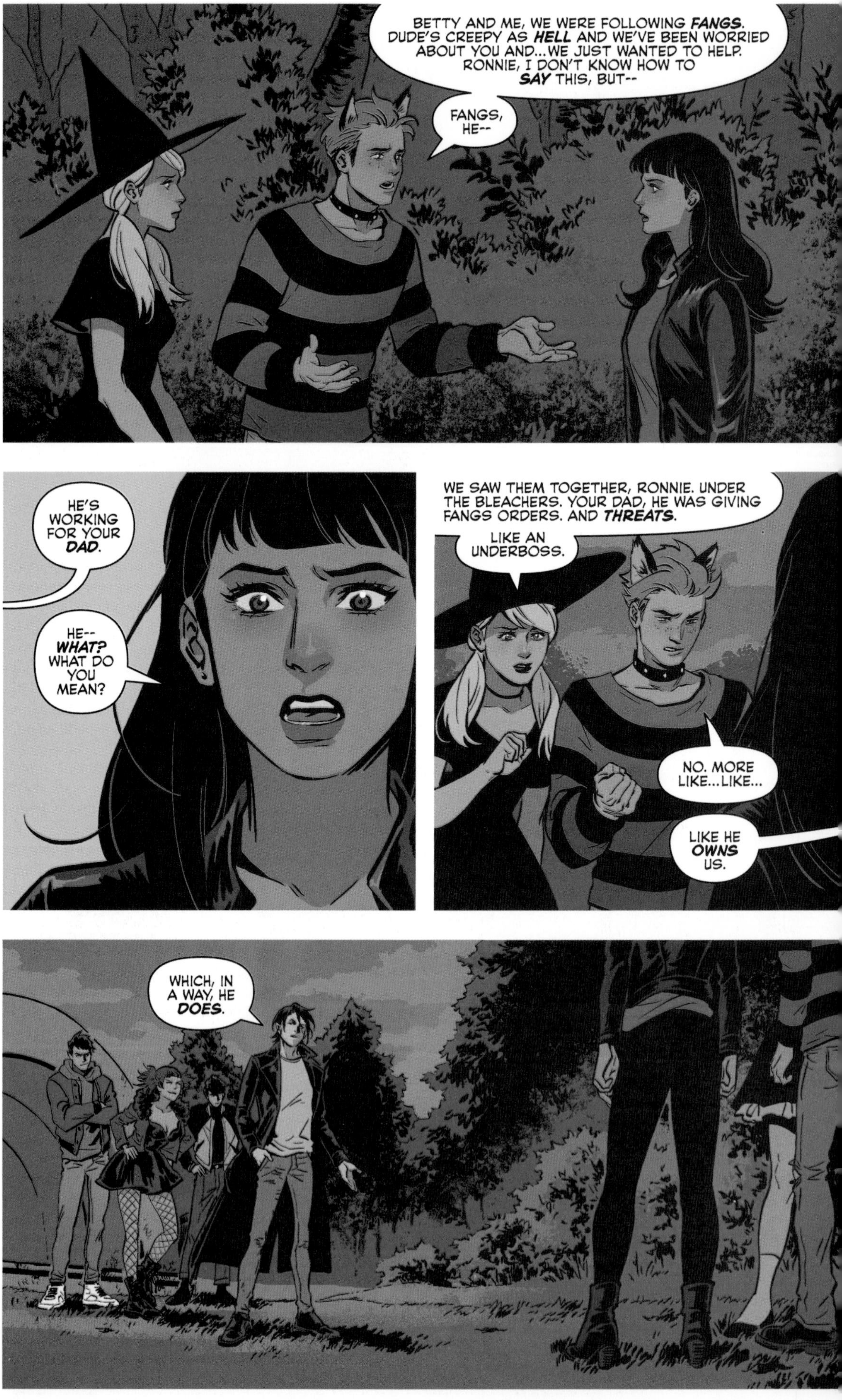
BETTY AND ME, WE WERE FOLLOWING **FANGS**. DUDE'S CREEPY AS **HELL** AND WE'VE BEEN WORRIED ABOUT YOU AND...WE JUST WANTED TO HELP. RONNIE, I DON'T KNOW HOW TO **SAY** THIS, BUT--
FANGS, HE--
HE'S WORKING FOR YOUR **DAD**.
HE-- **WHAT?** WHAT DO YOU MEAN?
WE SAW THEM TOGETHER, RONNIE. UNDER THE BLEACHERS. YOUR DAD, HE WAS GIVING FANGS ORDERS. AND **THREATS**.
LIKE AN UNDERBOSS.
NO. MORE LIKE...LIKE...
LIKE HE **OWNS** US.
WHICH, IN A WAY, HE **DOES**.

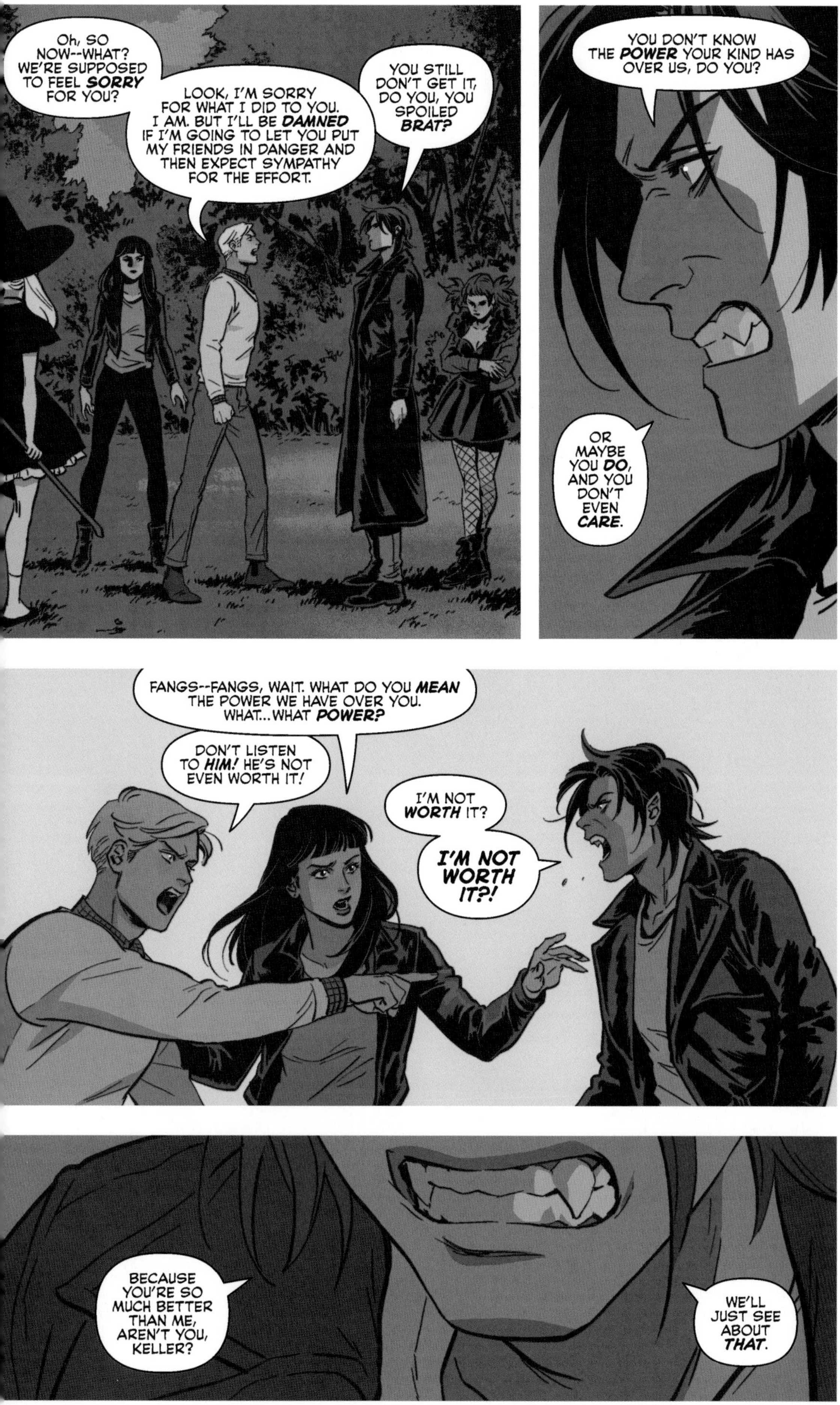
Oh, SO NOW--WHAT? WE'RE SUPPOSED TO FEEL **SORRY** FOR YOU?
LOOK, I'M SORRY FOR WHAT I DID TO YOU. I AM. BUT I'LL BE **DAMNED** IF I'M GOING TO LET YOU PUT MY FRIENDS IN DANGER AND THEN EXPECT SYMPATHY FOR THE EFFORT.
YOU STILL DON'T GET IT, DO YOU, YOU SPOILED **BRAT?**
YOU DON'T KNOW THE **POWER** YOUR KIND HAS OVER US, DO YOU?
OR MAYBE YOU **DO**, AND YOU DON'T EVEN **CARE**.
FANGS--FANGS, WAIT. WHAT DO YOU **MEAN** THE POWER WE HAVE OVER YOU. WHAT...WHAT **POWER?**
DON'T LISTEN TO **HIM!** HE'S NOT EVEN WORTH IT!
I'M NOT **WORTH** IT?
I'M NOT WORTH IT?!
BECAUSE YOU'RE SO MUCH BETTER THAN ME, AREN'T YOU, KELLER?
WE'LL JUST SEE ABOUT **THAT**.

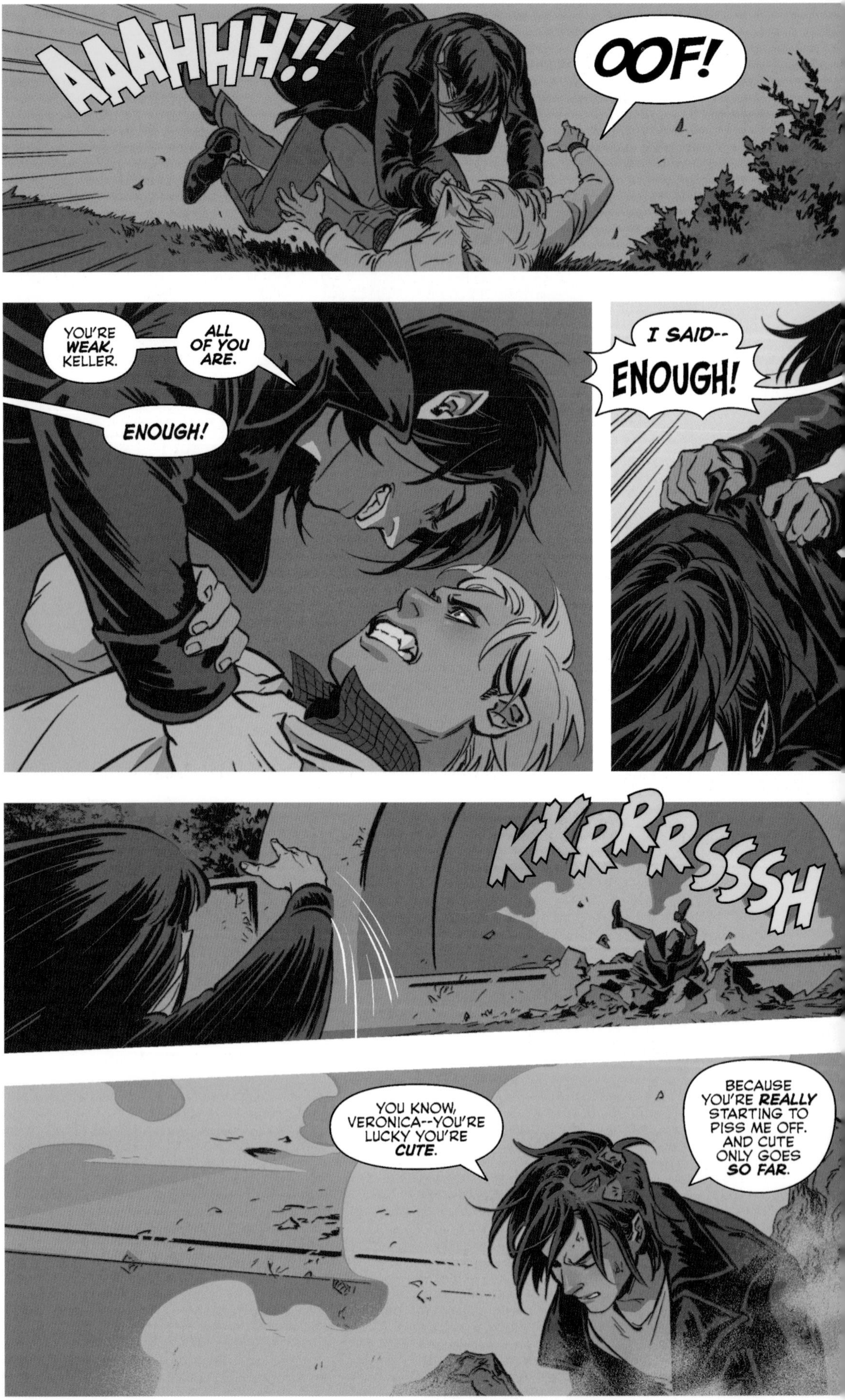
AAAHHH!!
OOF!
YOU'RE WEAK, KELLER.
ALL OF YOU ARE.
ENOUGH!
I SAID--
ENOUGH!
KKRRRSSSH
YOU KNOW, VERONICA--YOU'RE LUCKY YOU'RE CUTE.
BECAUSE YOU'RE REALLY STARTING TO PISS ME OFF. AND CUTE ONLY GOES SO FAR.

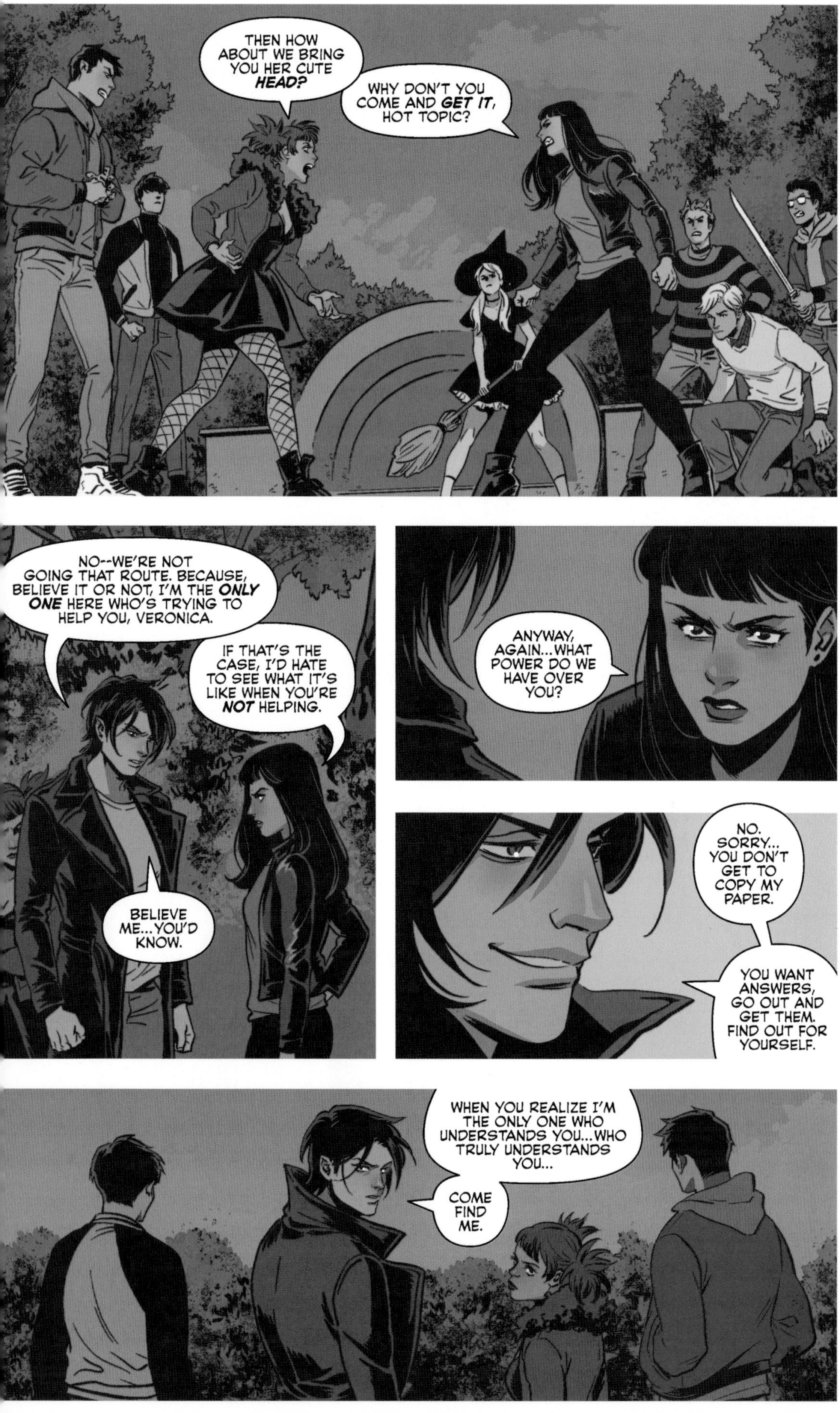
THEN HOW ABOUT WE BRING YOU HER CUTE **HEAD?**
WHY DON'T YOU COME AND **GET IT**, HOT TOPIC?
NO--WE'RE NOT GOING THAT ROUTE. BECAUSE, BELIEVE IT OR NOT, I'M THE **ONLY ONE** HERE WHO'S TRYING TO HELP YOU, VERONICA.
IF THAT'S THE CASE, I'D HATE TO SEE WHAT IT'S LIKE WHEN YOU'RE **NOT** HELPING.
BELIEVE ME...YOU'D KNOW.
ANYWAY, AGAIN...WHAT POWER DO WE HAVE OVER YOU?
NO. SORRY... YOU DON'T GET TO COPY MY PAPER.
YOU WANT ANSWERS, GO OUT AND GET THEM. FIND OUT FOR YOURSELF.
WHEN YOU REALIZE I'M THE ONLY ONE WHO UNDERSTANDS YOU...WHO TRULY UNDERSTANDS YOU...
COME FIND ME.

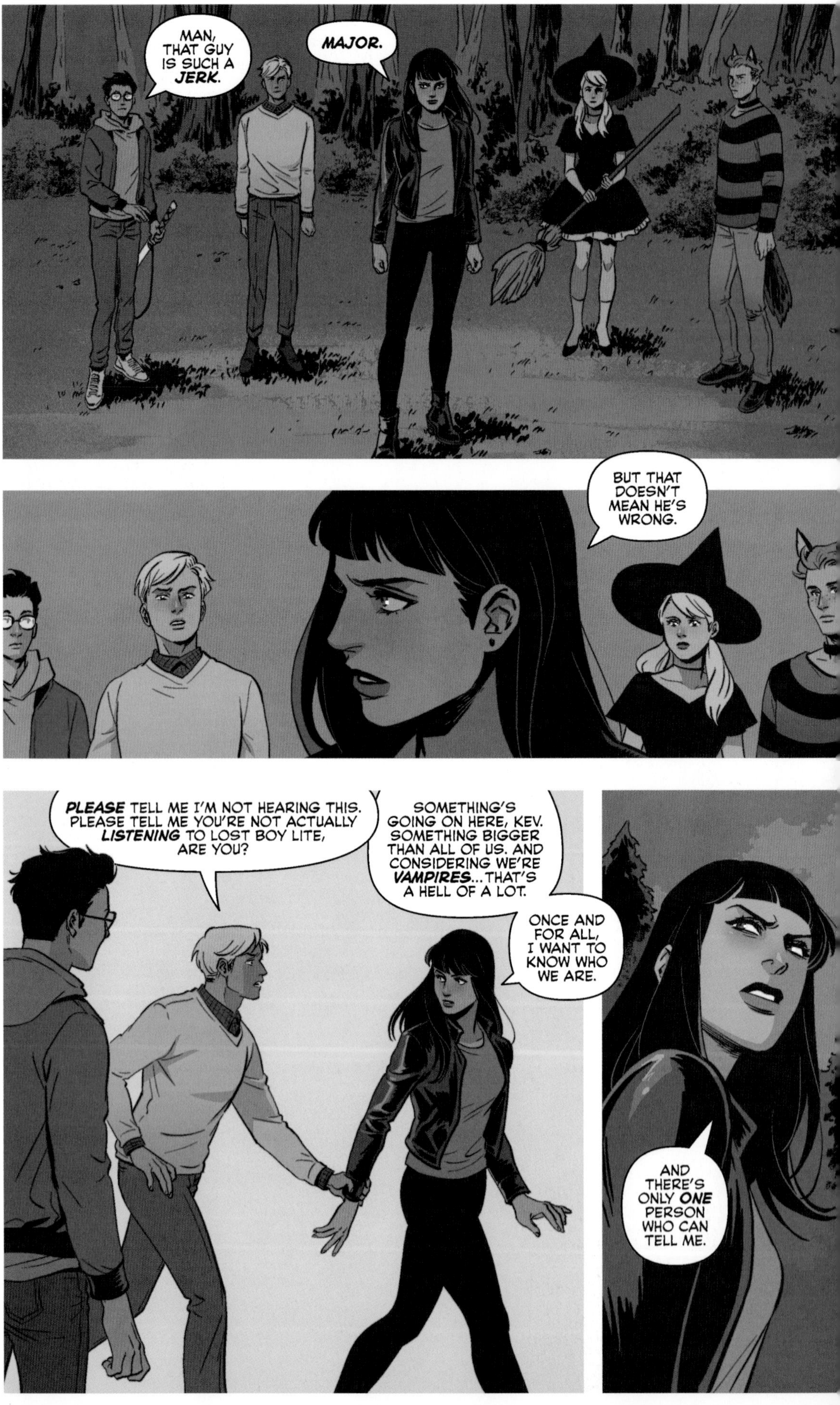

MAN, THAT GUY IS SUCH A **JERK**.
MAJOR.
BUT THAT DOESN'T MEAN HE'S WRONG.
PLEASE TELL ME I'M NOT HEARING THIS. PLEASE TELL ME YOU'RE NOT ACTUALLY ***LISTENING*** TO LOST BOY LITE, ARE YOU?
SOMETHING'S GOING ON HERE, KEV. SOMETHING BIGGER THAN ALL OF US. AND CONSIDERING WE'RE ***VAMPIRES***... THAT'S A HELL OF A LOT.
ONCE AND FOR ALL, I WANT TO KNOW WHO WE ARE.
AND THERE'S ONLY ***ONE*** PERSON WHO CAN TELL ME.

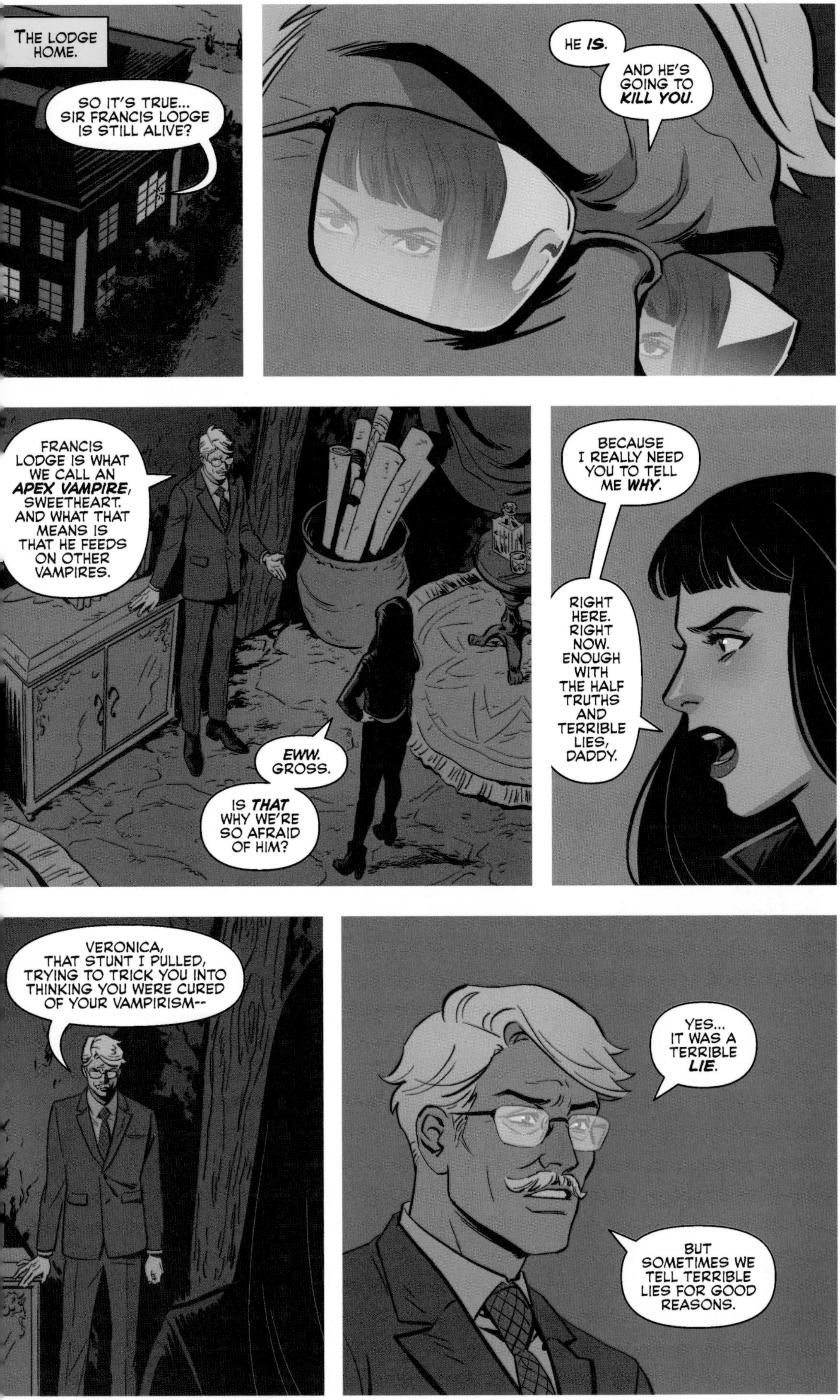
THE LODGE HOME.
SO IT'S TRUE... SIR FRANCIS LODGE IS STILL ALIVE?
HE IS.
AND HE'S GOING TO KILL YOU.
FRANCIS LODGE IS WHAT WE CALL AN APEX VAMPIRE, SWEETHEART. AND WHAT THAT MEANS IS THAT HE FEEDS ON OTHER VAMPIRES.
EWW. GROSS.
IS THAT WHY WE'RE SO AFRAID OF HIM?
BECAUSE I REALLY NEED YOU TO TELL ME WHY.
RIGHT HERE. RIGHT NOW. ENOUGH WITH THE HALF TRUTHS AND TERRIBLE LIES, DADDY.
VERONICA, THAT STUNT I PULLED, TRYING TO TRICK YOU INTO THINKING YOU WERE CURED OF YOUR VAMPIRISM--
YES... IT WAS A TERRIBLE LIE.
BUT SOMETIMES WE TELL TERRIBLE LIES FOR GOOD REASONS.

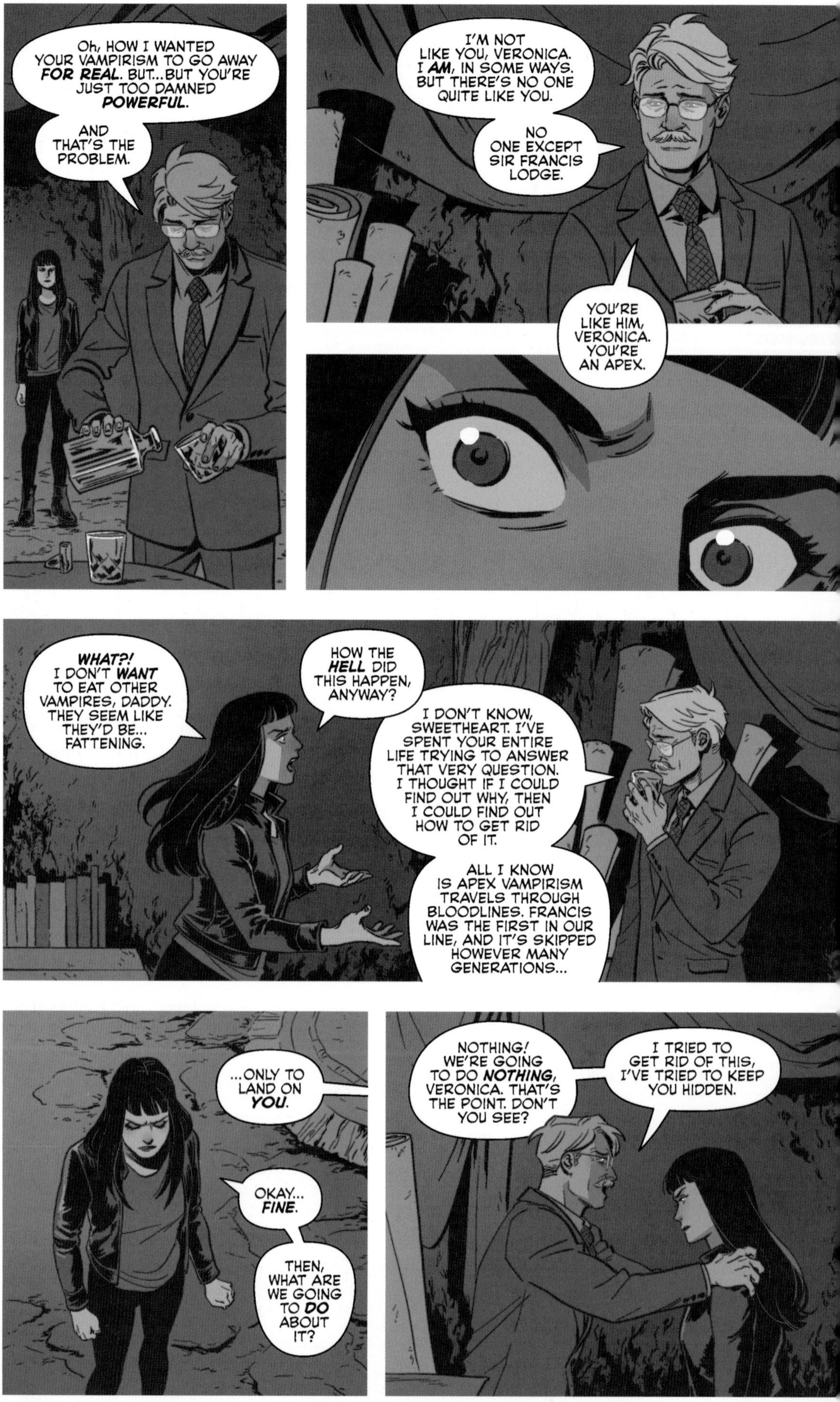
Oh, HOW I WANTED YOUR VAMPIRISM TO GO AWAY **FOR REAL**. BUT...BUT YOU'RE JUST TOO DAMNED **POWERFUL**.
AND THAT'S THE PROBLEM.
I'M NOT LIKE YOU, VERONICA. I **AM**, IN SOME WAYS. BUT THERE'S NO ONE QUITE LIKE YOU.
NO ONE EXCEPT SIR FRANCIS LODGE.
YOU'RE LIKE HIM, VERONICA. YOU'RE AN APEX.
WHAT?! I DON'T **WANT** TO EAT OTHER VAMPIRES, DADDY. THEY SEEM LIKE THEY'D BE... FATTENING.
HOW THE **HELL** DID THIS HAPPEN, ANYWAY?
I DON'T KNOW, SWEETHEART. I'VE SPENT YOUR ENTIRE LIFE TRYING TO ANSWER THAT VERY QUESTION. I THOUGHT IF I COULD FIND OUT WHY, THEN I COULD FIND OUT HOW TO GET RID OF IT.
ALL I KNOW IS APEX VAMPIRISM TRAVELS THROUGH BLOODLINES. FRANCIS WAS THE FIRST IN OUR LINE, AND IT'S SKIPPED HOWEVER MANY GENERATIONS...
...ONLY TO LAND ON **YOU**.
OKAY... **FINE**.
THEN, WHAT ARE WE GOING TO **DO** ABOUT IT?
NOTHING! WE'RE GOING TO DO **NOTHING**, VERONICA. THAT'S THE POINT. DON'T YOU SEE?
I TRIED TO GET RID OF THIS, I'VE TRIED TO KEEP YOU HIDDEN.

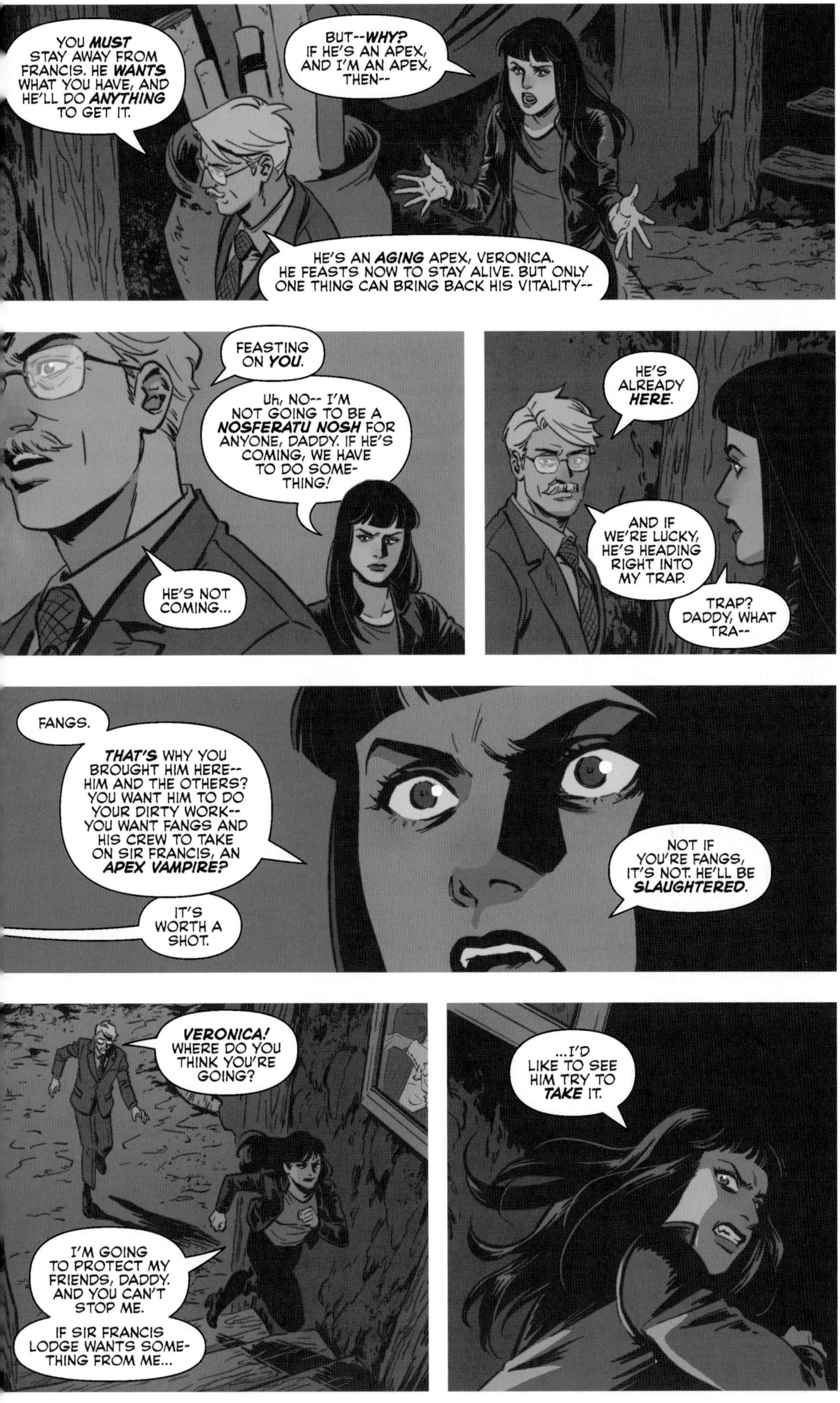

YOU MUST STAY AWAY FROM FRANCIS. HE WANTS WHAT YOU HAVE, AND HE'LL DO ANYTHING TO GET IT.
BUT--WHY? IF HE'S AN APEX, AND I'M AN APEX, THEN--
HE'S AN AGING APEX, VERONICA. HE FEASTS NOW TO STAY ALIVE. BUT ONLY ONE THING CAN BRING BACK HIS VITALITY--
FEASTING ON YOU.
Uh, NO-- I'M NOT GOING TO BE A NOSFERATU NOSH FOR ANYONE, DADDY. IF HE'S COMING, WE HAVE TO DO SOME-THING!
HE'S NOT COMING...
HE'S ALREADY HERE.
AND IF WE'RE LUCKY, HE'S HEADING RIGHT INTO MY TRAP.
TRAP? DADDY, WHAT TRA--
FANGS.
THAT'S WHY YOU BROUGHT HIM HERE-- HIM AND THE OTHERS? YOU WANT HIM TO DO YOUR DIRTY WORK-- YOU WANT FANGS AND HIS CREW TO TAKE ON SIR FRANCIS, AN APEX VAMPIRE?
IT'S WORTH A SHOT.
NOT IF YOU'RE FANGS, IT'S NOT. HE'LL BE SLAUGHTERED.
VERONICA! WHERE DO YOU THINK YOU'RE GOING?
I'M GOING TO PROTECT MY FRIENDS, DADDY. AND YOU CAN'T STOP ME.
IF SIR FRANCIS LODGE WANTS SOME-THING FROM ME...
...I'D LIKE TO SEE HIM TRY TO TAKE IT.

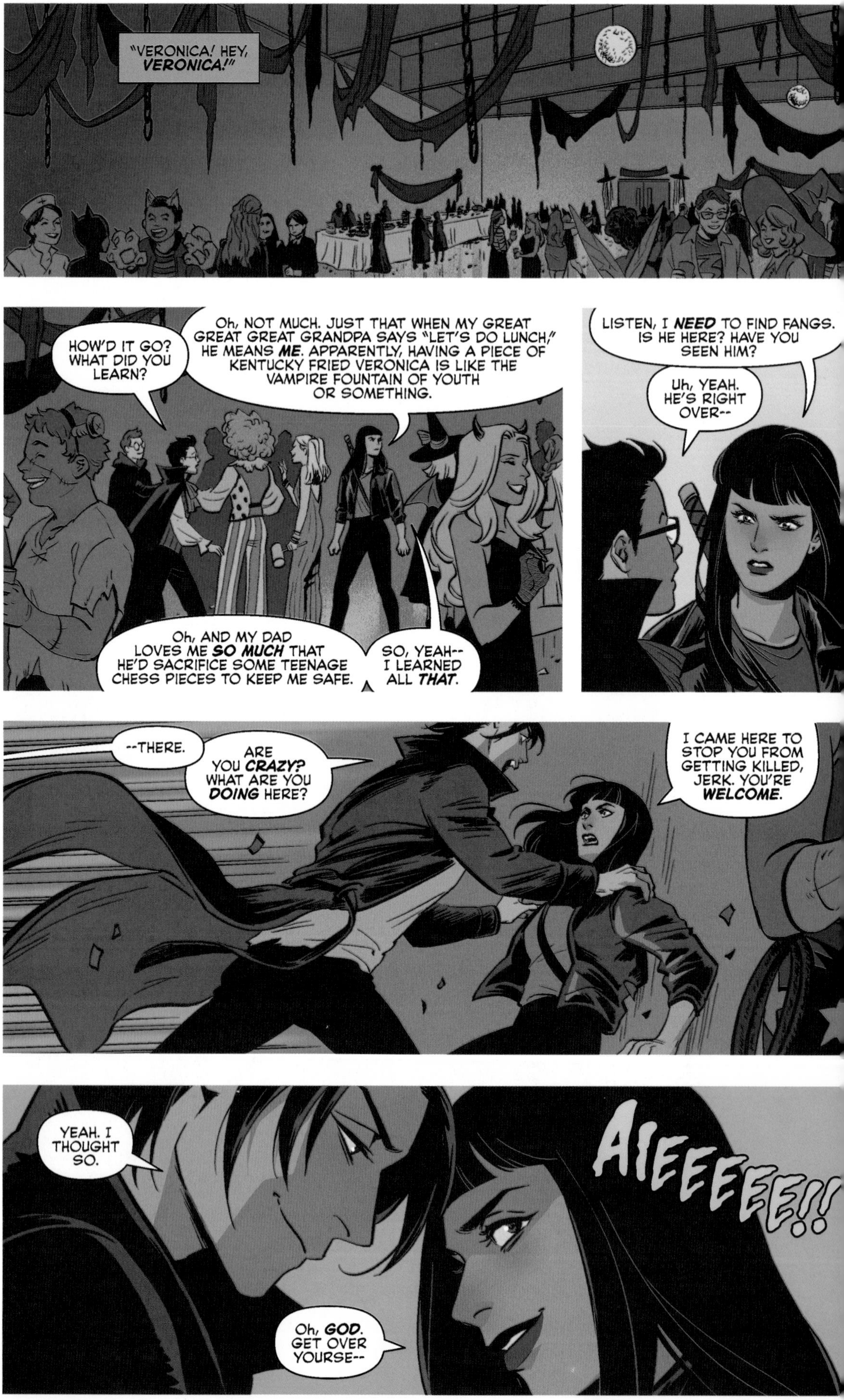
"VERONICA! HEY, VERONICA!"
HOW'D IT GO? WHAT DID YOU LEARN?
Oh, NOT MUCH. JUST THAT WHEN MY GREAT GREAT GREAT GRANDPA SAYS "LET'S DO LUNCH," HE MEANS ME. APPARENTLY, HAVING A PIECE OF KENTUCKY FRIED VERONICA IS LIKE THE VAMPIRE FOUNTAIN OF YOUTH OR SOMETHING.
Oh, AND MY DAD LOVES ME SO MUCH THAT HE'D SACRIFICE SOME TEENAGE CHESS PIECES TO KEEP ME SAFE.
SO, YEAH-- I LEARNED ALL THAT.
LISTEN, I NEED TO FIND FANGS. IS HE HERE? HAVE YOU SEEN HIM?
Uh, YEAH. HE'S RIGHT OVER--
--THERE.
ARE YOU CRAZY? WHAT ARE YOU DOING HERE?
I CAME HERE TO STOP YOU FROM GETTING KILLED, JERK. YOU'RE WELCOME.
YEAH. I THOUGHT SO.
AIEEEEEE!!
Oh, GOD. GET OVER YOURSE--

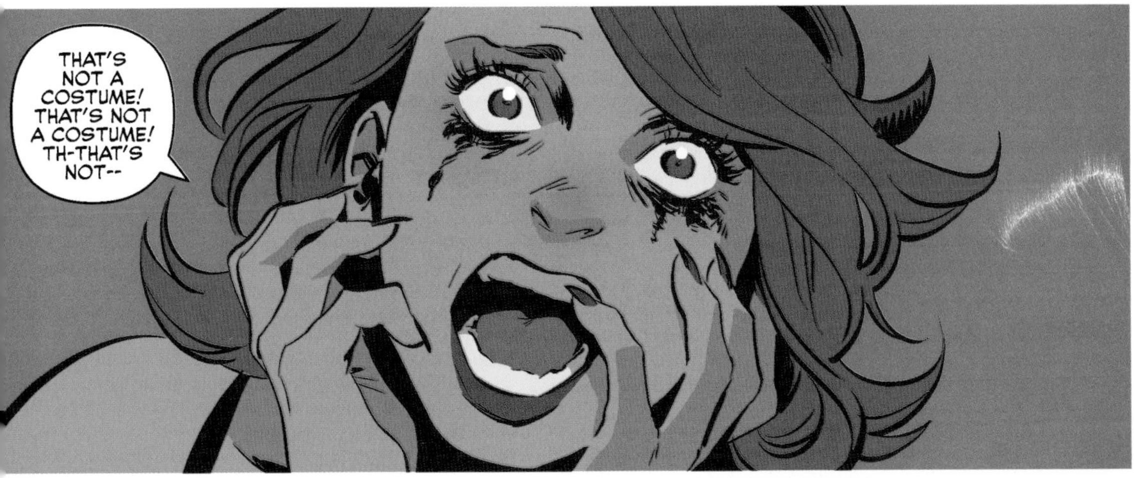
THAT'S NOT A COSTUME! THAT'S NOT A COSTUME! TH-THAT'S NOT--

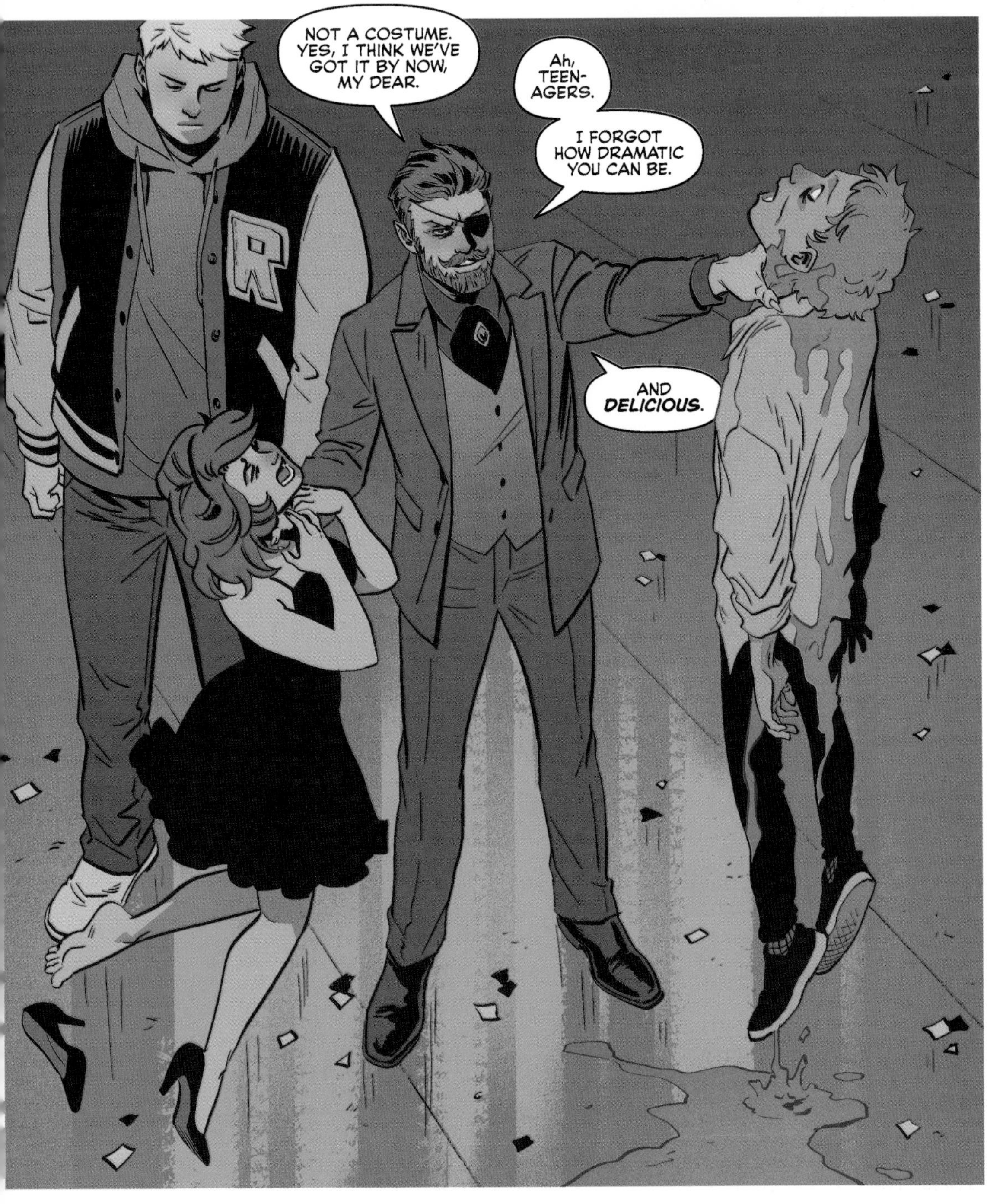
NOT A COSTUME. YES, I THINK WE'VE GOT IT BY NOW, MY DEAR.
Ah, TEEN-AGERS.
I FORGOT HOW DRAMATIC YOU CAN BE.
AND *DELICIOUS*.

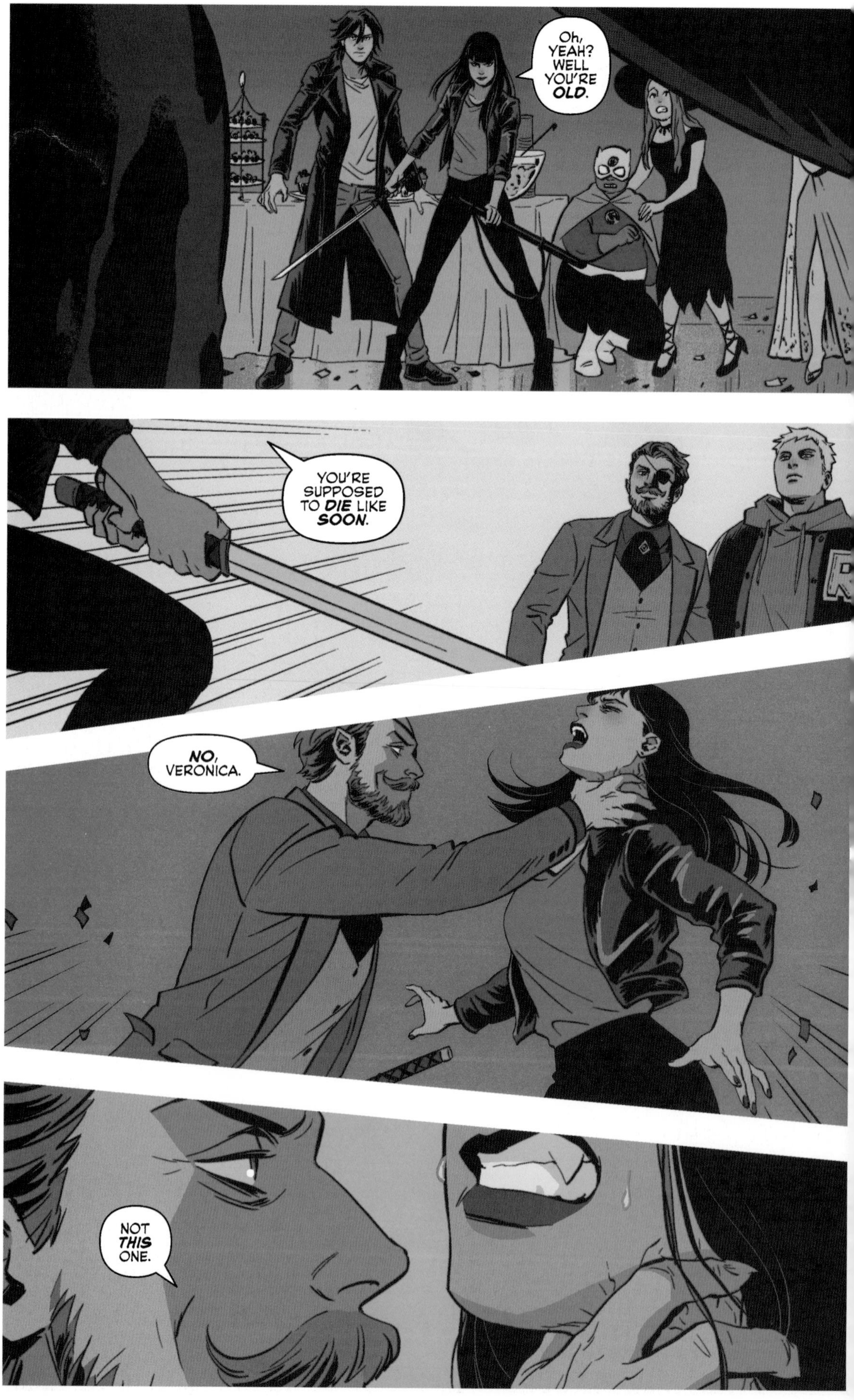
Oh, YEAH? WELL YOU'RE OLD.
YOU'RE SUPPOSED TO DIE LIKE SOON.
NO, VERONICA.
NOT THIS ONE.

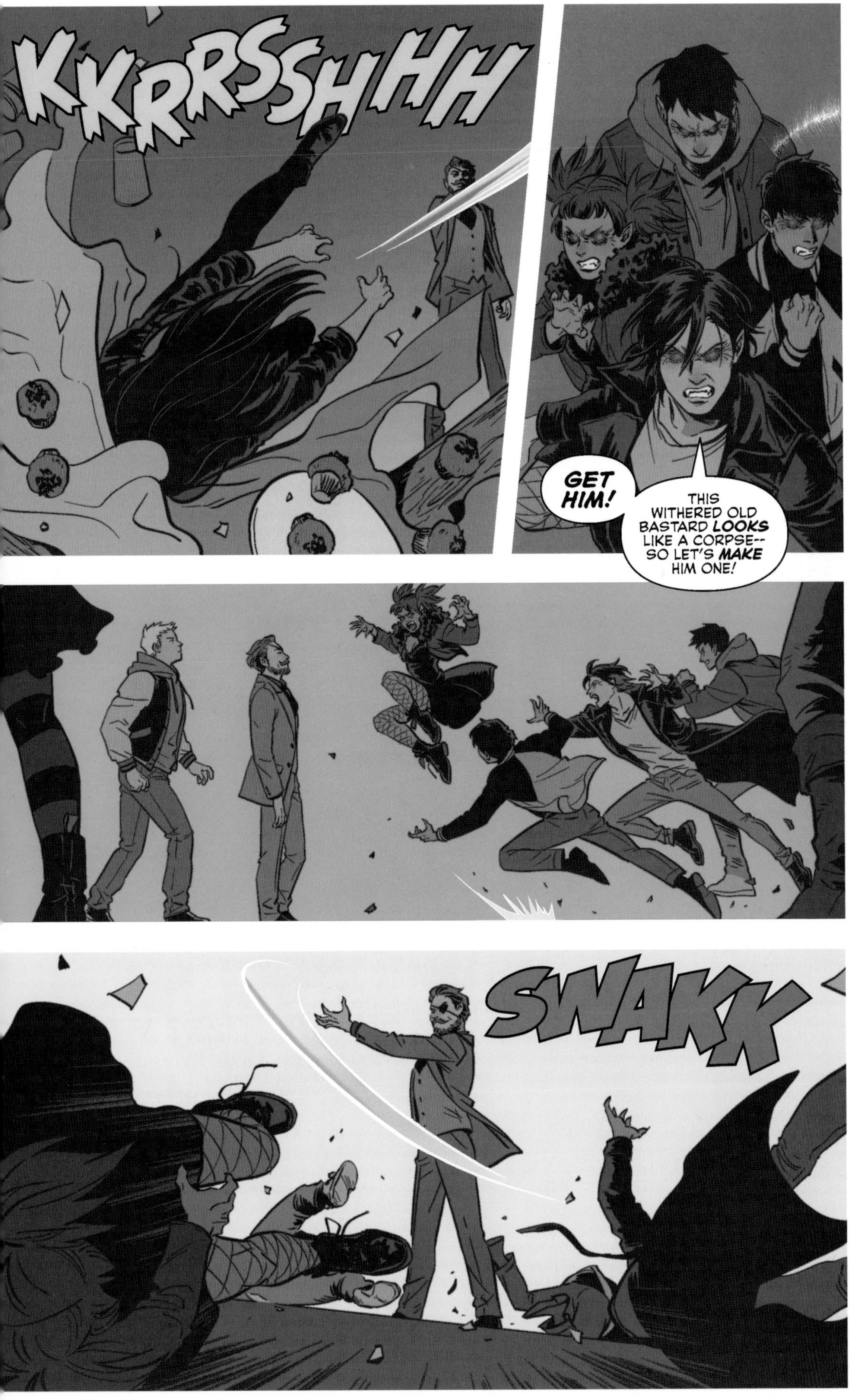
KKRRSSHHH
GET HIM!
THIS WITHERED OLD BASTARD **LOOKS** LIKE A CORPSE-- SO LET'S **MAKE** HIM ONE!
SWAKK

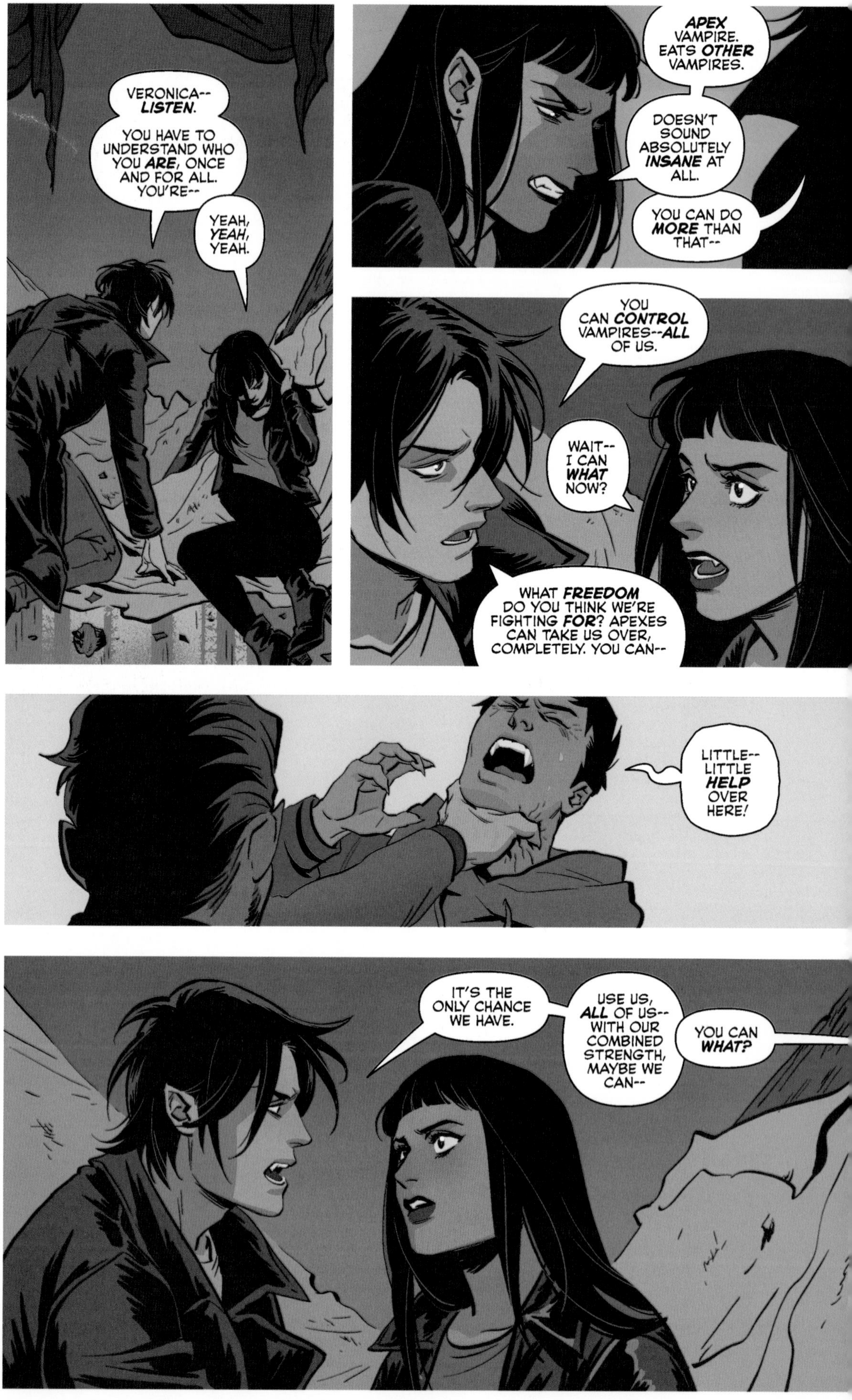
VERONICA-- LISTEN.
YOU HAVE TO UNDERSTAND WHO YOU ARE, ONCE AND FOR ALL. YOU'RE--
YEAH, YEAH, YEAH.
APEX VAMPIRE. EATS OTHER VAMPIRES.
DOESN'T SOUND ABSOLUTELY INSANE AT ALL.
YOU CAN DO MORE THAN THAT--
YOU CAN CONTROL VAMPIRES--ALL OF US.
WAIT-- I CAN WHAT NOW?
WHAT FREEDOM DO YOU THINK WE'RE FIGHTING FOR? APEXES CAN TAKE US OVER, COMPLETELY. YOU CAN--
LITTLE-- LITTLE HELP OVER HERE!
IT'S THE ONLY CHANCE WE HAVE.
USE US, ALL OF US-- WITH OUR COMBINED STRENGTH, MAYBE WE CAN--
YOU CAN WHAT?

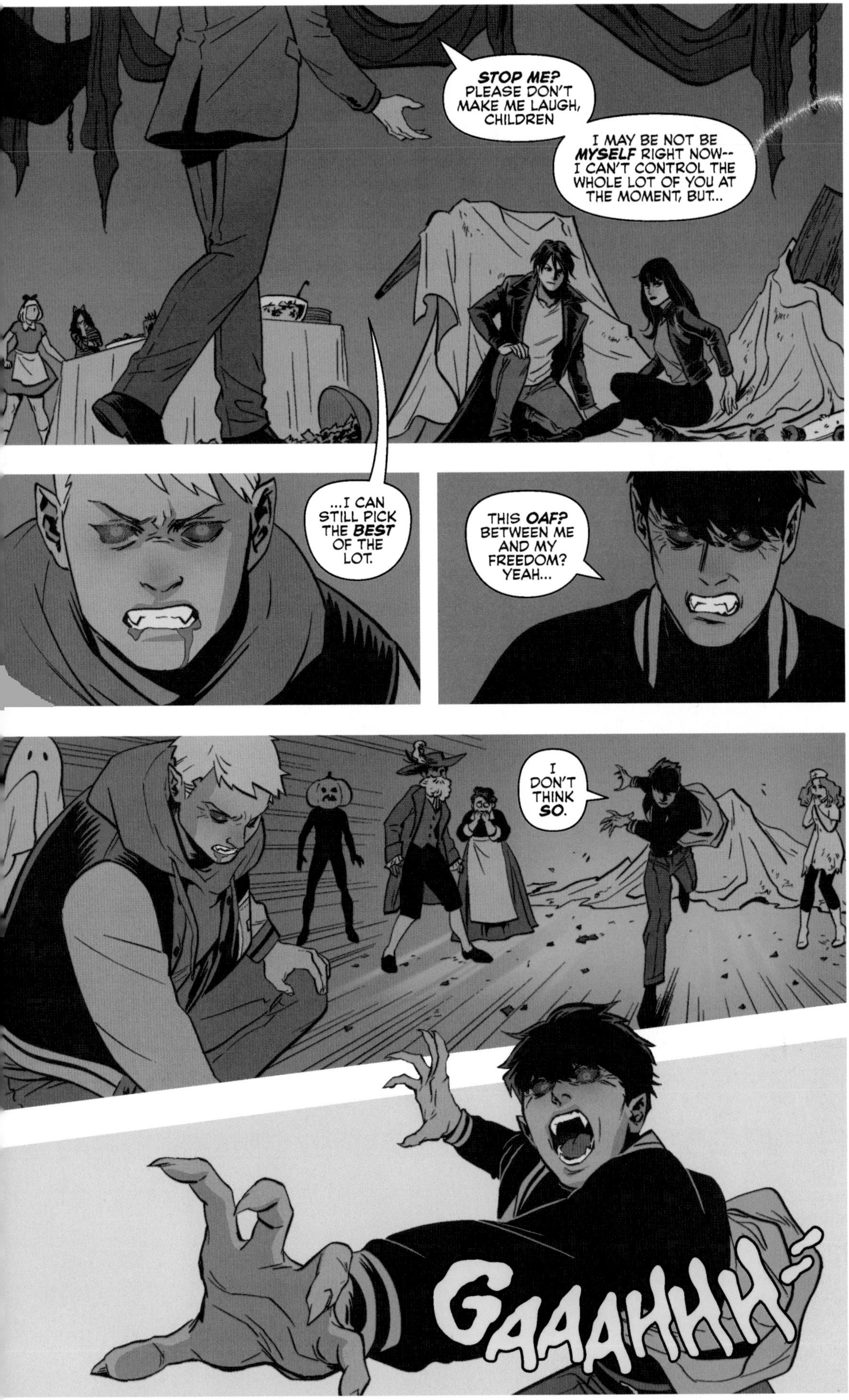
STOP ME? PLEASE DON'T MAKE ME LAUGH, CHILDREN
I MAY BE NOT BE MYSELF RIGHT NOW-- I CAN'T CONTROL THE WHOLE LOT OF YOU AT THE MOMENT, BUT...
...I CAN STILL PICK THE BEST OF THE LOT.
THIS OAF? BETWEEN ME AND MY FREEDOM? YEAH...
I DON'T THINK SO.
GAAHHH-

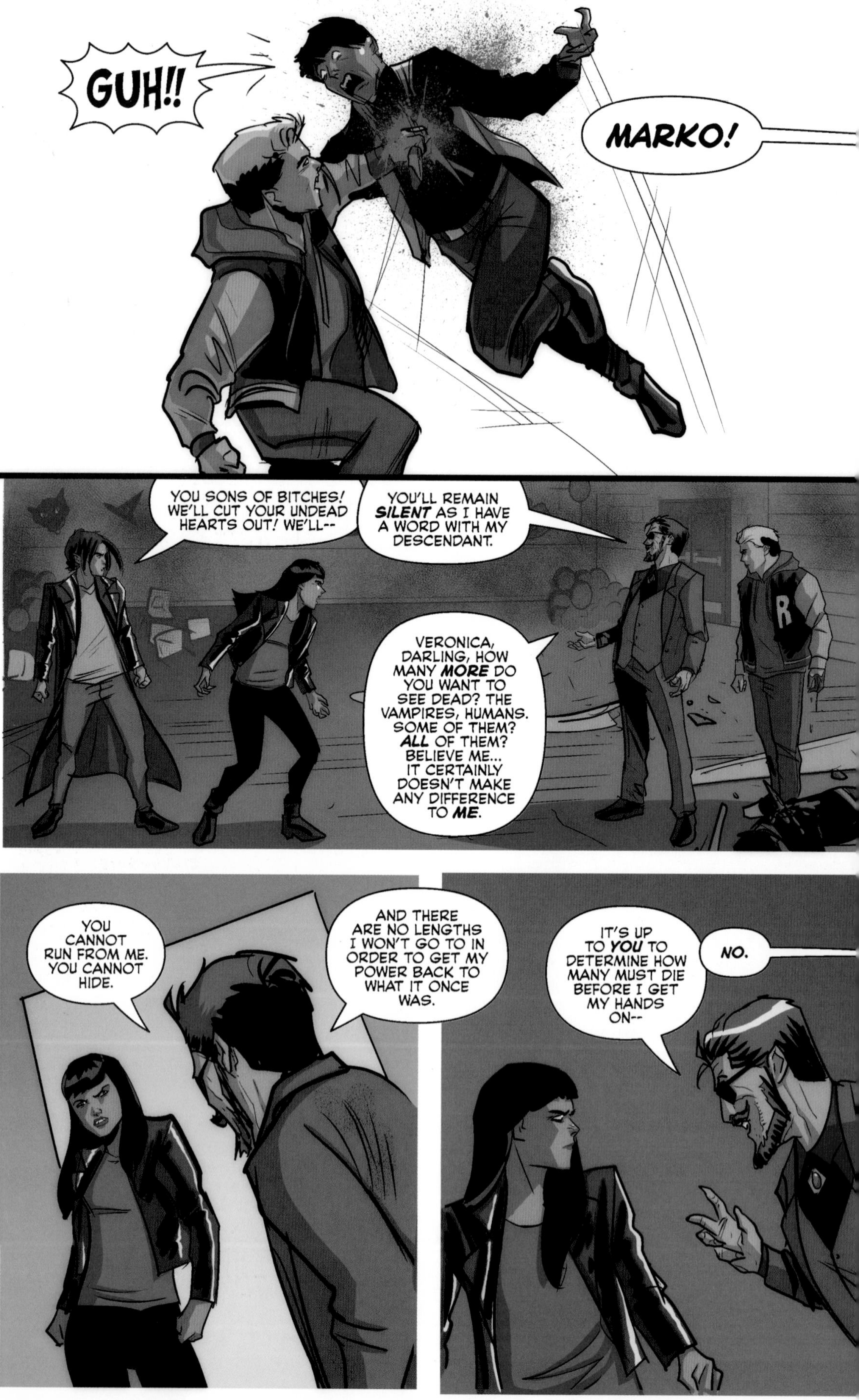
GUH!!
MARKO!
YOU SONS OF BITCHES! WE'LL CUT YOUR UNDEAD HEARTS OUT! WE'LL--
YOU'LL REMAIN SILENT AS I HAVE A WORD WITH MY DESCENDANT.
VERONICA, DARLING, HOW MANY MORE DO YOU WANT TO SEE DEAD? THE VAMPIRES, HUMANS. SOME OF THEM? ALL OF THEM? BELIEVE ME... IT CERTAINLY DOESN'T MAKE ANY DIFFERENCE TO ME.
YOU CANNOT RUN FROM ME. YOU CANNOT HIDE.
AND THERE ARE NO LENGTHS I WON'T GO TO IN ORDER TO GET MY POWER BACK TO WHAT IT ONCE WAS.
IT'S UP TO YOU TO DETERMINE HOW MANY MUST DIE BEFORE I GET MY HANDS ON--
NO.

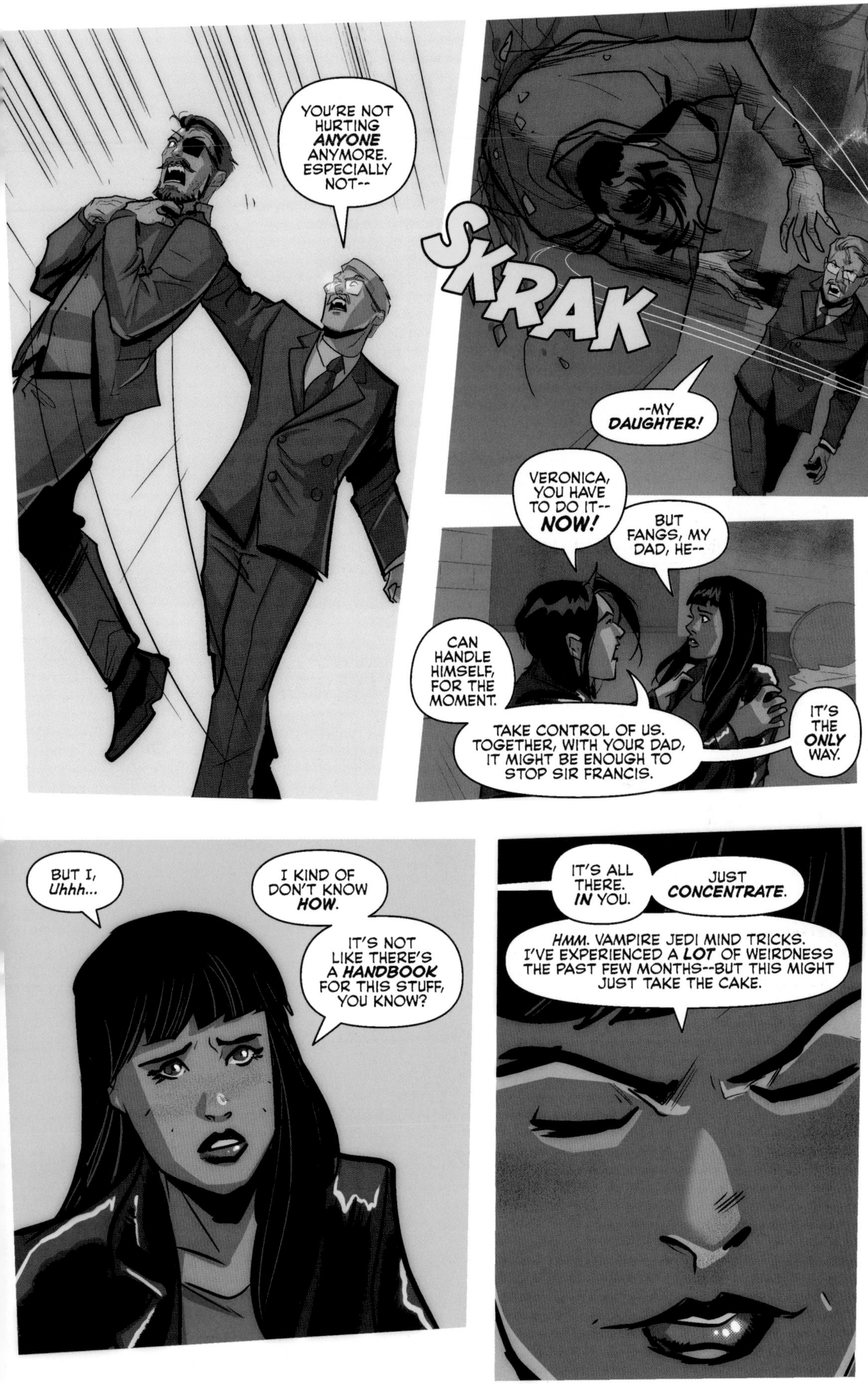
YOU'RE NOT HURTING ***ANYONE*** ANYMORE. ESPECIALLY NOT--
SKRAK
--MY ***DAUGHTER!***
VERONICA, YOU HAVE TO DO IT-- ***NOW!***
BUT FANGS, MY DAD, HE--
CAN HANDLE HIMSELF, FOR THE MOMENT.
TAKE CONTROL OF US. TOGETHER, WITH YOUR DAD, IT MIGHT BE ENOUGH TO STOP SIR FRANCIS.
IT'S THE ***ONLY*** WAY.
BUT I, *Uhhh...*
I KIND OF DON'T KNOW ***HOW***.
IT'S NOT LIKE THERE'S A ***HANDBOOK*** FOR THIS STUFF, YOU KNOW?
IT'S ALL THERE. ***IN*** YOU.
JUST ***CONCENTRATE***.
HMM. VAMPIRE JEDI MIND TRICKS. I'VE EXPERIENCED A ***LOT*** OF WEIRDNESS THE PAST FEW MONTHS--BUT THIS MIGHT JUST TAKE THE CAKE.

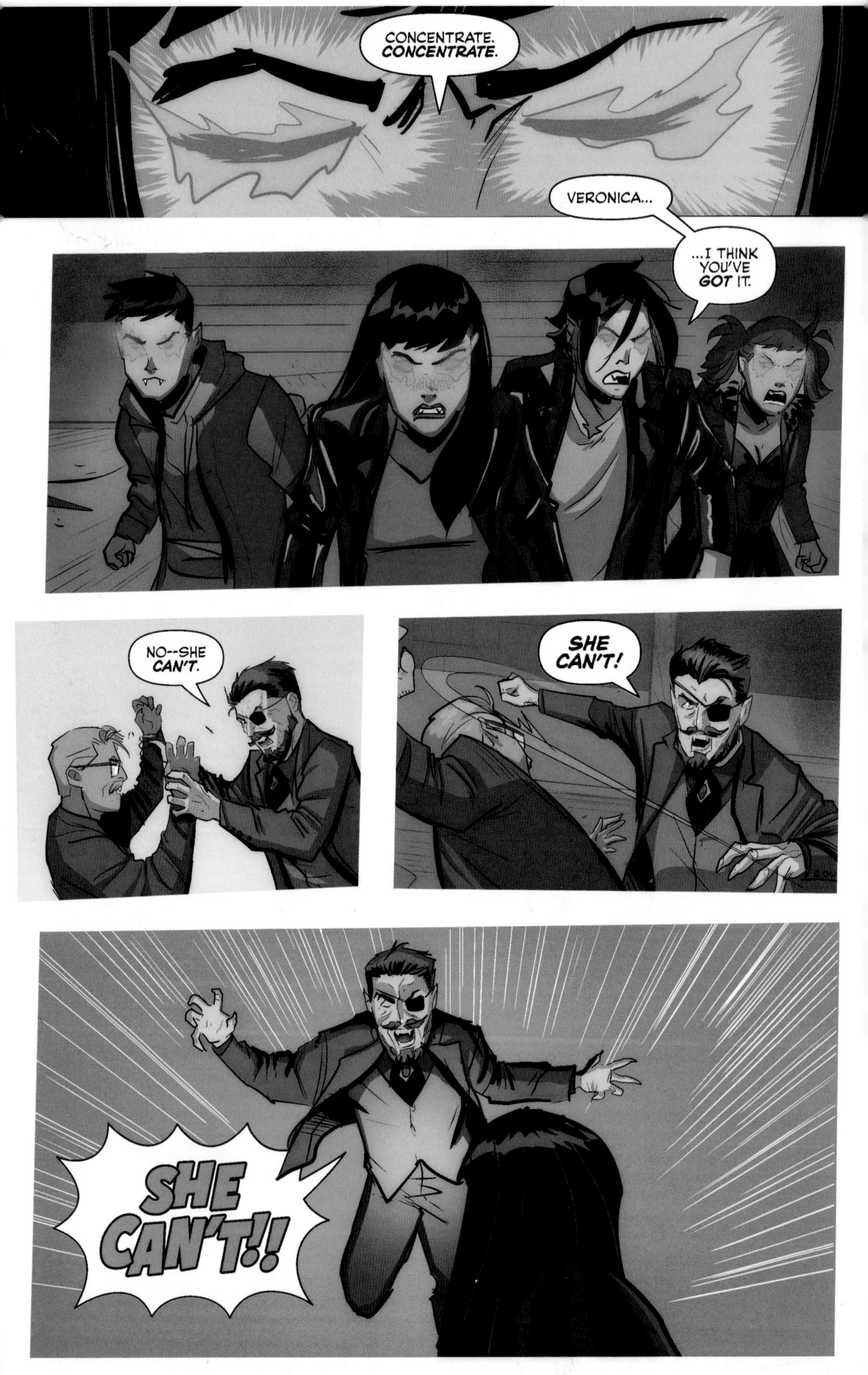
CONCENTRATE. CONCENTRATE.
VERONICA...
...I THINK YOU'VE GOT IT.
NO--SHE CAN'T.
SHE CAN'T!
SHE CAN'T!!

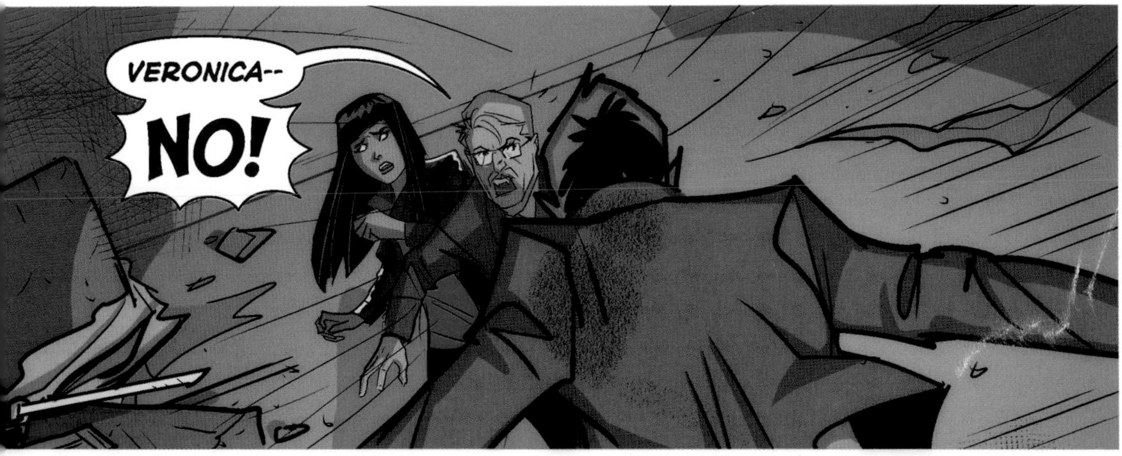
VERONICA--
NO!

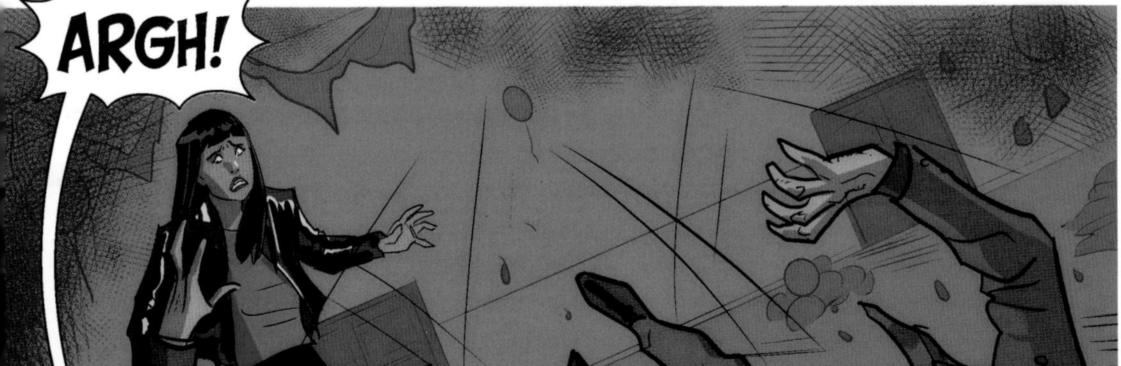
ARGH!
SHUNK

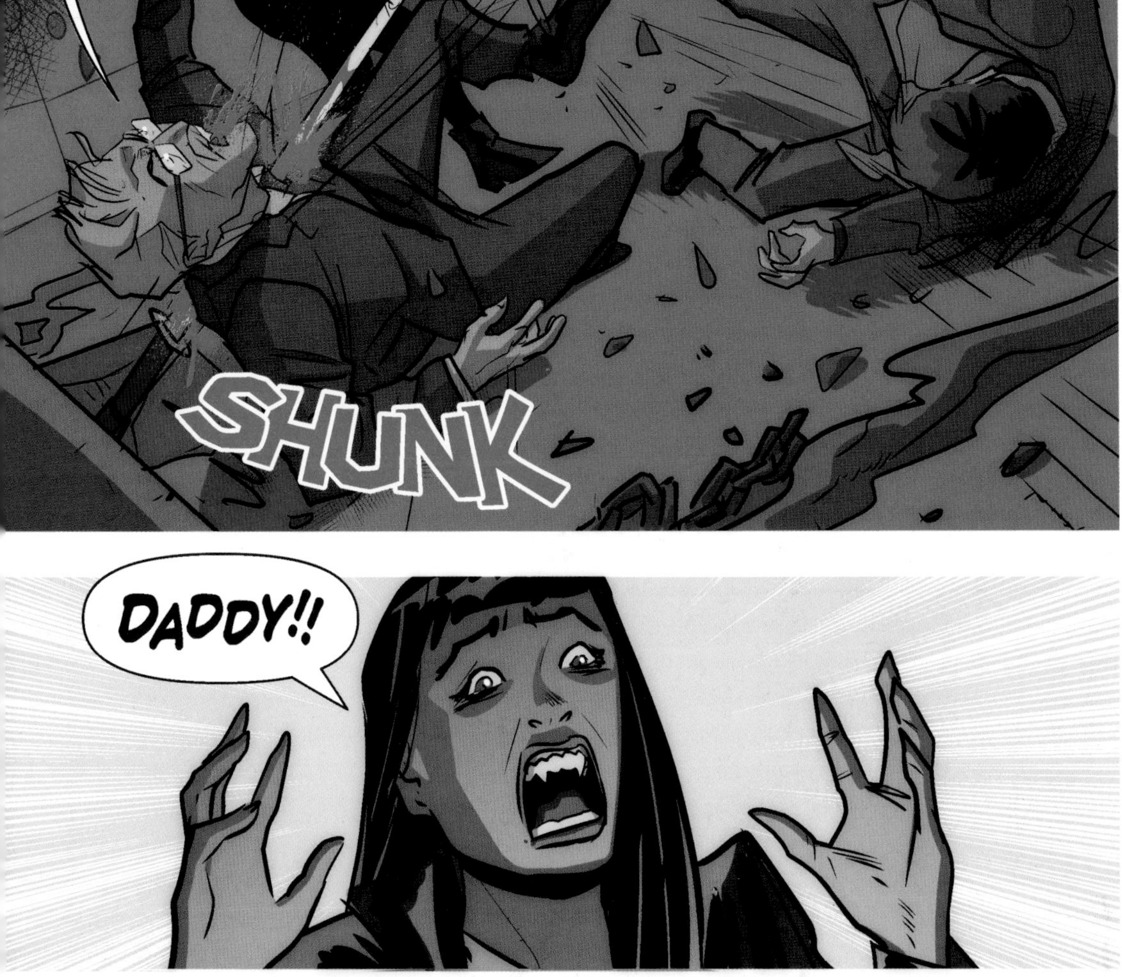
DADDY!!

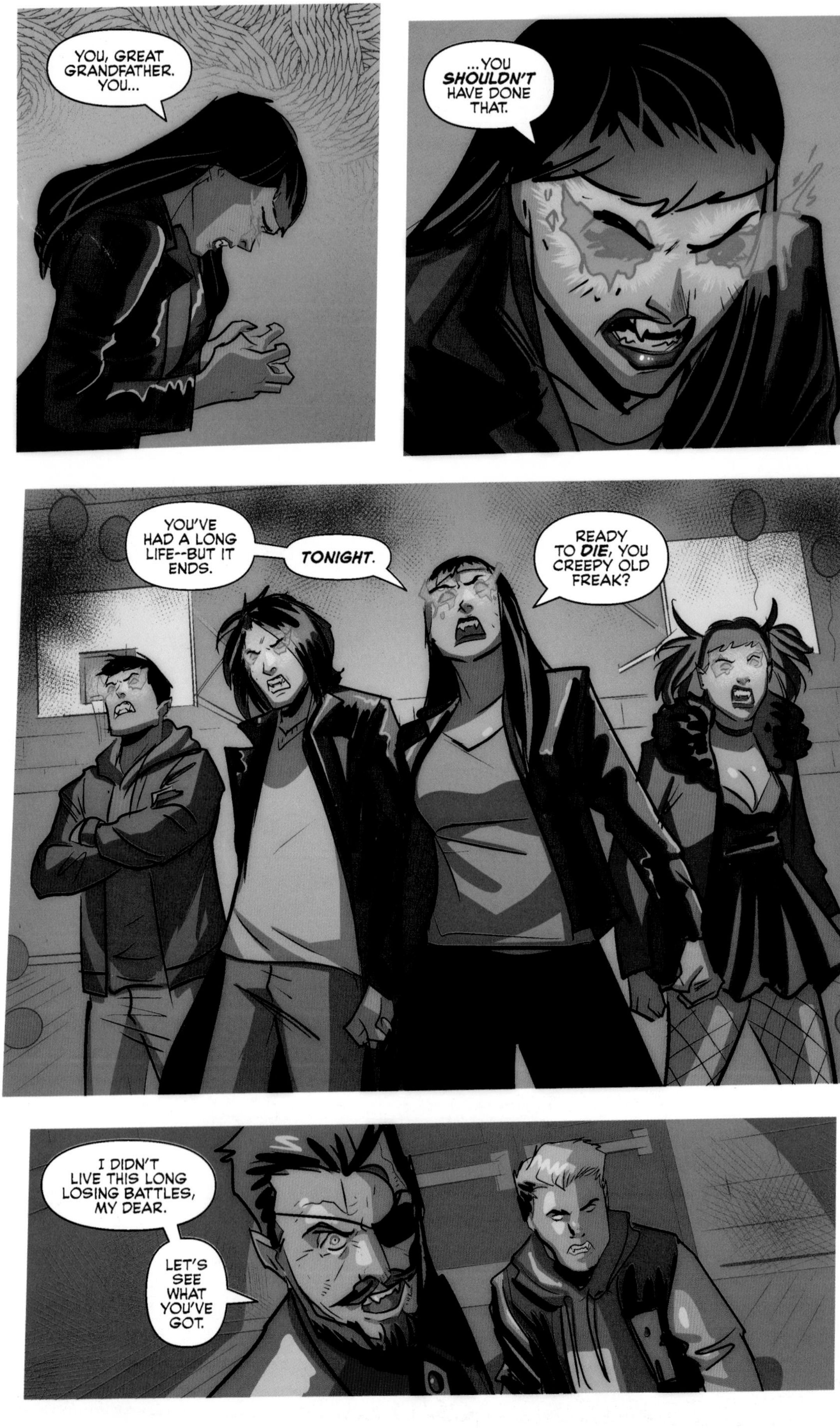
YOU, GREAT GRANDFATHER. YOU...
...YOU *SHOULDN'T* HAVE DONE THAT.
YOU'VE HAD A LONG LIFE--BUT IT ENDS.
TONIGHT.
READY TO *DIE*, YOU CREEPY OLD FREAK?
I DIDN'T LIVE THIS LONG LOSING BATTLES, MY DEAR.
LET'S SEE WHAT YOU'VE GOT.

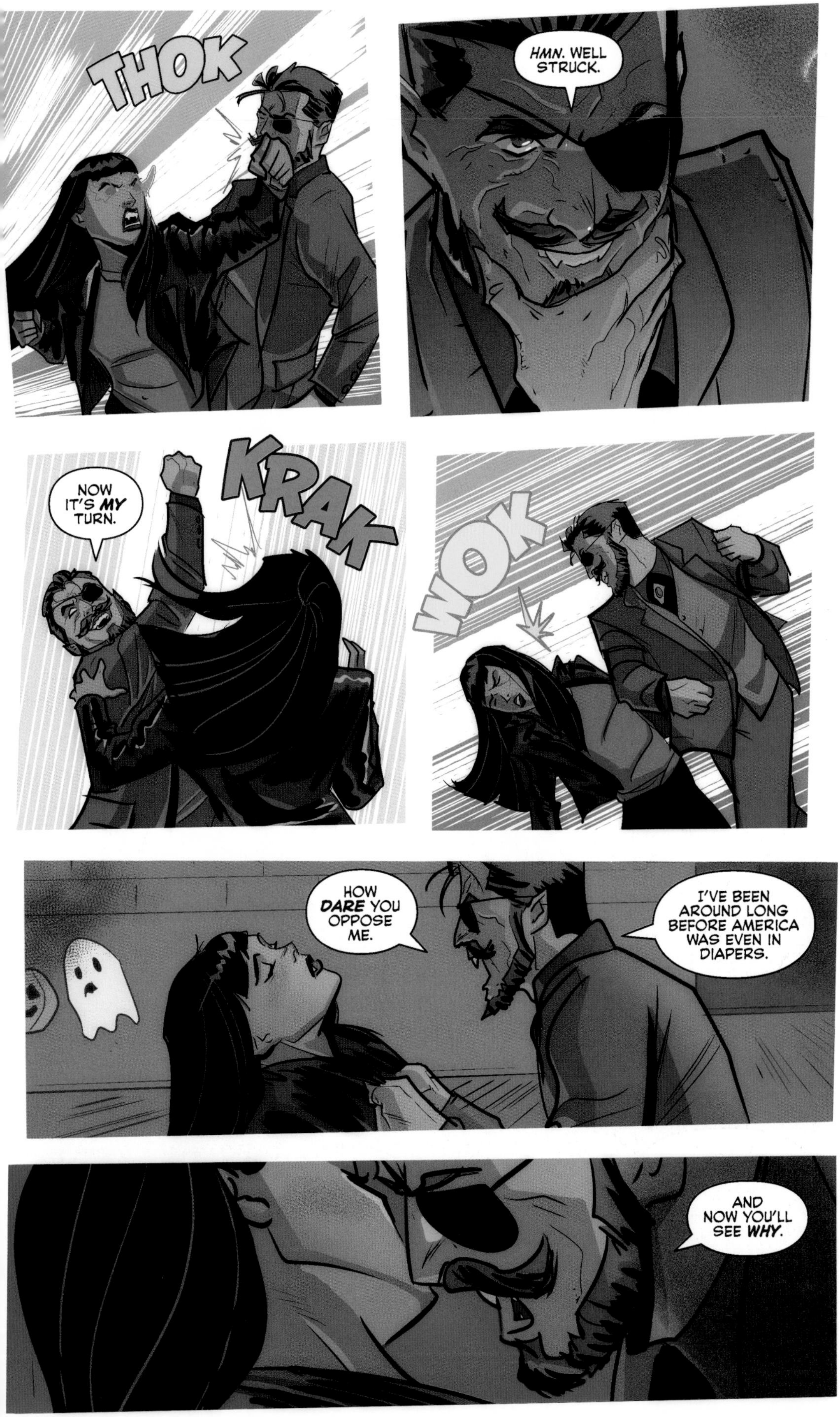
THOK
HMN. WELL STRUCK.
NOW IT'S MY TURN.
KRAK
WOK
HOW DARE YOU OPPOSE ME.
I'VE BEEN AROUND LONG BEFORE AMERICA WAS EVEN IN DIAPERS.
AND NOW YOU'LL SEE WHY.

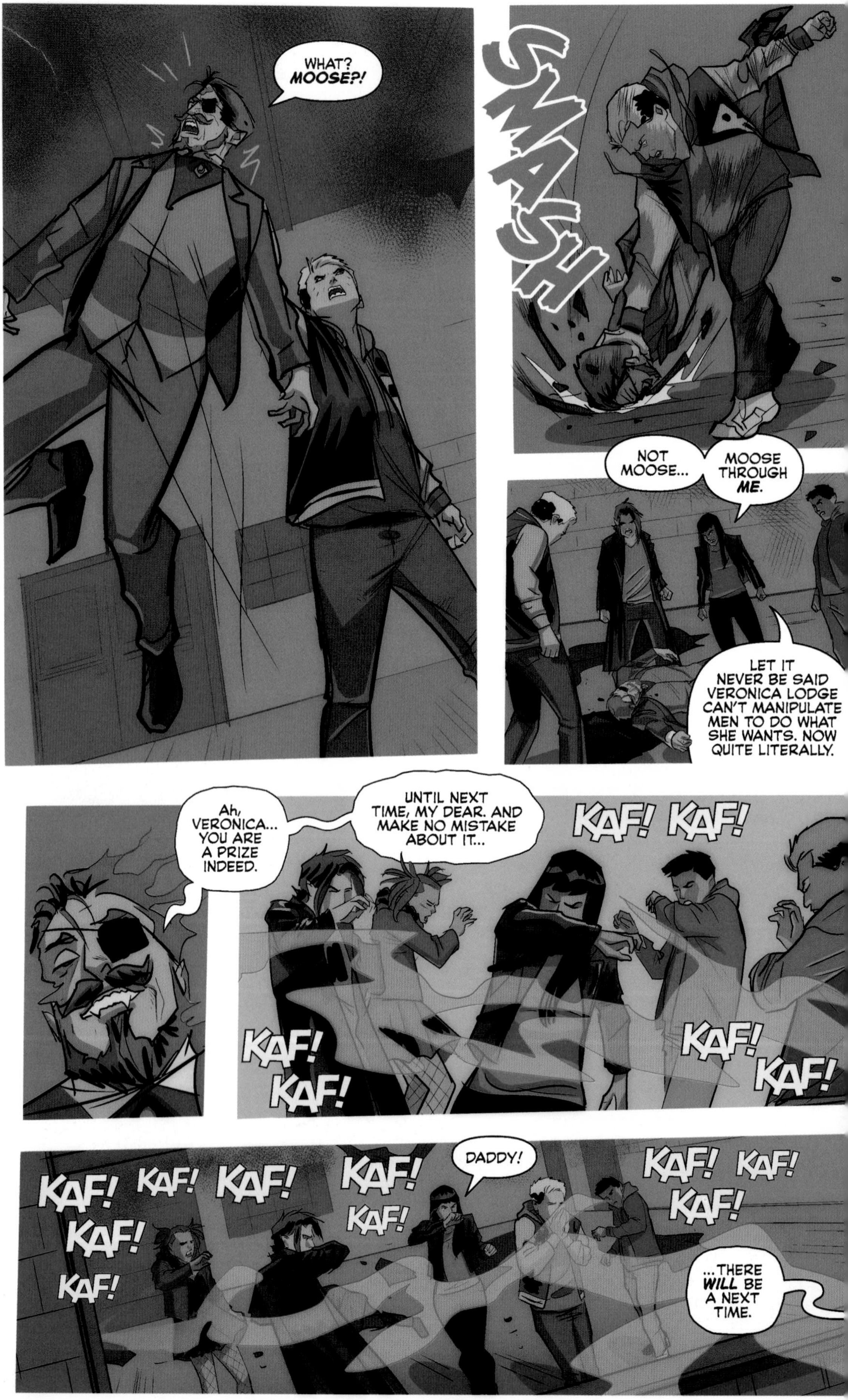

WHAT? MOOSE?!
SMASH
NOT MOOSE...
MOOSE THROUGH ME.
LET IT NEVER BE SAID VERONICA LODGE CAN'T MANIPULATE MEN TO DO WHAT SHE WANTS. NOW QUITE LITERALLY.
Ah, VERONICA... YOU ARE A PRIZE INDEED.
UNTIL NEXT TIME, MY DEAR. AND MAKE NO MISTAKE ABOUT IT...
KAF! KAF!
KAF! KAF!
KAF! KAF!
KAF! KAF! KAF!
KAF! KAF!
KAF!
KAF! KAF!
DADDY!
KAF! KAF! KAF!
...THERE WILL BE A NEXT TIME.

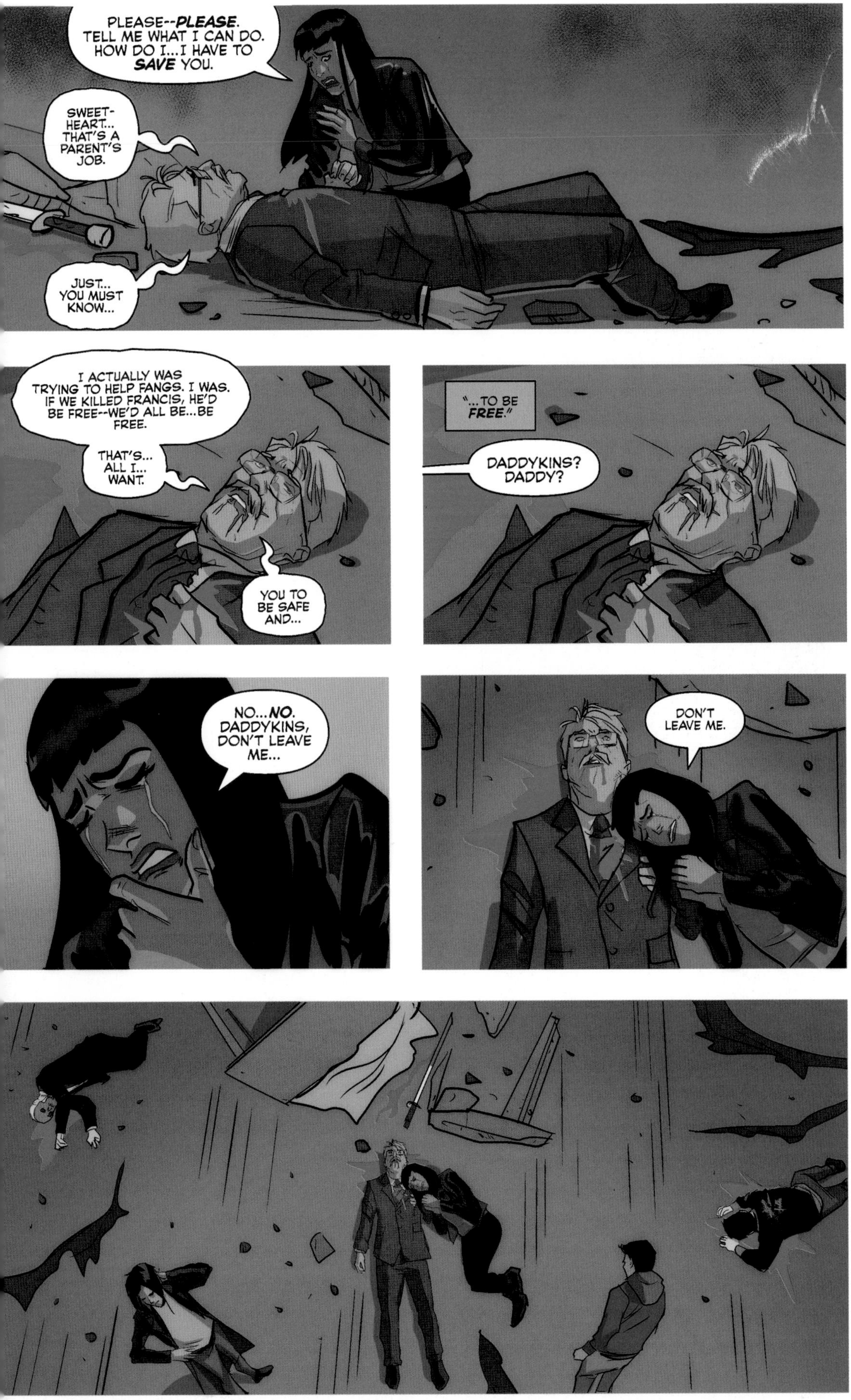

PLEASE--PLEASE. TELL ME WHAT I CAN DO. HOW DO I...I HAVE TO SAVE YOU.
SWEET-HEART... THAT'S A PARENT'S JOB.
JUST... YOU MUST KNOW...
I ACTUALLY WAS TRYING TO HELP FANGS. I WAS. IF WE KILLED FRANCIS, HE'D BE FREE--WE'D ALL BE...BE FREE.
THAT'S... ALL I... WANT.
YOU TO BE SAFE AND...
"...TO BE FREE."
DADDYKINS? DADDY?
NO...NO. DADDYKINS, DON'T LEAVE ME...
DON'T LEAVE ME.

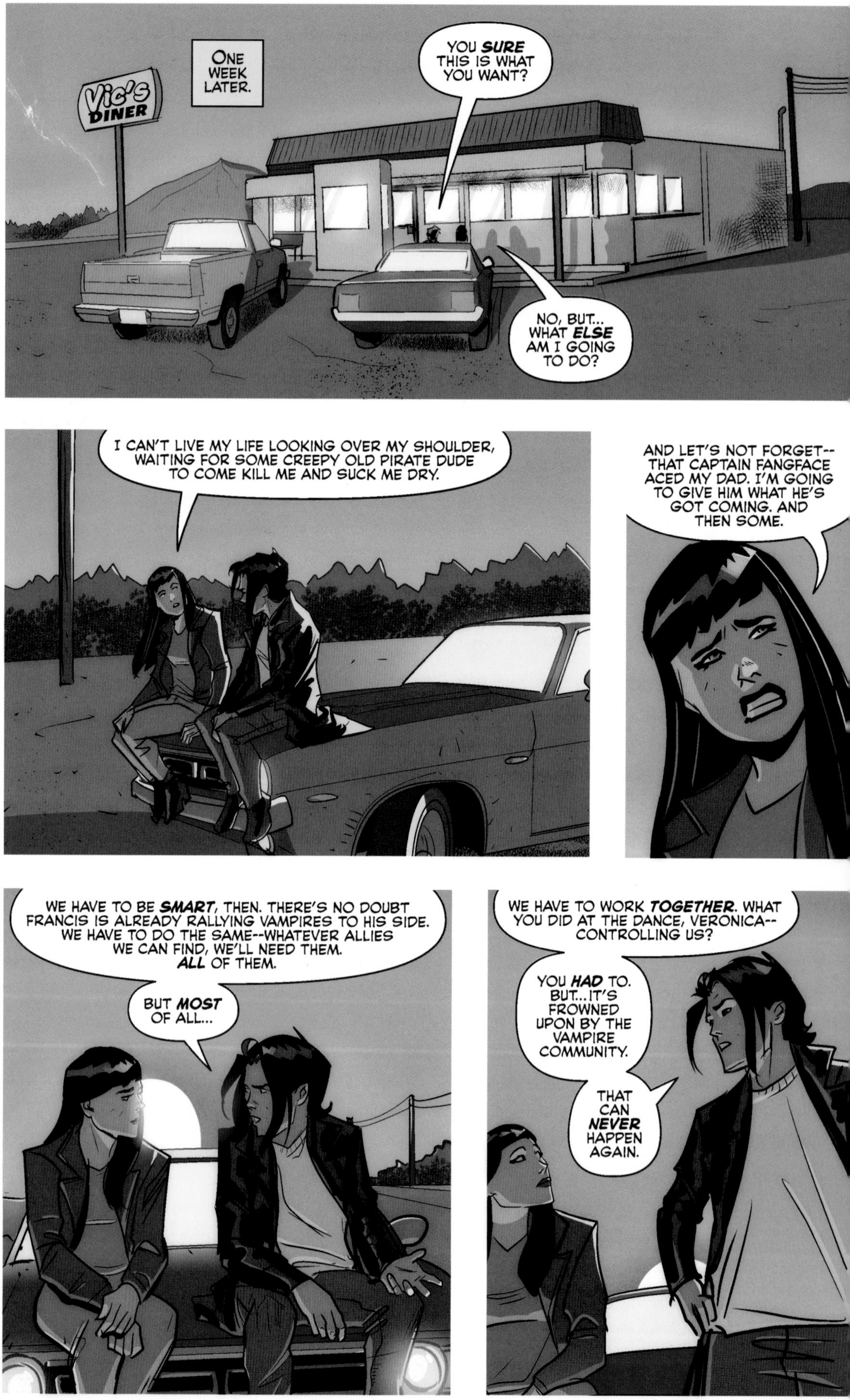

Vic's DINER
ONE WEEK LATER.
YOU SURE THIS IS WHAT YOU WANT?
NO, BUT... WHAT ELSE AM I GOING TO DO?
I CAN'T LIVE MY LIFE LOOKING OVER MY SHOULDER, WAITING FOR SOME CREEPY OLD PIRATE DUDE TO COME KILL ME AND SUCK ME DRY.
AND LET'S NOT FORGET-- THAT CAPTAIN FANGFACE ACED MY DAD. I'M GOING TO GIVE HIM WHAT HE'S GOT COMING. AND THEN SOME.
WE HAVE TO BE SMART, THEN. THERE'S NO DOUBT FRANCIS IS ALREADY RALLYING VAMPIRES TO HIS SIDE. WE HAVE TO DO THE SAME--WHATEVER ALLIES WE CAN FIND, WE'LL NEED THEM. ALL OF THEM.
BUT MOST OF ALL...
WE HAVE TO WORK TOGETHER. WHAT YOU DID AT THE DANCE, VERONICA-- CONTROLLING US?
YOU HAD TO. BUT...IT'S FROWNED UPON BY THE VAMPIRE COMMUNITY.
THAT CAN NEVER HAPPEN AGAIN.

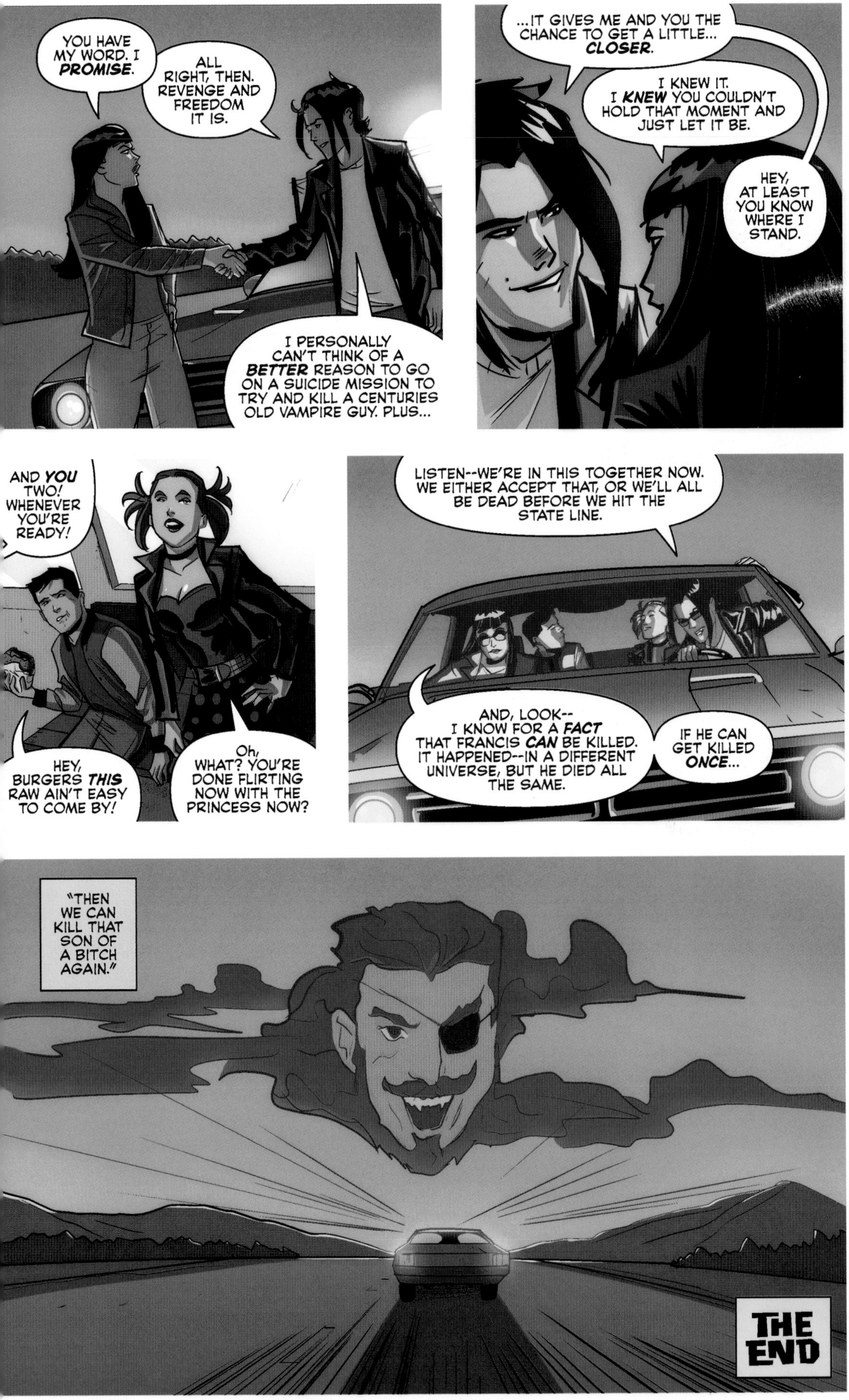
YOU HAVE MY WORD. I **PROMISE**.
ALL RIGHT, THEN. REVENGE AND FREEDOM IT IS.
I PERSONALLY CAN'T THINK OF A **BETTER** REASON TO GO ON A SUICIDE MISSION TO TRY AND KILL A CENTURIES OLD VAMPIRE GUY. PLUS...
...IT GIVES ME AND YOU THE CHANCE TO GET A LITTLE... **CLOSER**.
I KNEW IT. I **KNEW** YOU COULDN'T HOLD THAT MOMENT AND JUST LET IT BE.
HEY, AT LEAST YOU KNOW WHERE I STAND.
AND **YOU** TWO! WHENEVER YOU'RE READY!
HEY, BURGERS **THIS** RAW AIN'T EASY TO COME BY!
Oh, WHAT? YOU'RE DONE FLIRTING NOW WITH THE PRINCESS NOW?
LISTEN--WE'RE IN THIS TOGETHER NOW. WE EITHER ACCEPT THAT, OR WE'LL ALL BE DEAD BEFORE WE HIT THE STATE LINE.
AND, LOOK-- I KNOW FOR A **FACT** THAT FRANCIS **CAN** BE KILLED. IT HAPPENED--IN A DIFFERENT UNIVERSE, BUT HE DIED ALL THE SAME.
IF HE CAN GET KILLED **ONCE**...
"THEN WE CAN KILL THAT SON OF A BITCH AGAIN."
THE END

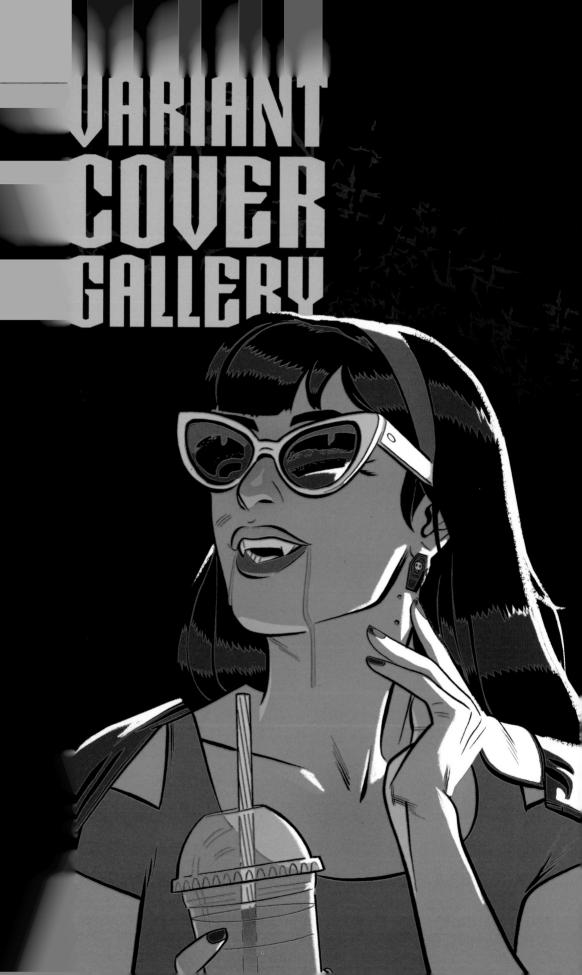

VARIANT COVER GALLERY

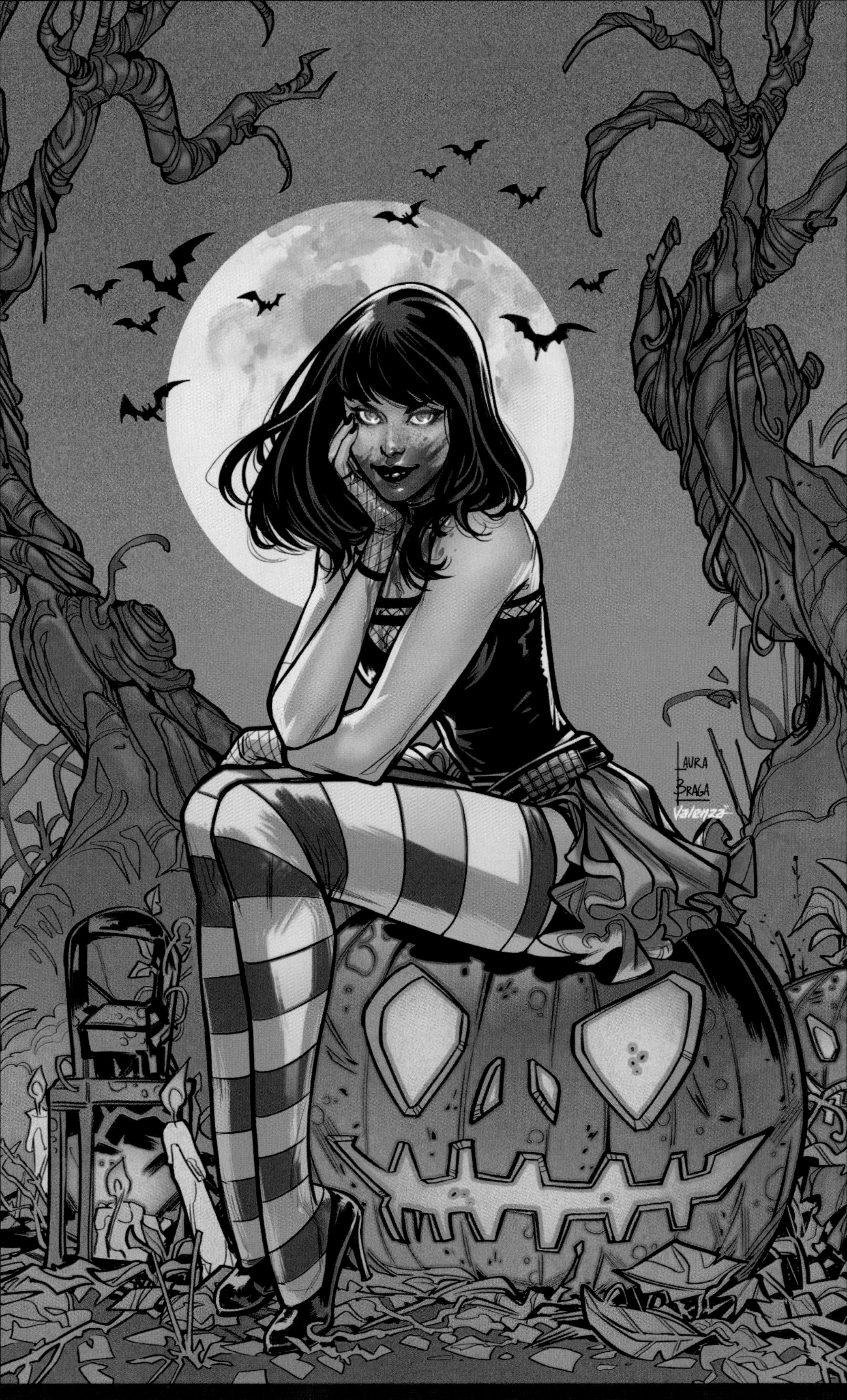
LAURA BRAGA
Valenza

ART BY LAURA BRAGA

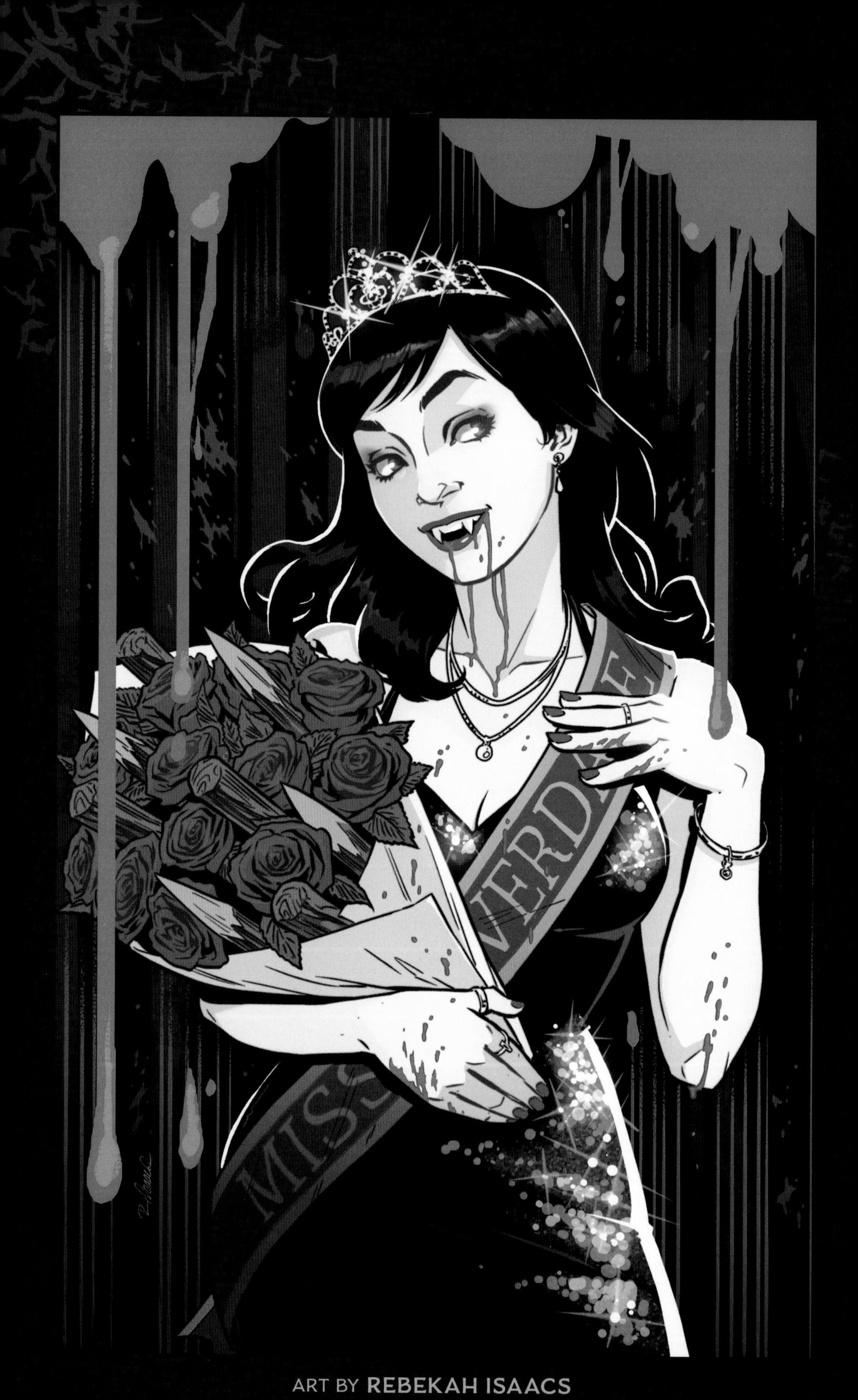
MISS

ART BY **REBEKAH ISAACS**

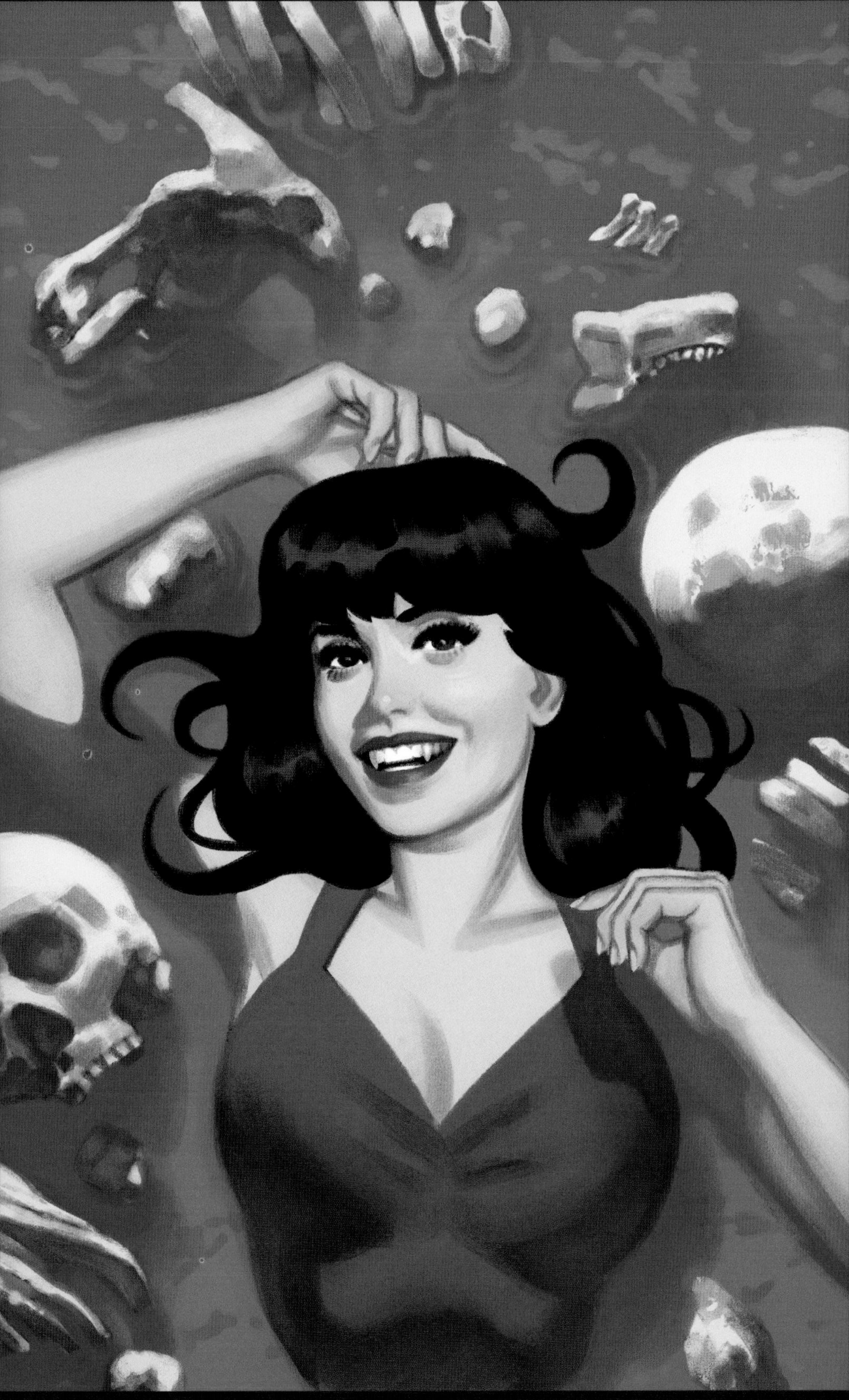

ART BY **GREG SMALLWOOD**

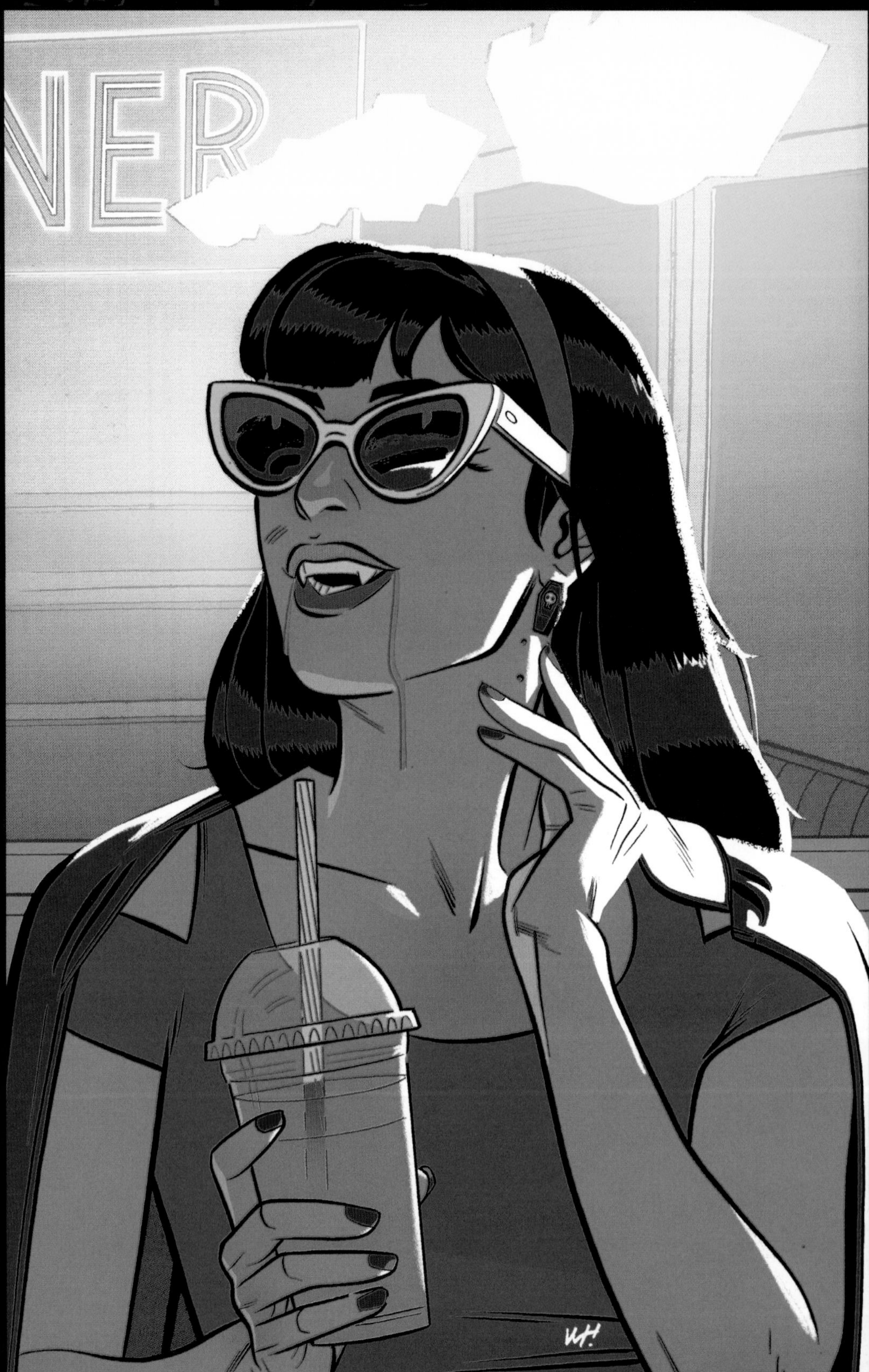

ART BY **WILFREDO TORRES**

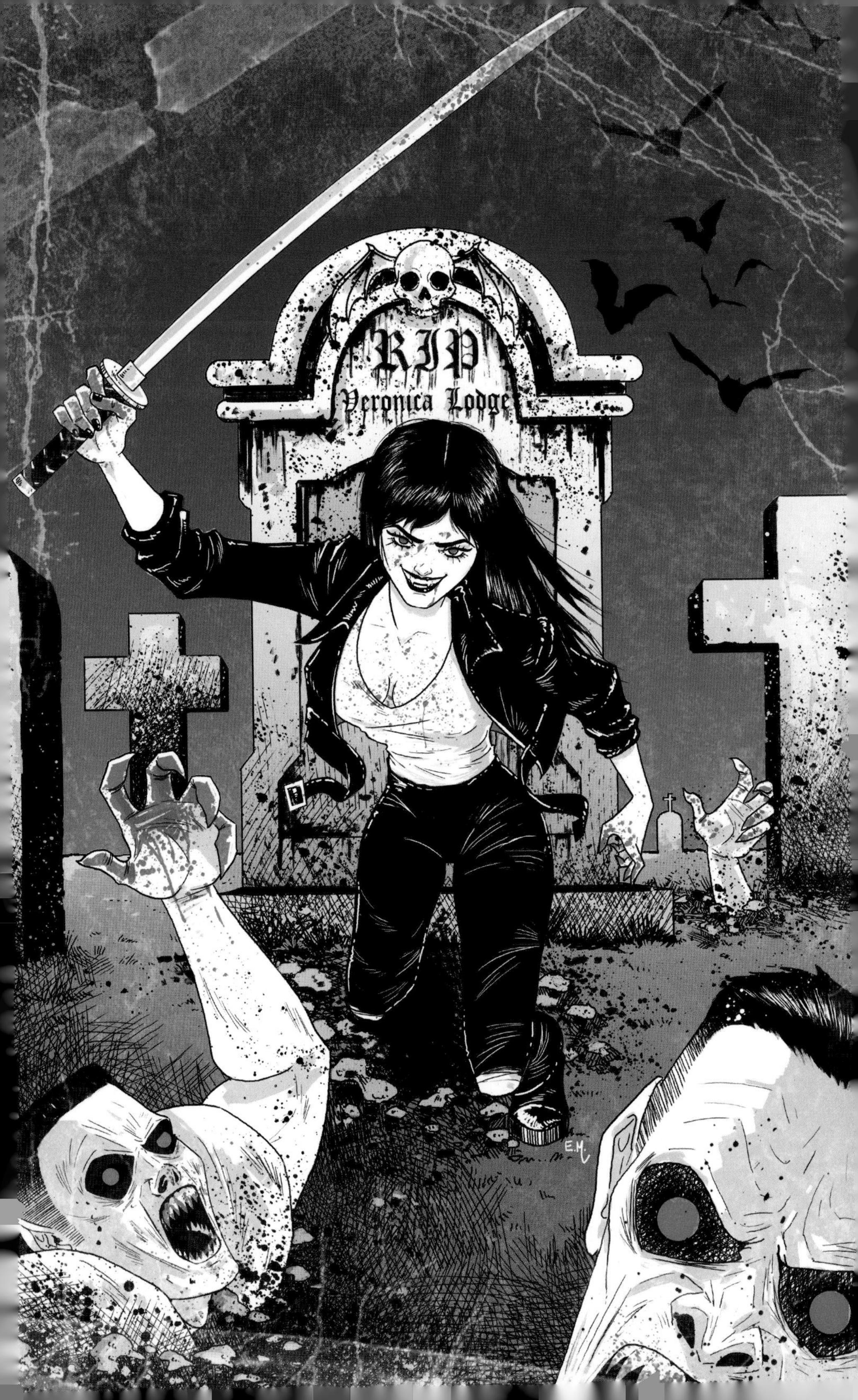
RIP
Veronica Lodge
E.M.

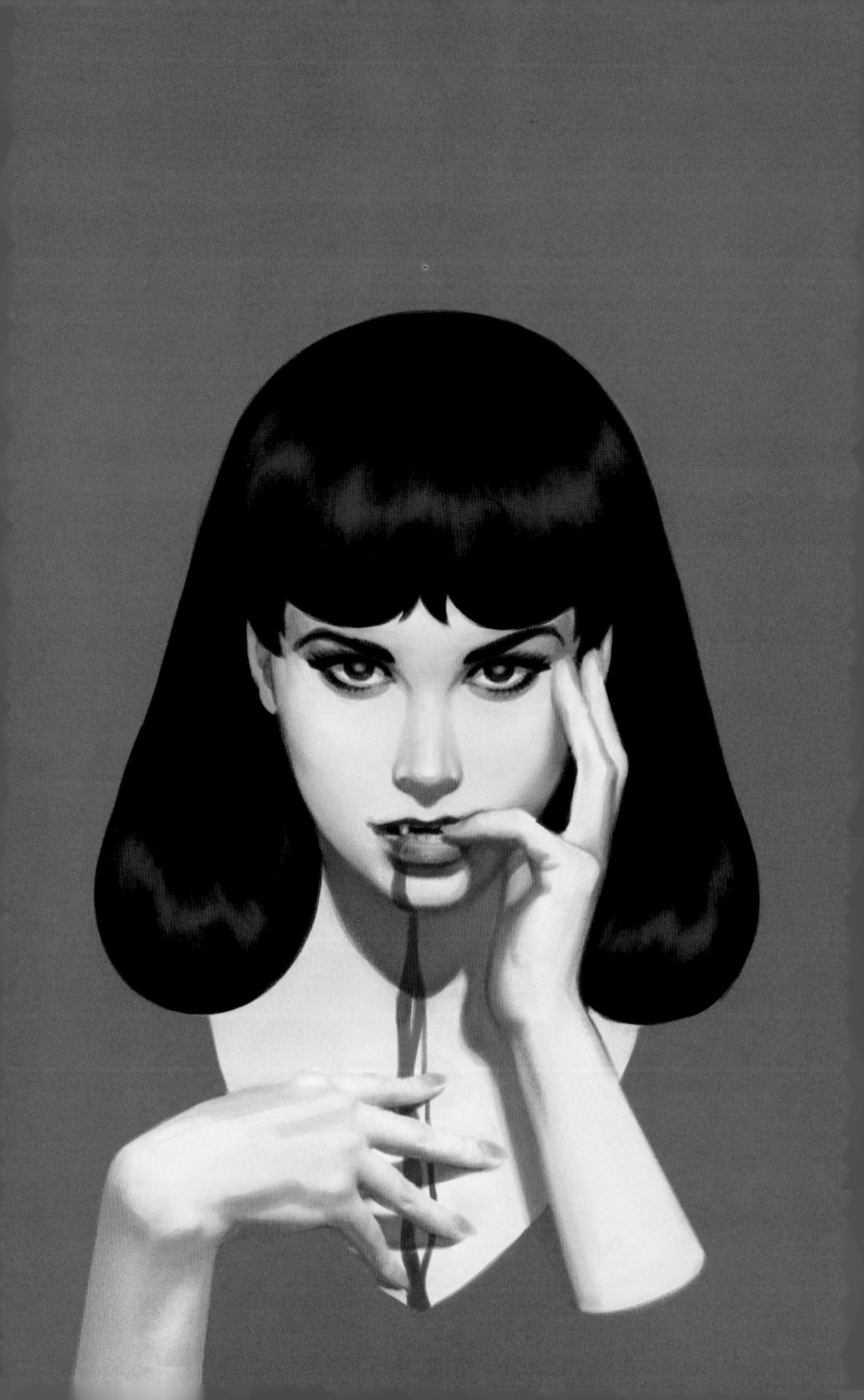

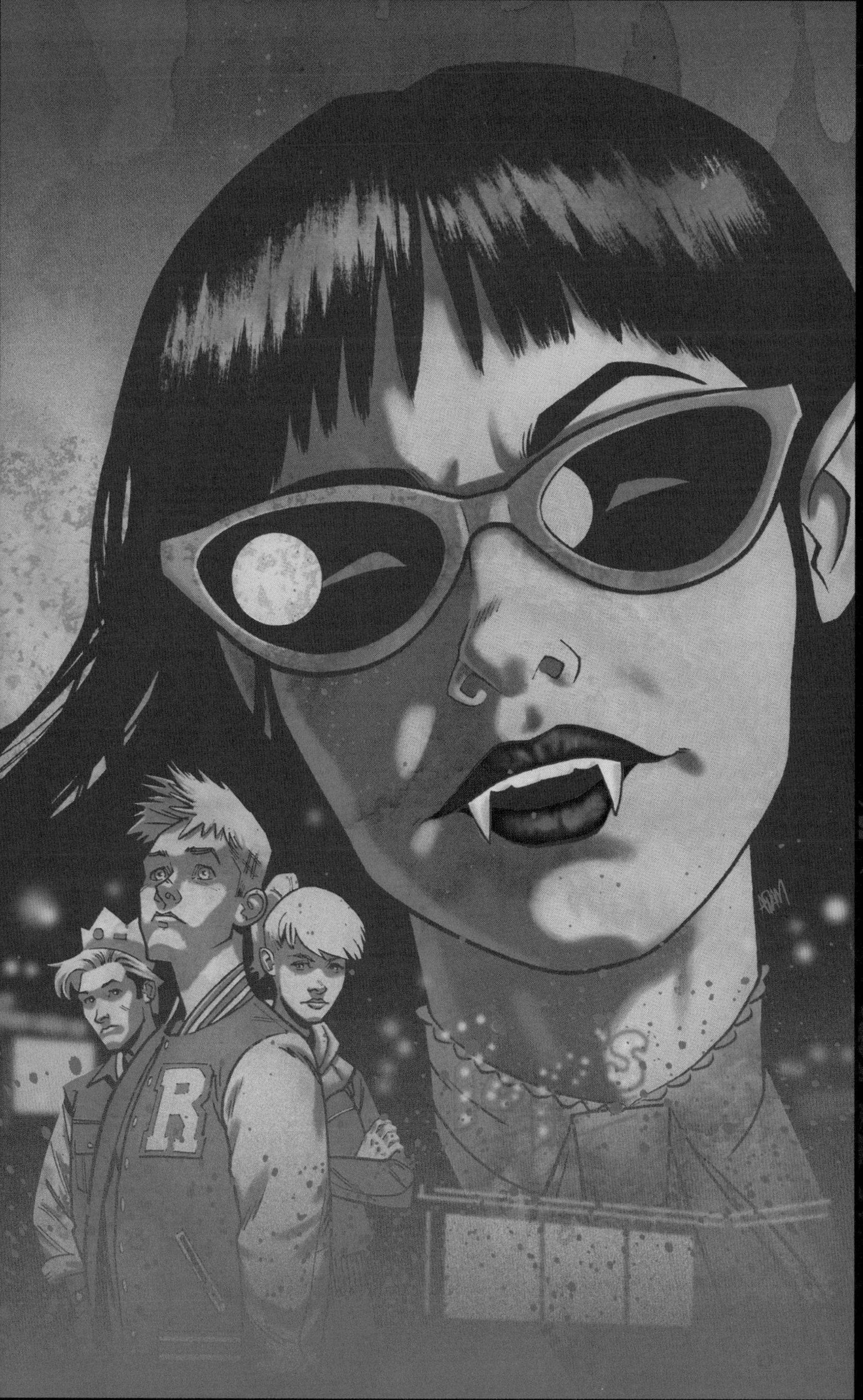

ART BY **ADAM GORHAM**

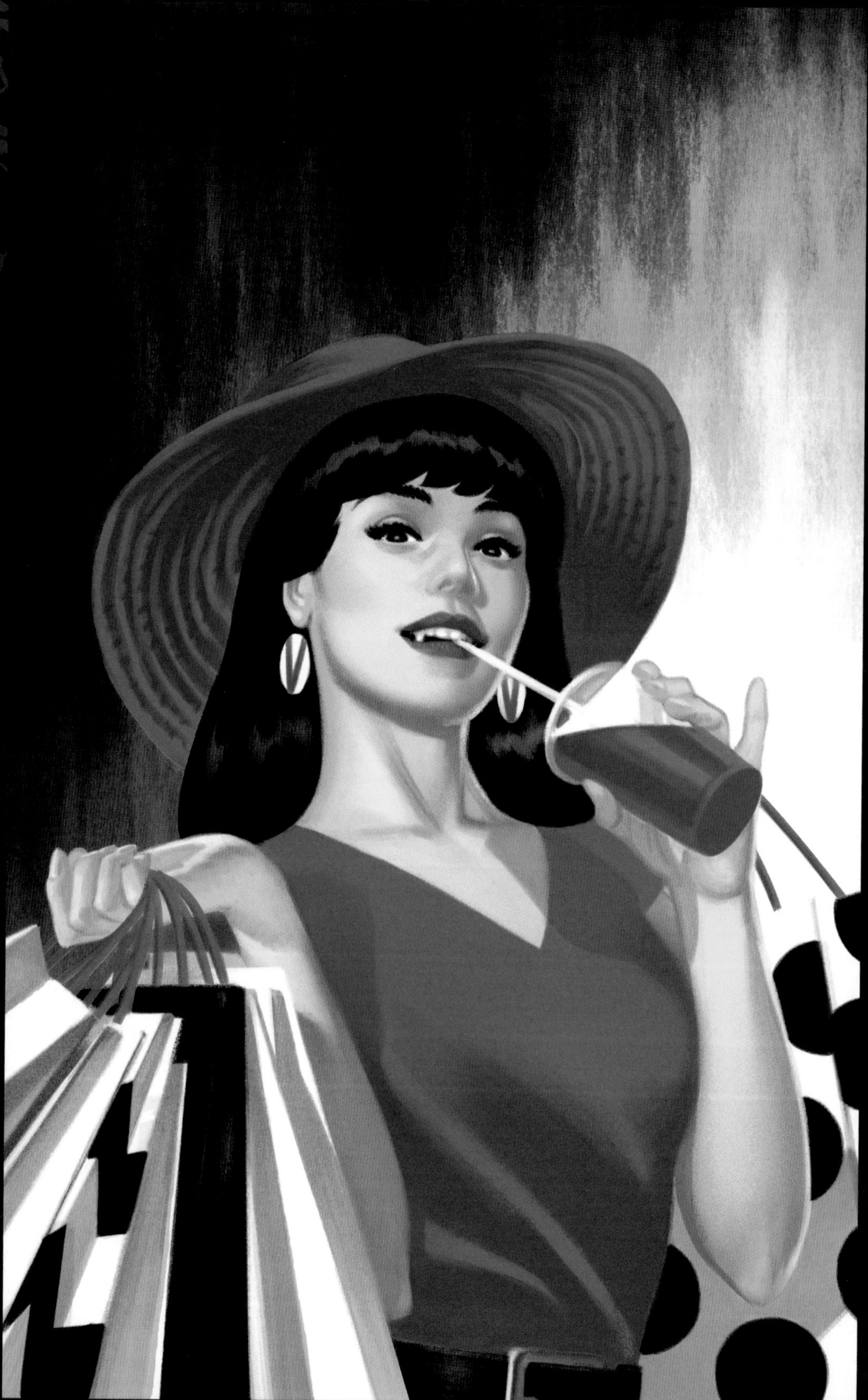

ART BY GREG SMALLWOOD

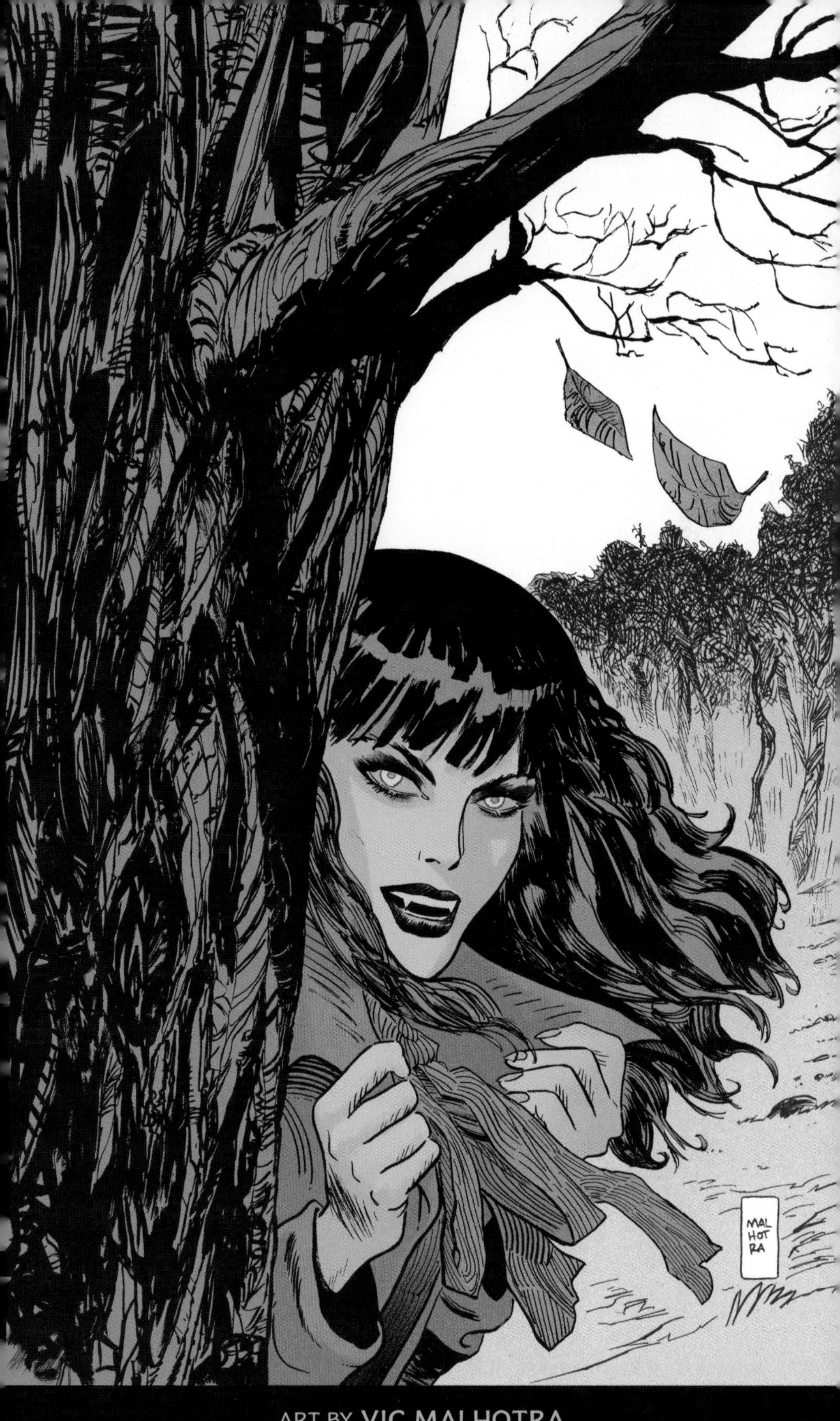
MAL
HOT
RA

ART BY VIC MALHOTRA

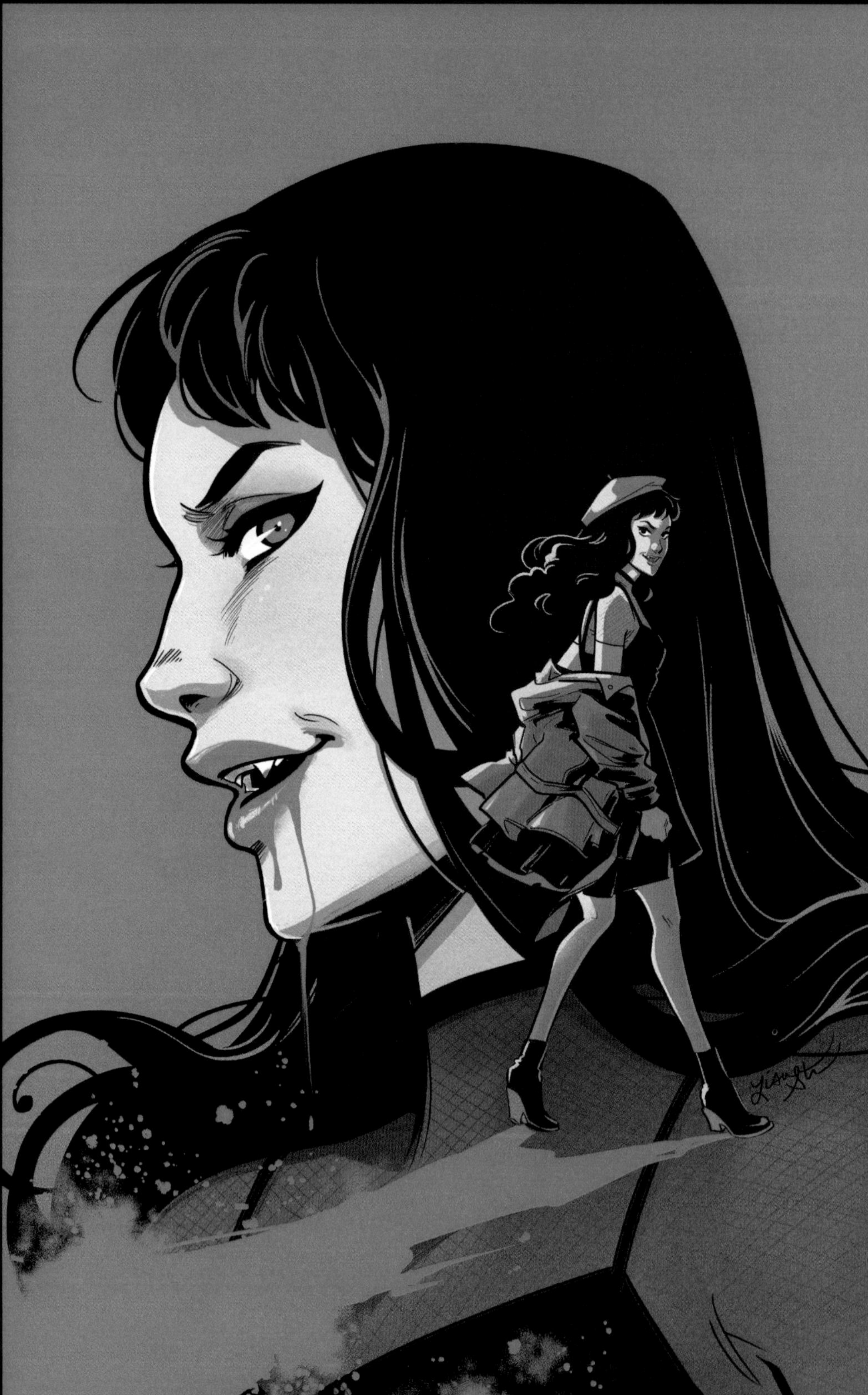

ART BY **LISA STERLE**

COVER SKETCHES

Before going ahead with the final cover, series artist Audrey Mok submits cover sketches for the editorial team to review.

Take a look at the sketches and final cover art for *Vampironica: New Blood*.

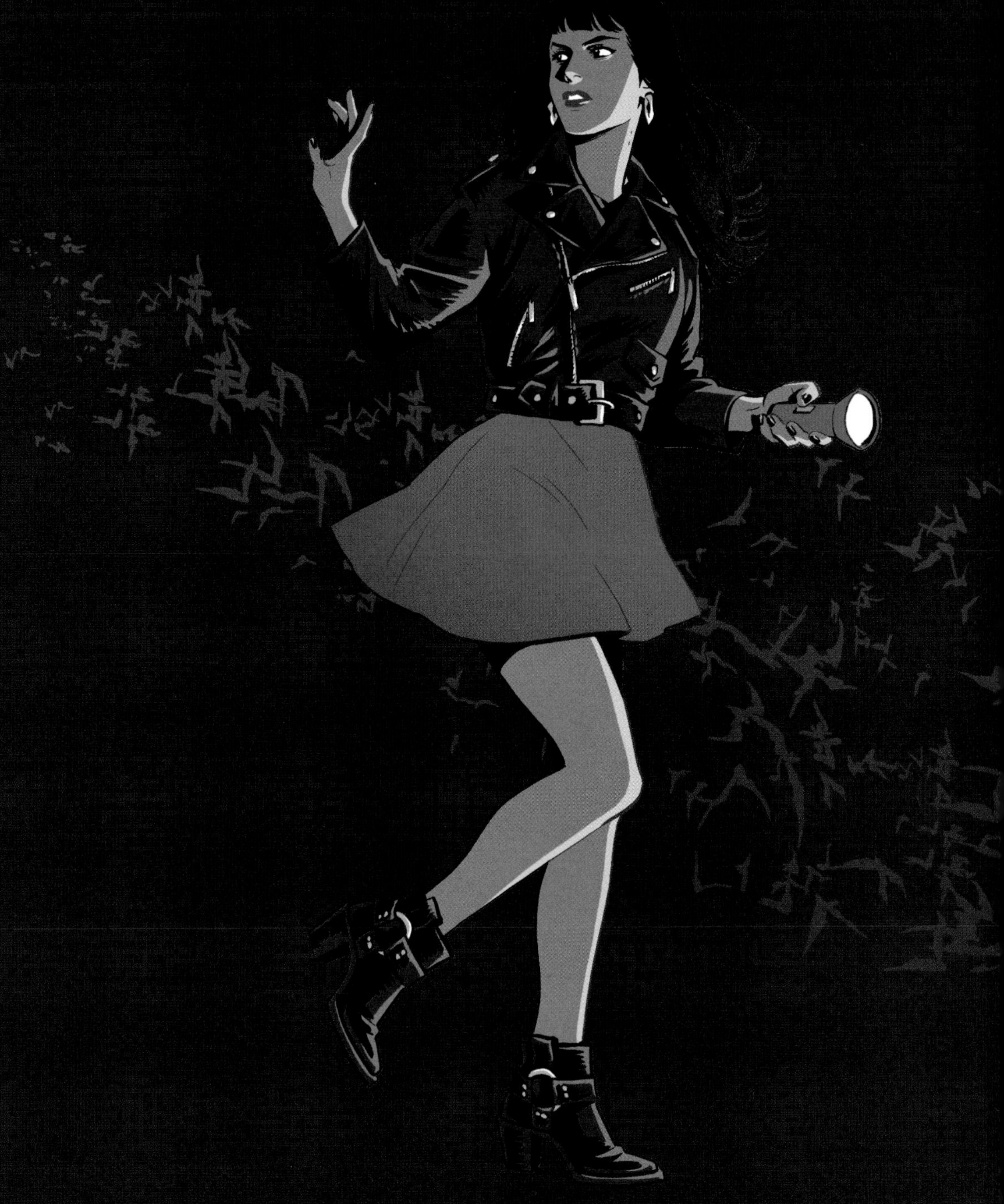

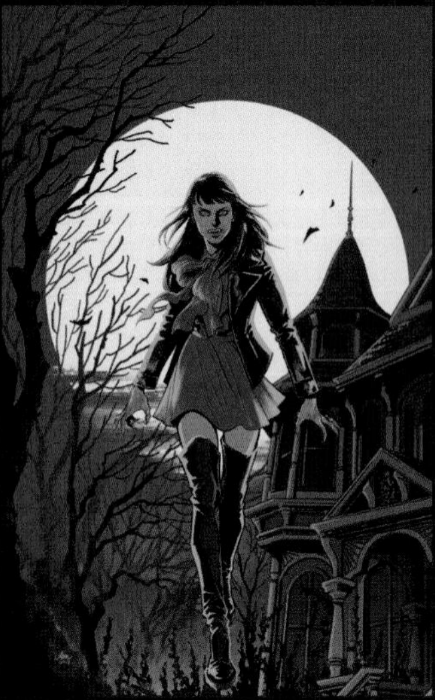

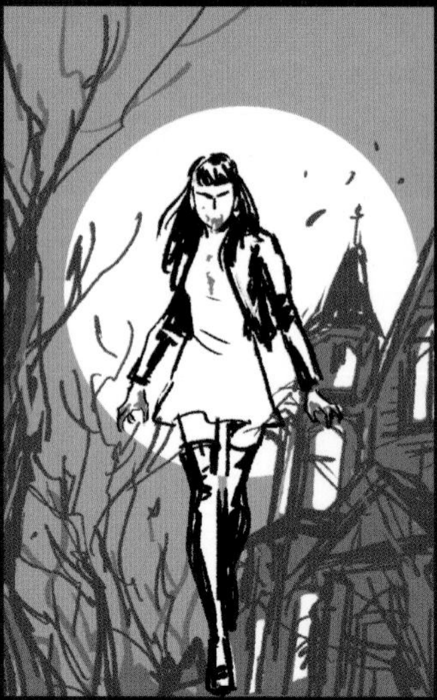

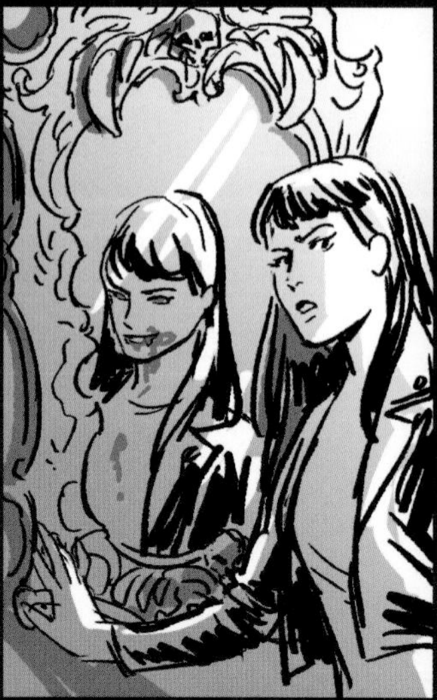

FINAL ART

COVER SKETCHES

ISSUE TWO

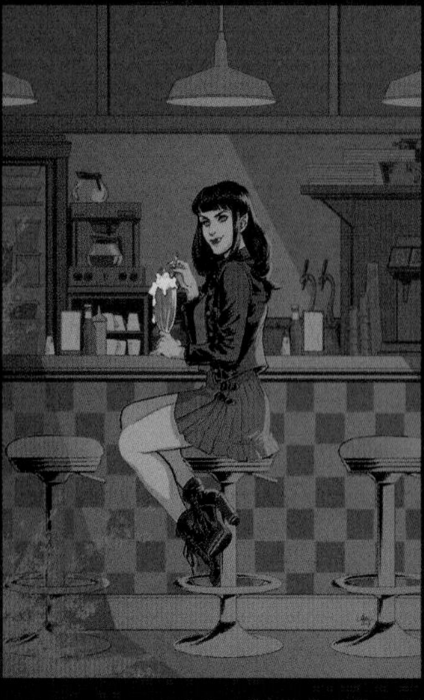

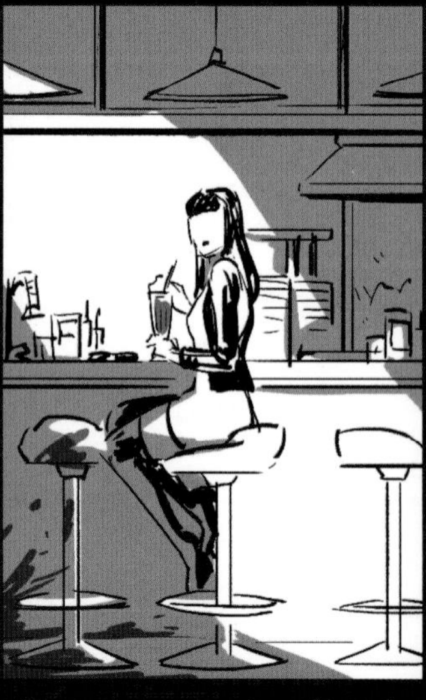

ISSUE THREE

COVER SKETCH   FINAL ART

ISSUE FOUR

COVER SKETCHES   FINAL ART

BONUS COMIC: ARCHIE & KATY KEENE

There's a new girl in Riverdale and she's turning everyone's heads—and NOT everyone is happy about that! Who is Katy Keene and why is she so Insta-famous and beloved in Riverdale? And, moreover, why is she quickly becoming Archie's biggest competition? Find out in this bonus peek of the all-new story arc with the characters that inspired The CW series *Katy Keene*!

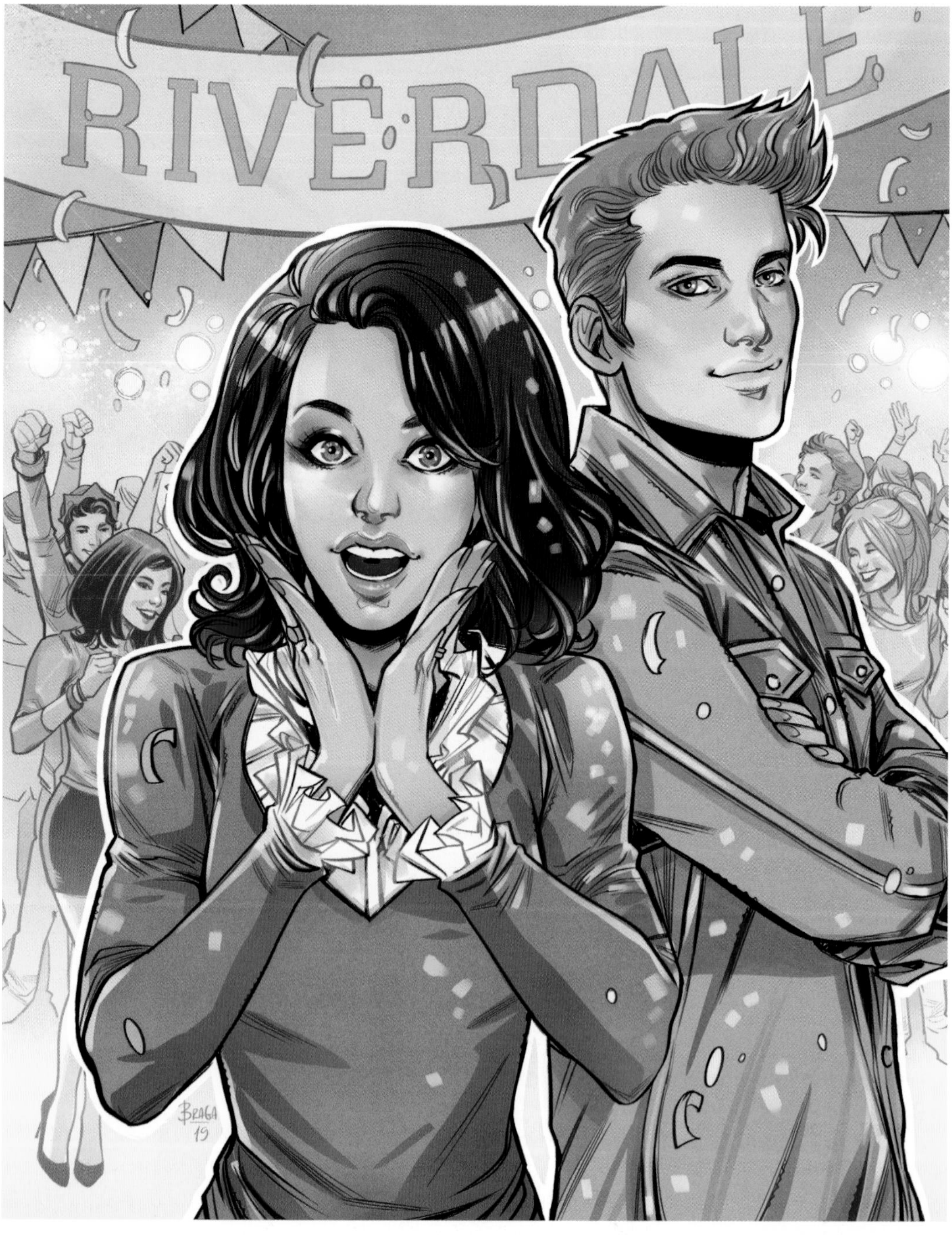
BRAGA
19

STORY BY MARIKO TAMAKI & KEVIN PANETTA ART BY LAURA BRAGA
COLORING BY MATT HERMS LETTERING BY JACK MORELLI

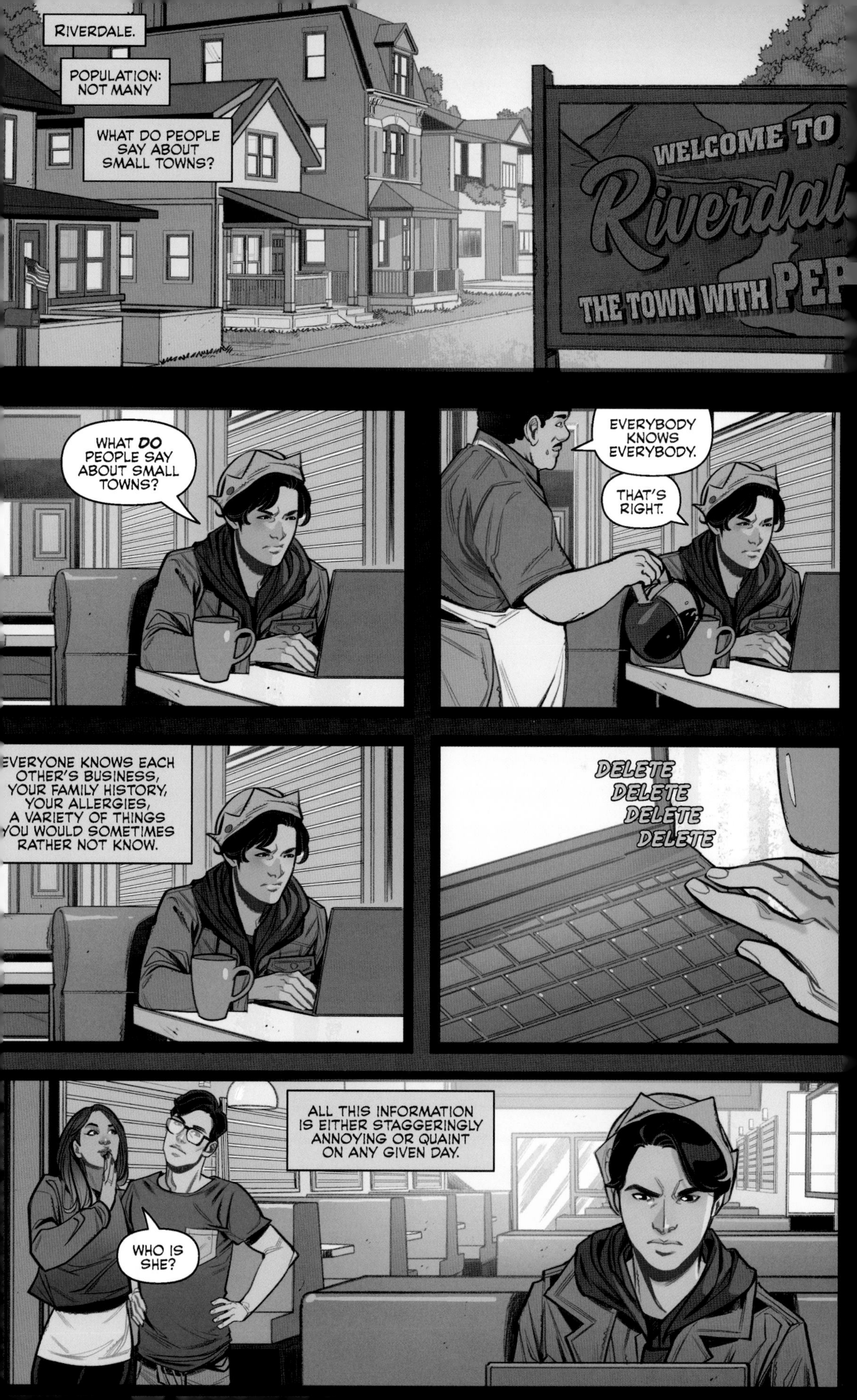
RIVERDALE.
POPULATION: NOT MANY
WHAT DO PEOPLE SAY ABOUT SMALL TOWNS?
WELCOME TO
Riverdal
THE TOWN WITH PEP
WHAT DO PEOPLE SAY ABOUT SMALL TOWNS?
EVERYBODY KNOWS EVERYBODY.
THAT'S RIGHT.
EVERYONE KNOWS EACH OTHER'S BUSINESS, YOUR FAMILY HISTORY, YOUR ALLERGIES, A VARIETY OF THINGS YOU WOULD SOMETIMES RATHER NOT KNOW.
DELETE
DELETE
DELETE
DELETE
ALL THIS INFORMATION IS EITHER STAGGERINGLY ANNOYING OR QUAINT ON ANY GIVEN DAY.
WHO IS SHE?

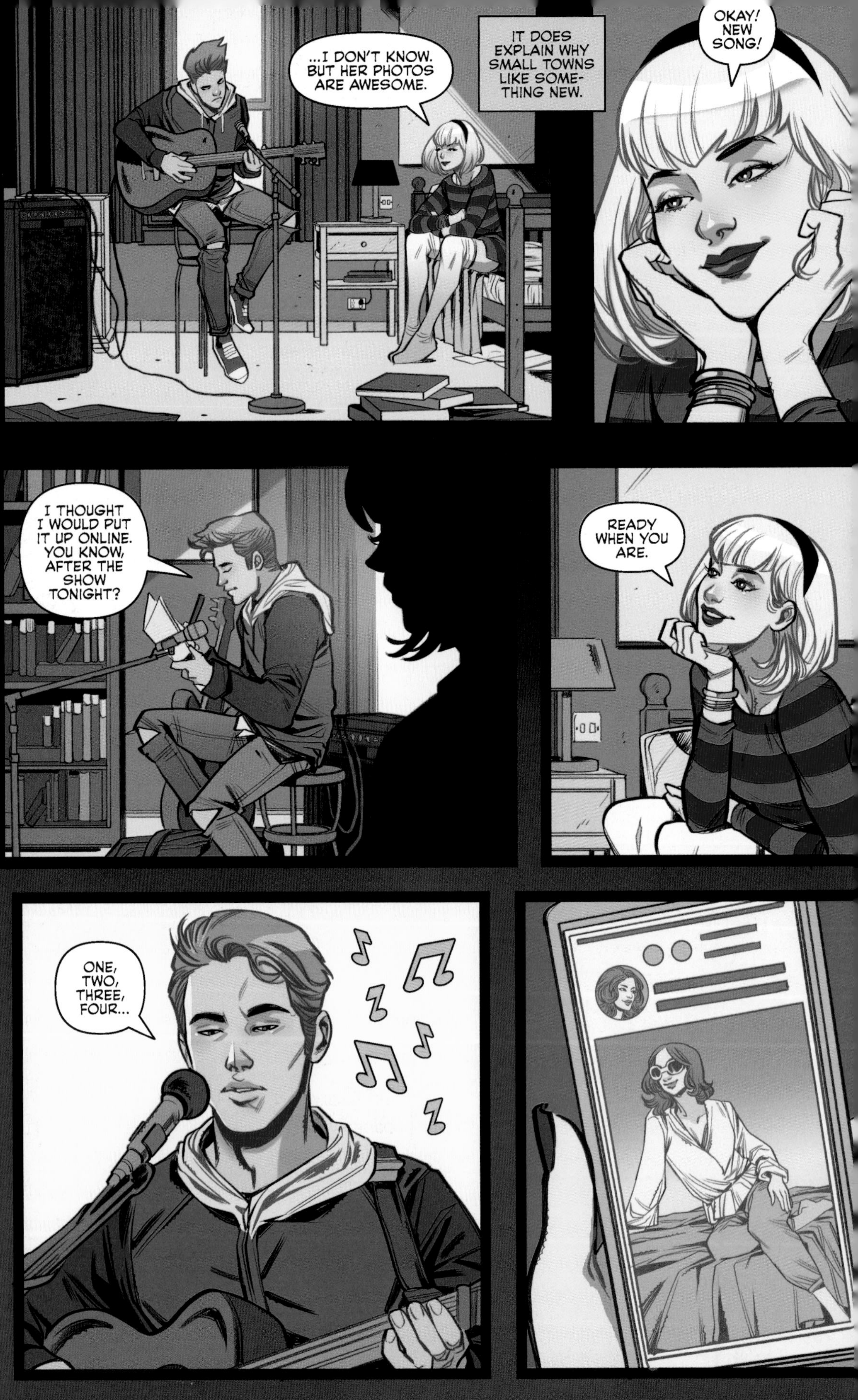
...I DON'T KNOW. BUT HER PHOTOS ARE AWESOME.
IT DOES EXPLAIN WHY SMALL TOWNS LIKE SOME-THING NEW.
OKAY! NEW SONG!
I THOUGHT I WOULD PUT IT UP ONLINE. YOU KNOW, AFTER THE SHOW TONIGHT?
READY WHEN YOU ARE.
ONE, TWO, THREE, FOUR...

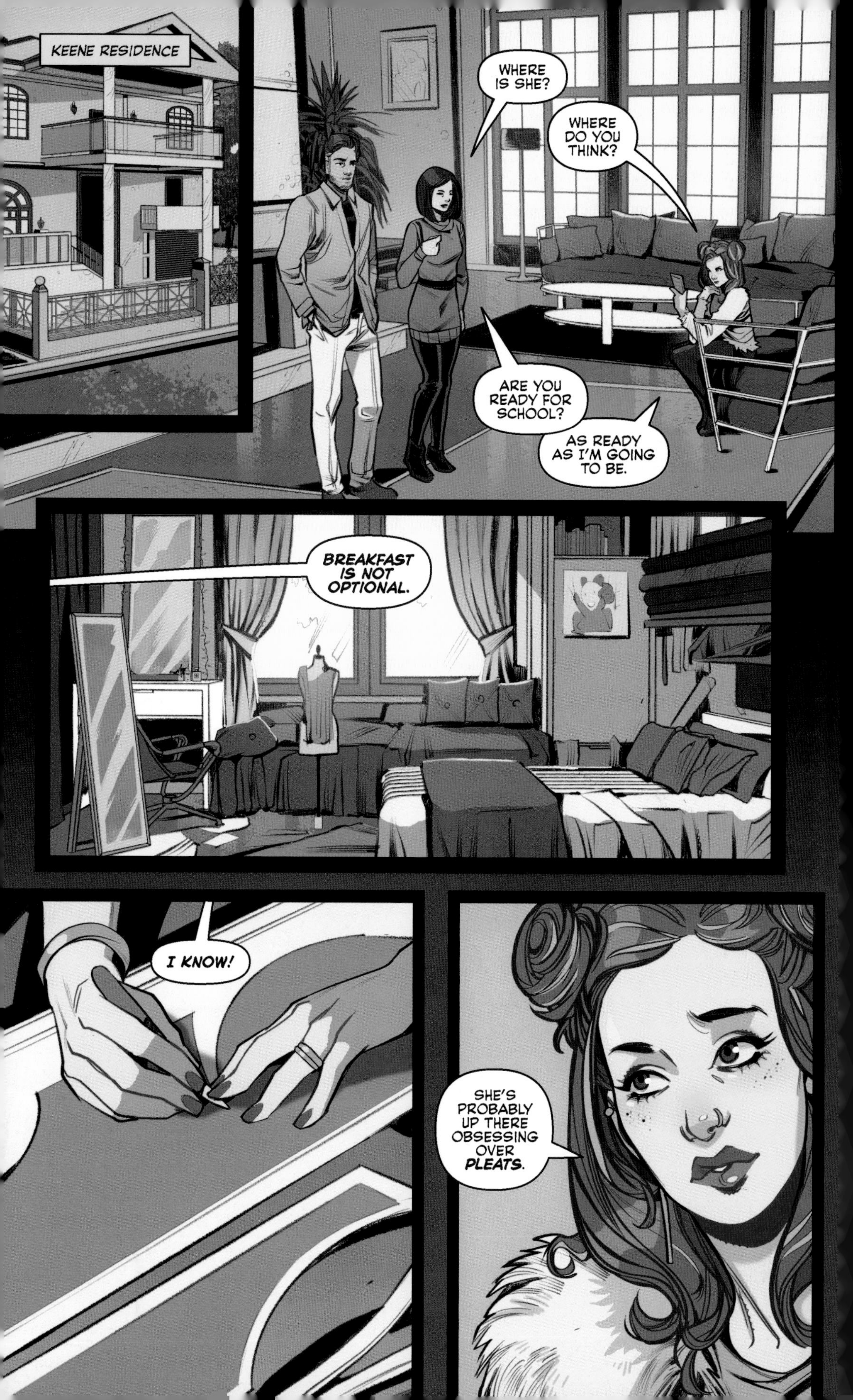
KEENE RESIDENCE
WHERE IS SHE?
WHERE DO YOU THINK?
ARE YOU READY FOR SCHOOL?
AS READY AS I'M GOING TO BE.
BREAKFAST IS NOT OPTIONAL.
I KNOW!
SHE'S PROBABLY UP THERE OBSESSING OVER PLEATS.

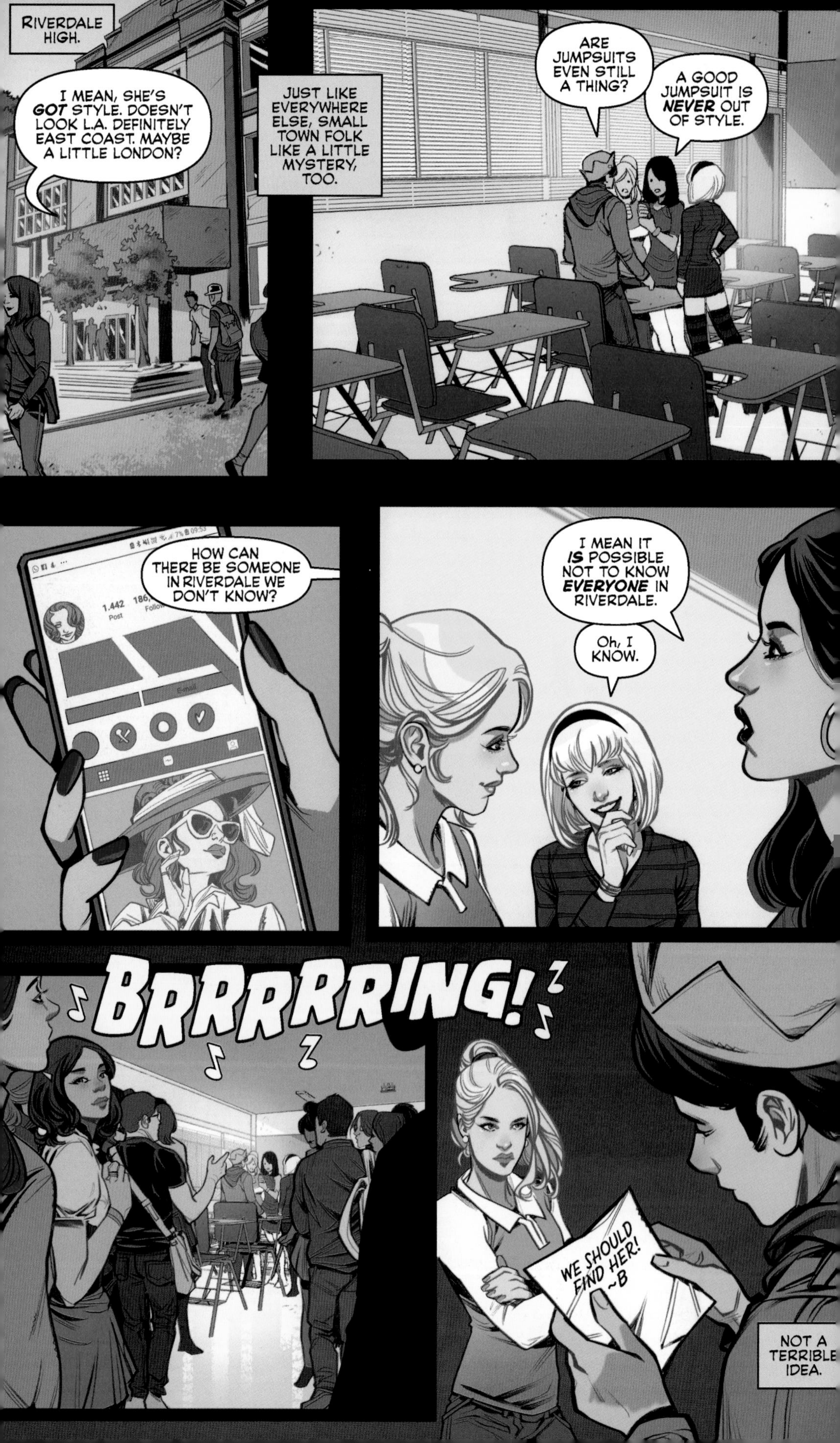
RIVERDALE HIGH.
I MEAN, SHE'S GOT STYLE. DOESN'T LOOK L.A. DEFINITELY EAST COAST. MAYBE A LITTLE LONDON?
JUST LIKE EVERYWHERE ELSE, SMALL TOWN FOLK LIKE A LITTLE MYSTERY, TOO.
ARE JUMPSUITS EVEN STILL A THING?
A GOOD JUMPSUIT IS NEVER OUT OF STYLE.
HOW CAN THERE BE SOMEONE IN RIVERDALE WE DON'T KNOW?
I MEAN IT IS POSSIBLE NOT TO KNOW EVERYONE IN RIVERDALE.
Oh, I KNOW.
BRRRRRING!
WE SHOULD FIND HER! ~B
NOT A TERRIBLE IDEA.

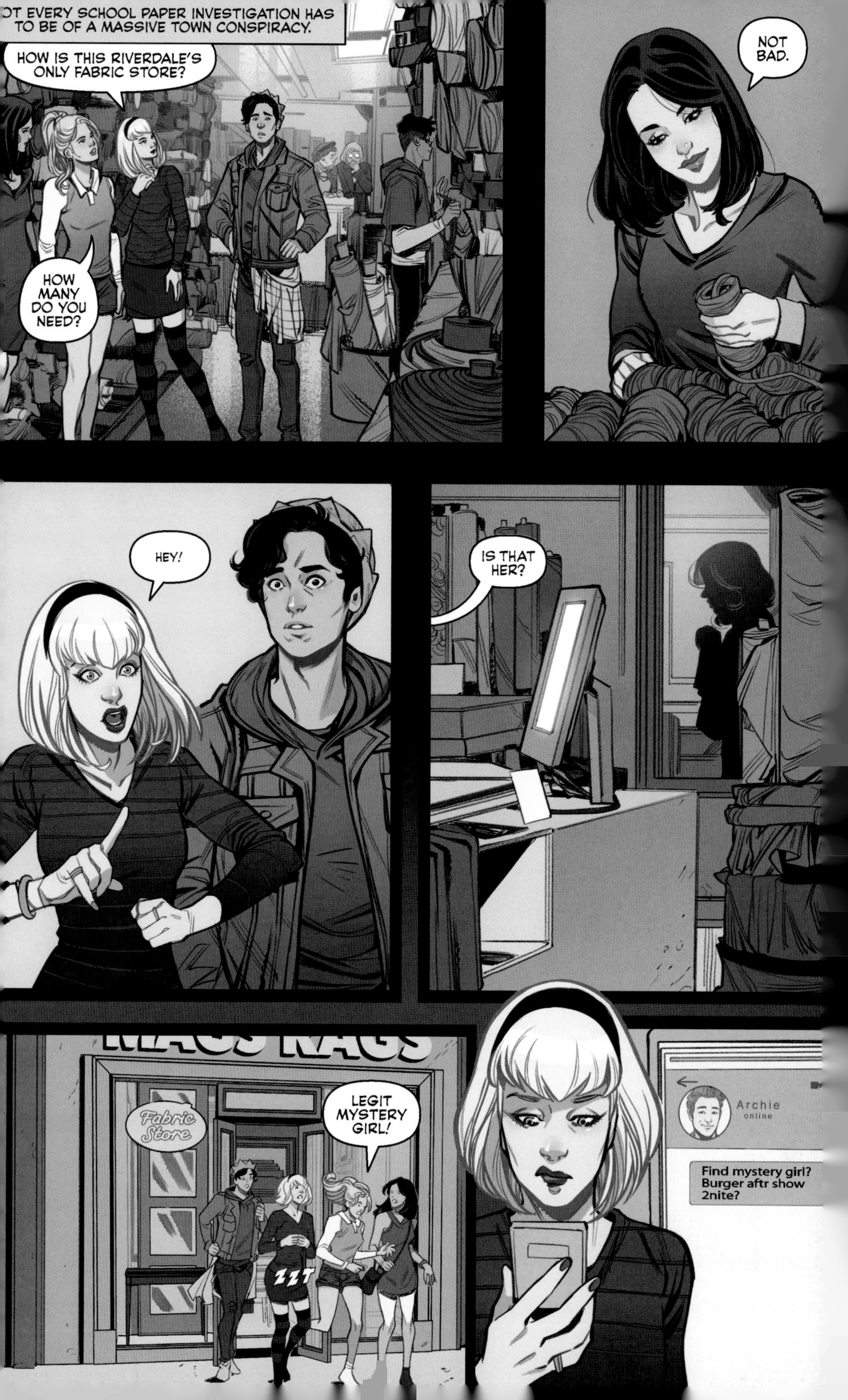
OT EVERY SCHOOL PAPER INVESTIGATION HAS TO BE OF A MASSIVE TOWN CONSPIRACY.
HOW IS THIS RIVERDALE'S ONLY FABRIC STORE?
HOW MANY DO YOU NEED?
NOT BAD.
HEY!
IS THAT HER?
MAGS RAGS
Fabric Store
LEGIT MYSTERY GIRL!
ZZT
Archie
online
Find mystery girl? Burger aftr show 2nite?

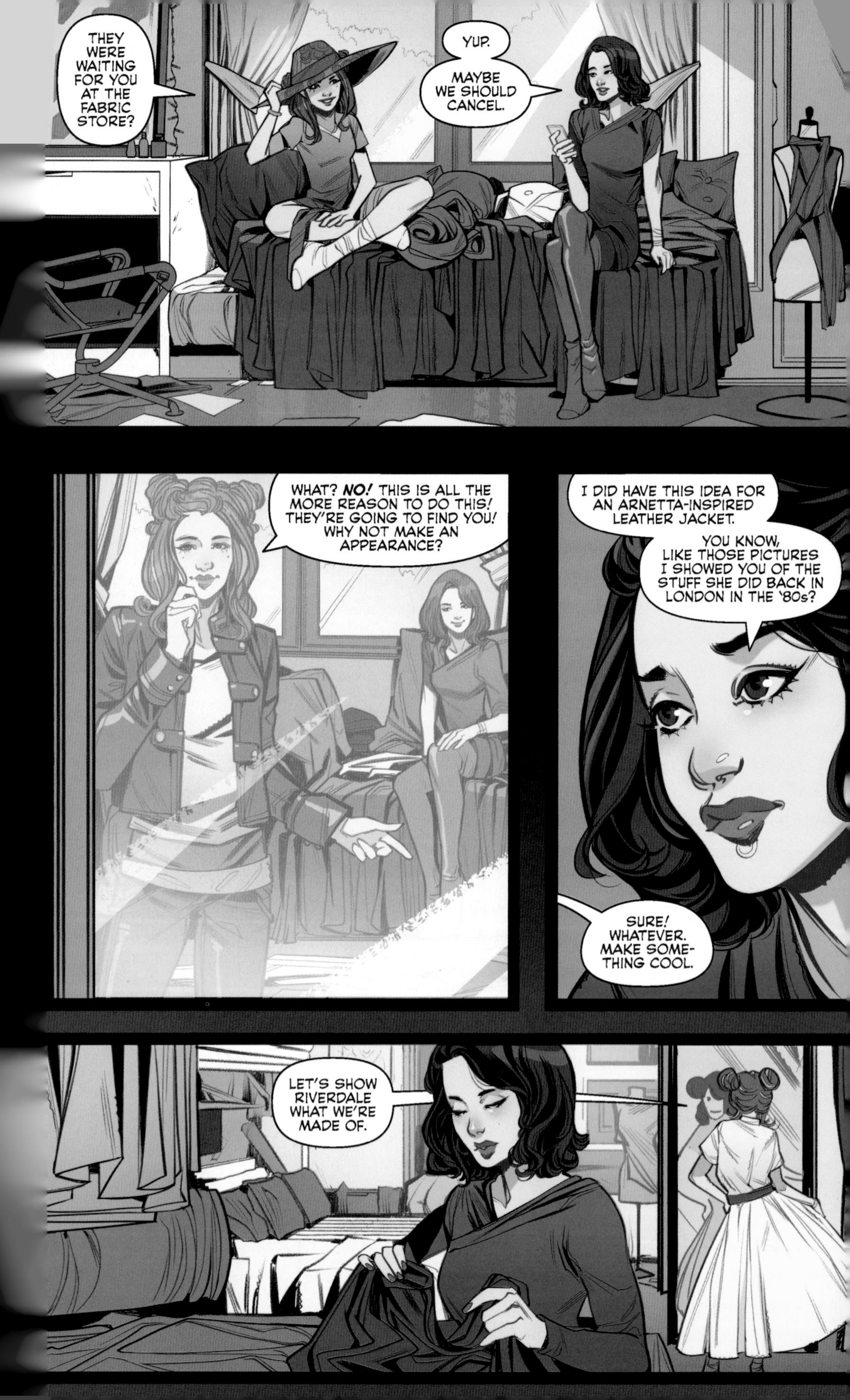
THEY WERE WAITING FOR YOU AT THE FABRIC STORE?
YUP.
MAYBE WE SHOULD CANCEL.
WHAT? NO! THIS IS ALL THE MORE REASON TO DO THIS! THEY'RE GOING TO FIND YOU! WHY NOT MAKE AN APPEARANCE?
I DID HAVE THIS IDEA FOR AN ARNETTA-INSPIRED LEATHER JACKET.
YOU KNOW, LIKE THOSE PICTURES I SHOWED YOU OF THE STUFF SHE DID BACK IN LONDON IN THE '80s?
SURE! WHATEVER. MAKE SOME-THING COOL.
LET'S SHOW RIVERDALE WHAT WE'RE MADE OF.

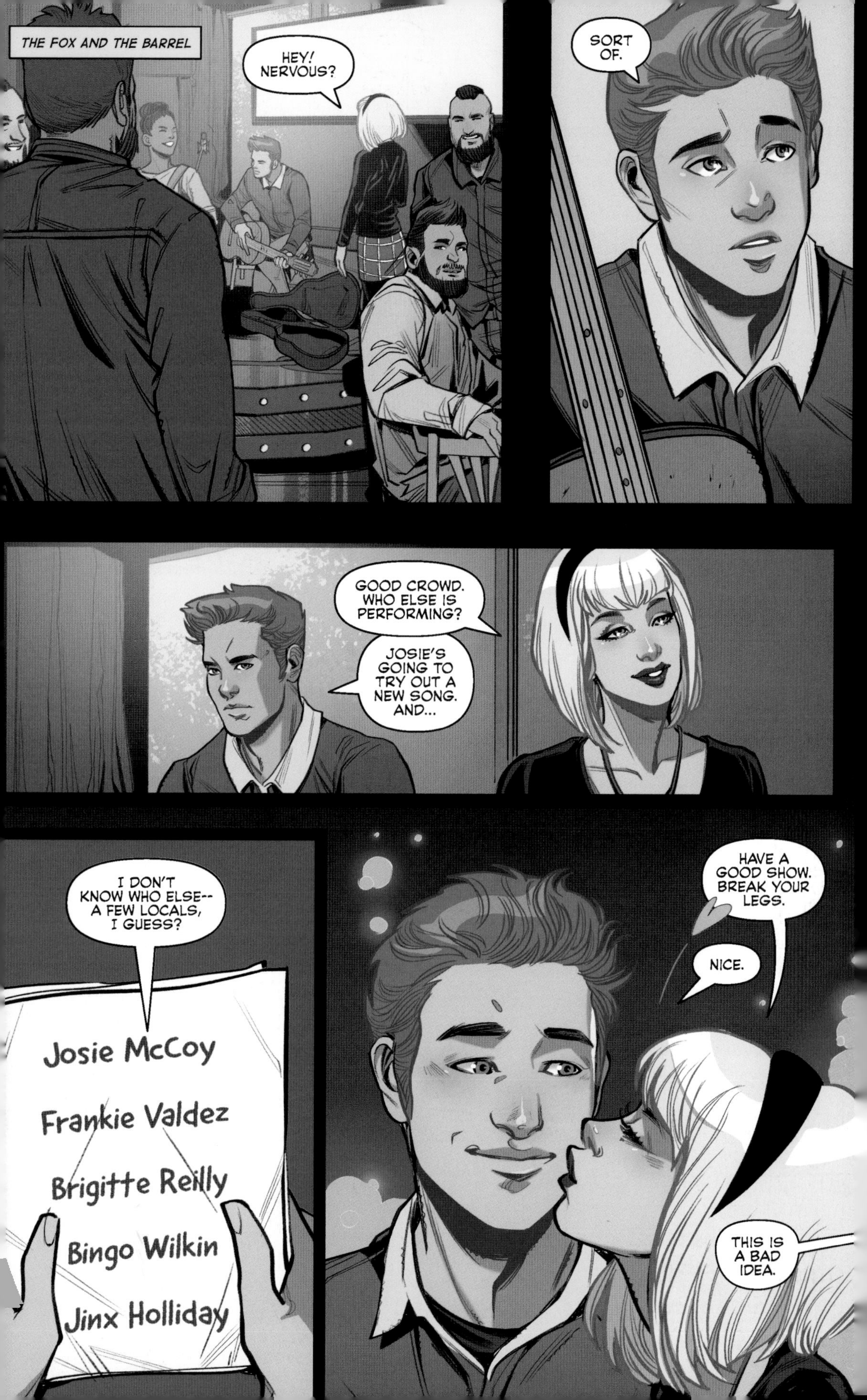
THE FOX AND THE BARREL
HEY! NERVOUS?
SORT OF.
GOOD CROWD. WHO ELSE IS PERFORMING?
JOSIE'S GOING TO TRY OUT A NEW SONG. AND...
I DON'T KNOW WHO ELSE-- A FEW LOCALS, I GUESS?
Josie McCoy
Frankie Valdez
Brigitte Reilly
Bingo Wilkin
Jinx Holliday
HAVE A GOOD SHOW. BREAK YOUR LEGS.
NICE.
THIS IS A BAD IDEA.

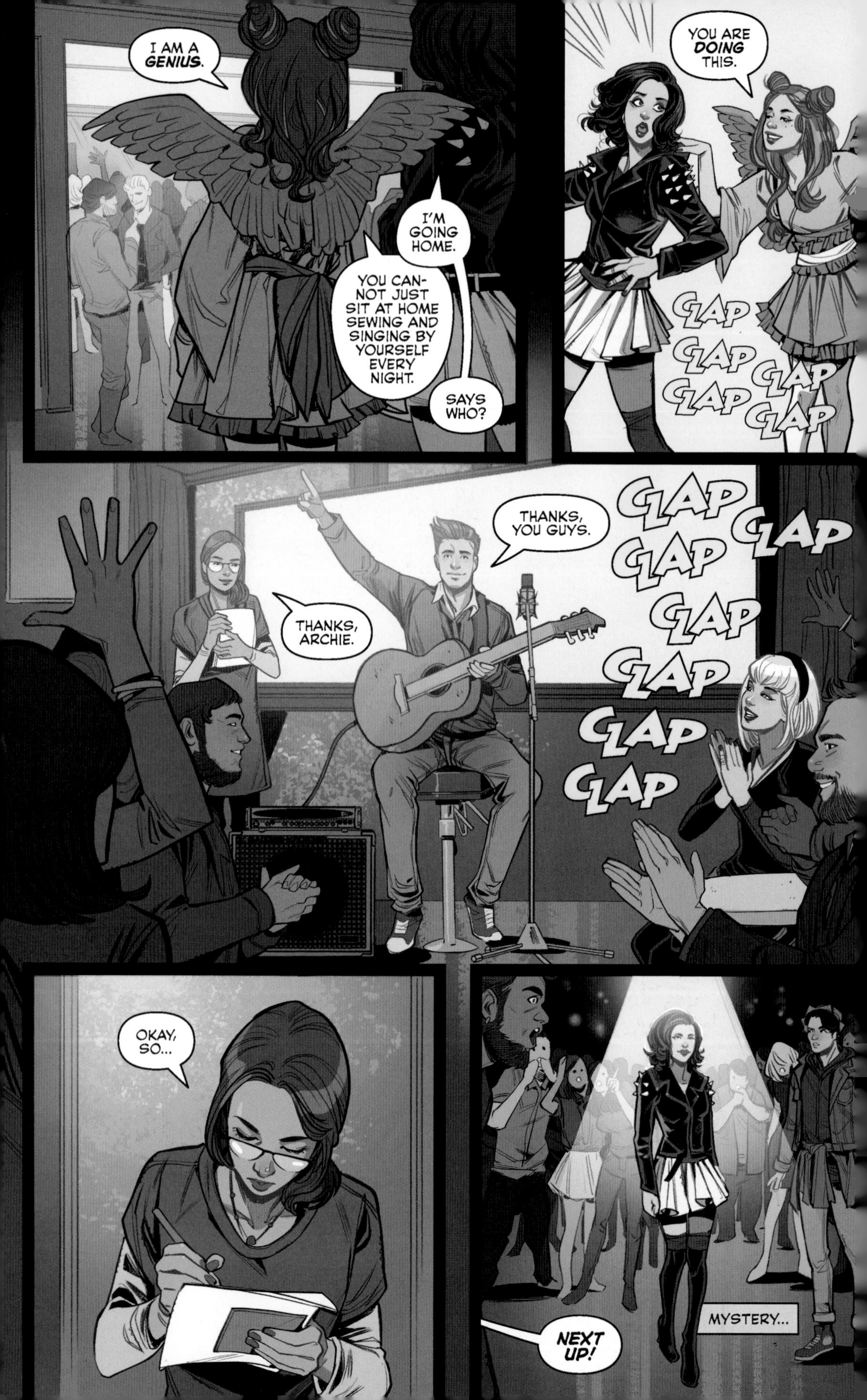
I AM A GENIUS.
I'M GOING HOME.
YOU CAN-NOT JUST SIT AT HOME SEWING AND SINGING BY YOURSELF EVERY NIGHT.
SAYS WHO?
YOU ARE DOING THIS.
CLAP CLAP CLAP CLAP CLAP
THANKS, YOU GUYS.
THANKS, ARCHIE.
CLAP CLAP CLAP CLAP CLAP CLAP CLAP
OKAY, SO...
MYSTERY...
NEXT UP!

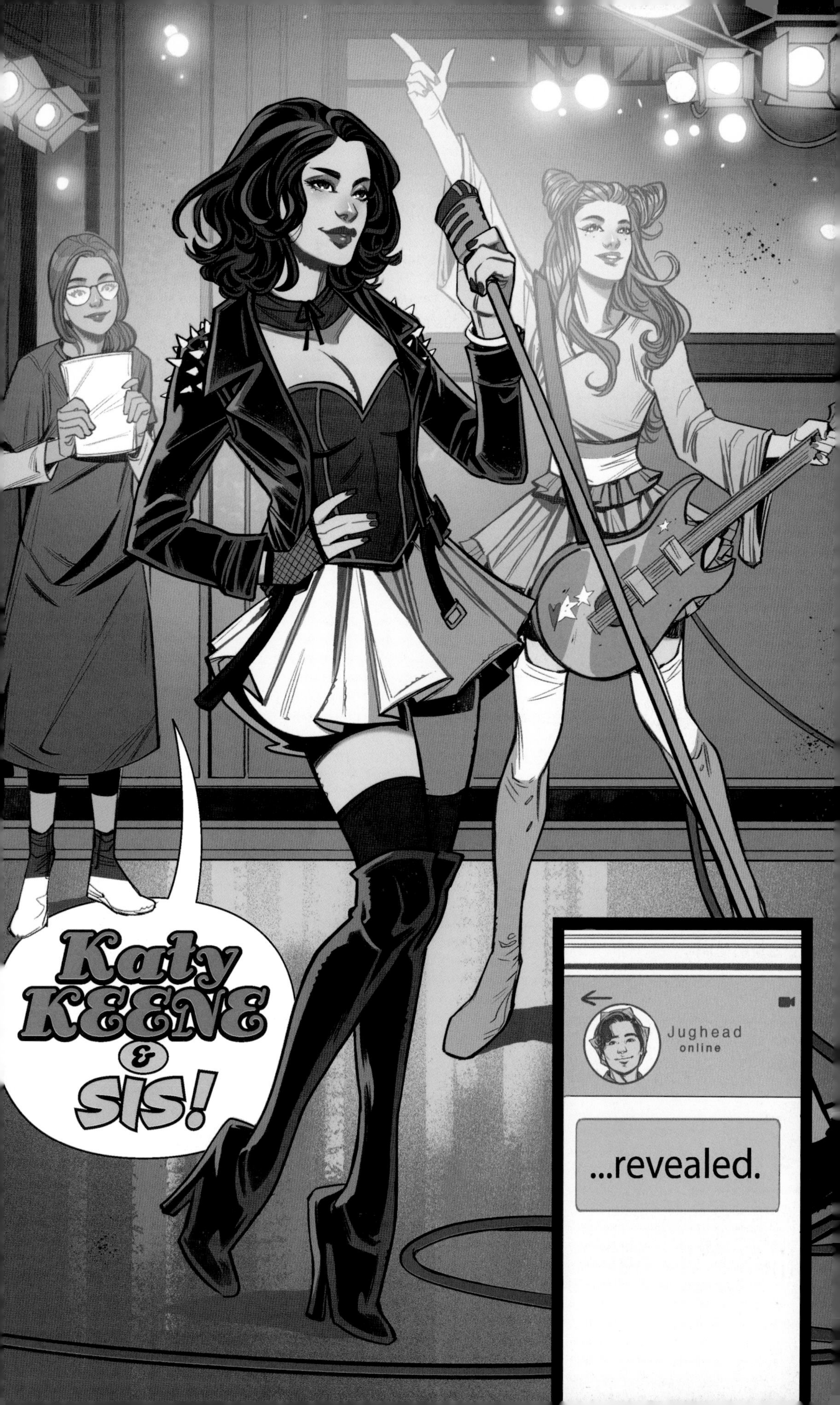
Katy KEENE & SIS!
Jughead
online
...revealed.

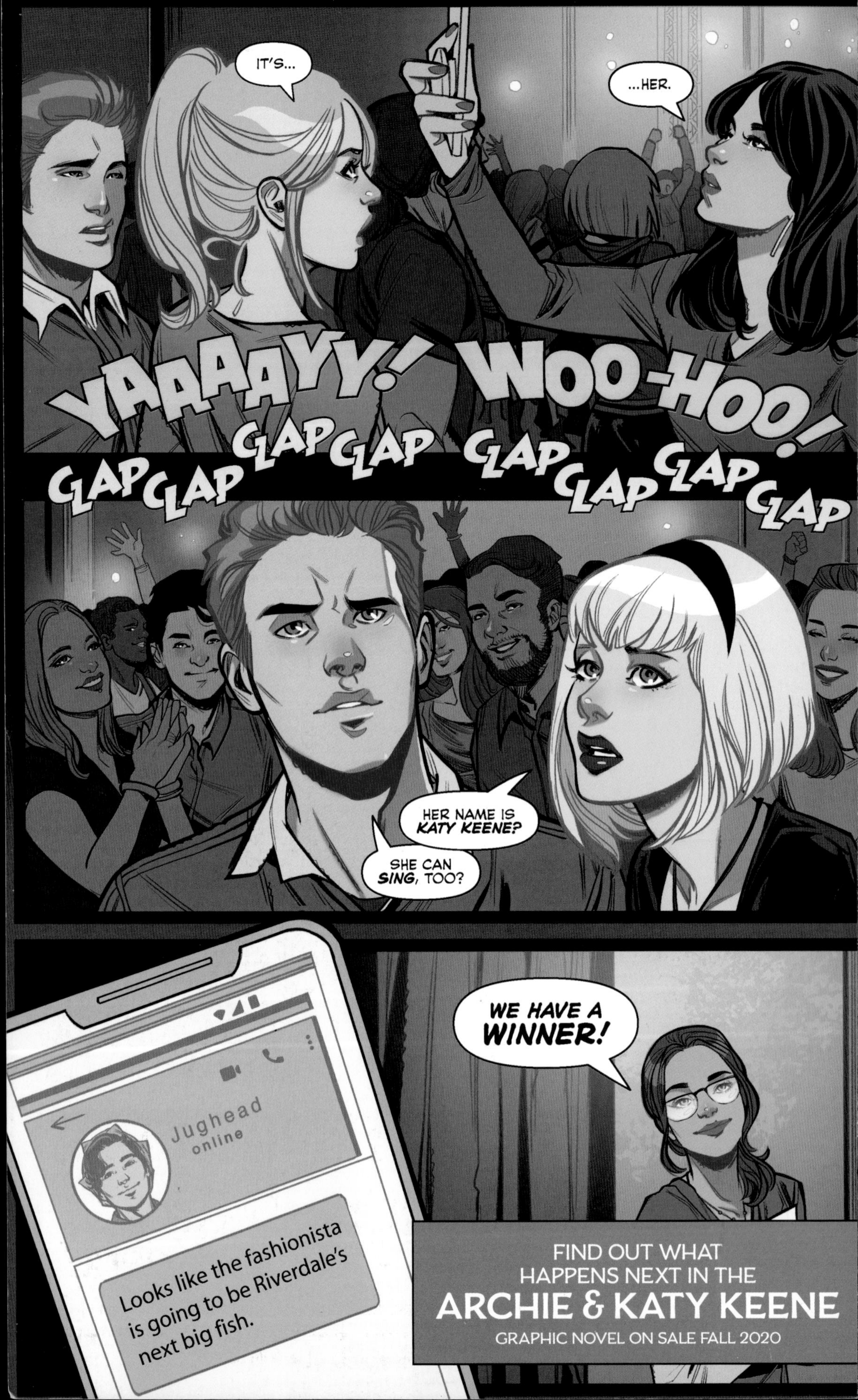
IT'S...
...HER.
YAAAAYY!
WOO-HOO!
CLAP CLAP CLAP CLAP CLAP CLAP CLAP CLAP
HER NAME IS KATY KEENE?
SHE CAN SING, TOO?
Jughead
online
Looks like the fashionista is going to be Riverdale's next big fish.
WE HAVE A WINNER!
FIND OUT WHAT HAPPENS NEXT IN THE
ARCHIE & KATY KEENE
GRAPHIC NOVEL ON SALE FALL 2020